Anti-Racist Scholarship

SUNY series, The Social Context of Education
Christine E. Sleeter, editor

ANTI-RACIST SCHOLARSHIP
An Advocacy

edited by
James Joseph Scheurich

State University of New York Press

Published by
State University of New York Press, Albany

Printed in the United States of America

For information, address State University of New York Press,
90 State Street, Suite 700, Albany, NY 12207

Production by Dana Foote
Marketing by Michael Campochiaro

Library of Congress Cataloging-in-Publication Data

Anti-racist scholarship : an advocacy / edited by James Joseph Scheurich.
p. cm. — (SUNY series, social context of education)
Includes bibliographical references and index.
ISBN 0-7914-5359-6 (alk. paper) — ISBN 0-7914-5360-X (pbk. : alk. paper)
1. Discrimination in higher education—United States. 2. Racism—Study and teaching—
United States. 3. Educational sociology—United States. I. Scheurich, James Joseph,
1944- II. Series.
LC212.42 .A58 2002
306.43—dc21
2002017643

10 9 8 7 6 5 4 3 2 1

This book is dedicated to
Julie Laible,
my first doctoral student,
an anti-racist scholar and activist,
and
a good friend.

We tragically lost a beloved sister.

We all truly miss her wonderfully loving spirit
and
her powerful, unrelenting dedication
to challenging white racism.

The answer is not in the good intentions,
it is in the critical discourse that must take place for change to happen.
—Miguel Guajardo, father and community activist

CONTENTS

Acknowledgments   xiii

Introduction   1

PART I
ANTI-RACIST CRITIQUE AND DIALOGUE

CHAPTER 1
Preface   23
Section 1: Toward a White Discourse on White Racism   25
  James Joseph Scheurich
Section 2: Response to a "White Discourse on White Racism"   37
  W. B. Allen
Section 3: Advancing a White Discourse: A Response to Scheurich   42
  Christine E. Sleeter
Section 4: A Difficult, Confusing, Painful Problem That Requires
  Many Voices, Many Perspectives   46
  James Joseph Scheurich

CHAPTER 2
Preface   49
Section 1: Coloring Epistemology: Are Our Research
  Epistemologies Racially Biased?   51
  James Joseph Scheurich and Michelle D. Young
Section 2: A Response to "Coloring Epistemology: Are Our Research
  Epistemologies Racially Biased?"   74
  Cynthia A. Tyson
Section 3: Coloring Within and Outside the Lines: Some Comments   78
  Steven I. Miller
Section 4: *Rejoinder:* In the United States of America, in Both
  Our Souls and Our Sciences, We Are Avoiding White Racism   86
  James Joseph Scheurich and Michelle D. Young

PART II
ANTI-RACIST RESPONSES TO THE SCHOLARSHIP OF OTHERS

CHAPTER 3
Preface   99
The Buck Stops Here in Our Preparations Programs:
     Educative Leadership for All Children (No Exceptions Allowed)   101
     James Joseph Scheurich and Julie Laible

CHAPTER 4
Preface   109
Section 1: Educational Leadership for Democratic Purpose:
     What Do We Mean?   111
     Carl D. Glickman
Section 2: Commentary: The Grave Dangers in the Discourse
     on Democracy   118
     James Joseph Scheurich
Section 3: Commentary: A Response to the Discourse on
     Democracy: A Dangerous Retreat   124
     Carl D. Glickman

CHAPTER 5
Preface   129
The Building Blocks of Educational Administration:
     A Dialogic Review of the First Three Chapters of
     the New *Handbook of Research in Educational Administration*   131
     Jay D. Scribner, Gerardo R. Lopéz, James W. Koschoreck,
     Kanya Mahitivanichcha, and James Joseph Scheurich

CHAPTER 6
Preface   151
The Destructive Desire for a Depoliticized Ethnographic Methodology:
     Response to Harry Wolcott   153
     James Joseph Scheurich

PART III
ANTI-RACIST REPRESENTATIONS OF THE RACIAL "OTHER"

CHAPTER 7
Preface   161
Highly Successful and Loving Public Elementary Schools
     Populated Mainly by Low SES Children of Color:
     Core Beliefs and Cultural Characteristics   163
     James Joseph Scheurich

CHAPTER 8
Preface   191
Windows/Ventanas: A Postmodern Re-Presentation
     of Children in Migrancy   193
     Gerardo R. Lopéz, Miguel A. Guajardo,
     and James Joseph Scheurich

CHAPTER 9
Preface   215
Racing Representation: A "Raza Realist" Narration of
     Migrant Students, Their *Educación* and Their *Contexto*   217
     Gerardo Lopéz, Miguel Guajardo, Maricela Oliva,
     and James Joseph Scheurich

CHAPTER 10
Preface   223
Labores de la Vida/The Labors of Life: A Description of a
     Video Documentary of Mexican-American Adults
     Who Were Migrant Agricultural Workers as Children
     and a Commentary by Miguel Guajardo   225
     Miguel Guajardo, Patricia Sánchez, Elissa Fineman,
     and James Joseph Scheurich

References   233

Contributors   253

Index   257

ACKNOWLEDGMENTS

Thanks to Patti Spencer for her unwavering love and support.

Thanks to Corinna and Jasper for teaching me to love more deeply and completely.

Thanks to Roo and Sid, just for being such a central part of what life is for me.

Thanks to Peter Wheat who as a staff member in my department did an extraordinary amount of work helping me assemble this book.

Thanks to Christine Sleeter, who has always been a good friend, a source of warm support since I first became a professor, and a sister in the struggle against white racism.

Thanks to Michelle D. Young, Cynthia Tyson, Christine Sleeter, Jay Scribner, Patricia Sánchez, Kanya Mahitivanichcha, Gerardo Lopéz, Julie Laible, Jim Koschoreck, Miguel Guajardo, Carl Glickman, and Elissa Fineman, each of whom has work that is included here to help white scholars become anti-racist scholars.

Thanks to my colleagues, Henry Trueba, Lonnie Wagstaff, Pedro Reyes, Jay Scribner, Linda Skrla, and Joe Johnson, each of whom has been a source of continuing support for my work and me.

Thanks to all of my students, those who have become professors, those who have become educational leaders, and those who have gone to other areas of work and life. The interactions with all of you have contributed significantly to my own understanding and thus to the work that is presented here.

Thanks to the American Educational Research Association for allowing me to reprint several articles from *Educational Researcher* (ER). All four pieces in Chapter 1 were in vol. 22:8, 1993. Also, all four pieces in Chapter 2 were in ER. "Coloring epistemology" was in vol. 26:4, 1997, while the other three pieces in Chapter 2 were in vol. 27:9, 1997.

Thanks to Taylor and Francis Ltd, PO Box 25, Abingdon, Oxfordshire, OX14 3UE, UK, for allowing me to reprint three articles of the *International Journal of Leadership in Education*. The first two pieces in Chapter three are from vol. 1:1, and the third is from vol. 2:1.

Thanks to Sage and Sage/Corwin for Chapters 3, 5, 7, and 8. Chapters 3, 5, and 8 appeared in the *Educational Administration Quarterly,* respectively, vol. 31:2, vol. 35:4, and vol. 34:3. Chapter 7 appeared in *Urban Education,* vol. 33:4.

INTRODUCTION

Becoming a white anti-racist scholar and **doing** anti-racist scholarship is what this book is about. I will be using my own scholarship, of several different sorts, the work I have co-authored with several others, and my own experiences to try to help other whites, particularly "new"/"young" white scholars, become anti-racist scholars. However, it should be clearly understood that my approach, my views, and/my experiences are only one partial, fragmented, ambiguous possibility. There are many others, and anyone who decides to become an anti-racist scholar should investigate several possibilities and then invent her or his own./It should also be clearly understood that this book is not about helping people of color become anti-racist scholars. While this book may have some uses for scholars of color, for a person of color to be an anti-racist scholar is a very different enterprise, an enterprise of which I have little knowledge, experience, or understanding—and certainly no advice.

Though the study of white racism by whites has a decent history (e.g., Silberman, 1964), white racism studies or critical white studies by whites have recently gained more attention (e.g., *Critical White Studies,* edited by Delgado & Stefancic, 1997). This is a significant development, especially if it is able to be sustained (white attention to white racism definitely waxes and wanes historically, with much more waning than waxing, unfortunately). However,/I prefer the label of "anti-racism" for this book because this label has a powerful history in the fight against white racism and because its use indicates, to me and I hope to others, a much more aggressive, outspoken stand against white racism.

Another marking of this book is that it is both "within" and "against" the academy. By this marking I mean that my anti-racist scholarship occurs *both* "within" the university environment *and* "against" the white racism of the university, though the university should not be seen as a singular, totalized environment. Instead, it is a shifting, dynamic, complex, conflictual multiplicity. Thus, in relationship to anti-racist scholarship, the university is "both/and," that is, the university is a space of "both" racism "and" anti-racism. There are, in fact, only a few other environments within the white dominated world in which *explicit* anti-racist work is possible. This possibility, though, does not mean that anti-racism is widely supported in all universities or in any particular university. This means that in some spaces within some universities, it is possible to survive and even succeed as a white anti-racist scholar, as witness my own career and that of other white anti-racist scholars, like Ruth Frankenberg (1993, 1997), though this surviving and succeeding by white anti-racist scholars is itself, to some significant degree, a function of white racism itself. That is, my white skin privilege provides some protection for my white anti-racist work. Scholars of color correctly contend (see, for example, Cynthia Tyson's response in chapter 2 in this book) that their anti-racist work is seen and treated much differently—much more negatively—within the university.

The main reason, in my view, for this difference in treatment of anti-racism scholarship is that the university is fundamentally a white racist institution, consciously or not, as are most mainstream institutions in the United States. And this is why the other term I use, "against," is so salient. The white anti-racist scholarship that I advocate is *also* against the white racism of the university. U.S. universities historically and contemporarily play a crucial role, in many complex ways, in the reproduction of white racism. This book, nonetheless, will not include an in-depth analysis of this reproduction, and unfortunately, I am not familiar with any book that does so, though such work is definitely needed.

Why Become an Anti-Racist Scholar?

Because I don't have any other choice. This Really Is My Answer.

In fact, in answering this question and addressing white racism, I find that I cannot contain my thoughts and feelings within the traditional academic use of words and sentences. Instead, the horror of my focus—white racism—and the threat to the status quo of anti-racism requires a somewhat disruptive or transgressive textual practice.

Why become an anti-racist scholar? Because I don't have any other choice.

If I believe that all human beings are equal and they are not being treated that way, then I don't have choice.

If I believe that democracy requires racial equity and yet this equity does not exist throughout democracy, then I don't have a choice.

If I believe that racism is ethically wrong and I see that it is happening constantly, then I don't have a choice.

If I believe that schools ought to treat every child equitably, but they persistently do not, then I don't have a choice.

If I believe that we are all God's children and I see that people of color are not being treated fairly, then I don't have a choice.

If I believe in any kind of spirituality that values all people and I see some not being valued or even some being disvalued, then I don't have a choice.

For me anti-racism is most fundamentally spiritual. I cannot imagine that it is spiritually acceptable for there to be racial inequalities, particularly patterns of racial inequalities,
of any kind
to any extent
anywhere.

In addition, from an ethical, political, and democratic viewpoint, I cannot accept racism. Actually, I cannot imagine any contemporary morality or ethics in which any kind or form of racism is acceptable. I also cannot imagine that any theory of democracy would support any version of racism.

Thus, I think that if racism exists, anyone, **everyone** should be **compelled —spiritually, morally, ethically, and democratically**—to work to remove it. I think most citizens of the United States, and certainly most educators and researchers, would agree that if there is significant or even substantial racism in any aspect of social life, especially public social life, it should be removed. I even think that most U.S. citizens, educators, and researchers would agree that there *is* significant racism in public social life, including schools and research, and that they would agree that this racism ought to be removed.

But most U.S. citizens, particularly most white citizens, are not anti-racist activists. In fact, most white citizens, educators, and researchers do not believe that racism is a sufficiently large problem such that they might be **compelled —spiritually, ethically, morally, politically, democratically**—to become anti-racists.

Why?

The answer, in my view, is white racism itself, its nature, and the way it works.

White racism is the DEEP, implicit, taken-for-granted dominance of whites and white cultural norms, standards, assumptions, philosophies, etc. as the *"natural" nature of "reality" itself*. As such, white racism positions people of color, their cultural norms, standards, assumptions, languages and dialects, philosophies, etc. as less, as negative, as weak, as uncivilized, as undeveloped, as less meaningful, as less important. As less.

However, white racism is not primarily individual acts or beliefs; those are only social effects. White racism is Onto-Logical; it is built into the very nature of the social reality. It is Epistemo-Logical; it is built into the very nature of accepted and legitimated assumptions about how we come to know reality. It is *institutional, societal, and civilizational*. U.S. institutions from the government to the schools are white racist ones. U.S. society is fundamentally white racist. Western Civilization is fundamentally white racist. But not so much in an intentional sense, but interwoven throughout.

White racism is like the oxygen molecule; it is a primary aspect in a vast range of the Semiotic Categories that compose social reality. But it is not only omnipresent, it is endemically dependent on the subjugation of the racial other, as with Hegel's dualistic master and slave. Whites and white racism literally **NEED** the racial other as a subjugated, lessor other, particularly one upon which it can project its own *hard cruelty* and upon which to play out whites' own Rejected Desires and Fantasies of Violence, such as that of the big, black, or dark, dangerous man. Again, though this NEED is not held in center consciousness, it is dispersed, deployed within movies, news reports, novels, schools, home choices, television programs, employment, retailing, law enforcement, etc.

⋇But I know that for most whites, this above judgment will seem Too Harsh, Too ExTreme, ImPossible. It can't be this bad; we can't be this terrible. The way, though, that white racism works for Us White People, including educators and re-searchers, is that we can deeply and comfortably believe that we are (mostly) a good, ethical, fair, upstanding people—certainly not racists, while, at the same time, we hide white racism and its consequences from our direct, central consciousness. It is true. We white U.S. citizens, including we white researchers, overwhelmingly be-lieve we are, for the most part, a Good ethical, Fair, upstanding, Likable people, and certainly not racists, *certainly not badly or seriously racists,* anyway.

The Fascinating fact is that we Ignore a whole pattern of Evidence that is re-peatedly and literally right BEFORE OUR EYES.

This IS the crux of the matter.

⋇The evidence of *deep and pervasive patterns* of white racism is Unquestion-able and fairly obvious, while, simultaneously, white people do not seem to "see" it in anything other than a minimized version. Because of this, white people are Very Defensive about racism, having developed a range of tactics to Avoid the topic (see, for example, Frankenburg, 1993, among many others). Thus, white people believe themselves to be basically good while ignoring the repeated in-stances of highly visible patterns of **WHITE** RACISM and while resisting, avoid-ing, any talk of racism. What does this mean? Why does it work this way? First, though, the pattern.

The almost_wholly_ignored pattern patterned patterning

⋇White people ignore Racialized Job Patterns that are *constantly before their eyes.* There is a racial employment hierarchy. It is like a Color Chart. As you start at the Bottom with those earning the least and doing the Least Desired work—like those who clean our hotel rooms or those who pick up our garbage—the color is more brown and black. As you Work Your Way Up the hierarchy toward the bet-ter paid and more satisfying jobs, the color slowly turns lighter, until by the time you get to the top, it is Almost ALL **WHITE**. This is not hidden. It is constantly apparent wherever you go.

White people Ignore that they choose the Location of their Housing to avoid living with people of color. White people ignore that the Housing Pattern of our towns and cities is Overwhelmingly Racially Segregated, with African Ameri-can and Hispanic Americans being largely relegated to the worst housing stock. Quite simply, our housing is *highly racially segregated.*

Our schools are equally Highly Se-Gre-Gated. Overwhelmingly children of color attend school with other children of color. However, even if children of color and whites are in the same school, segregation is maintained through academic tracking, special education, and discipline policies, among other means—a kind of

RACIAL PROFILING, a kind of *APARTHEID*. The highest track classes, just like the highest level jobs and the best neighborhoods, are dominated (have dominion, territory controlled by a sovereign) by white children. The lowest track classes, just like the lowest, worst paid jobs and the worst housing stock, are dominated by children of color. All whites know this. This is not hidden from them. We White People choose our housing, our schools, and the classes within our schools on this basis.

In addition, many other patterns of racism regularly appear in the newspaper. I always feel compelled to save them and cut them out, to put them in their own stack. The evidence stacks up, overwhelms doubt; it accumulates; it continuously murmurs to me. Almost once a week I find data about racism explicitly and directly presented in the newspaper. I am overwhelmed by how much there actually is, but white people Seemingly Don't Get The Message, seeminglydon'tgetit.

Racism in the Law (dominion) Enforcement system is constantly in the newspaper and on television. There is considerable evidence that local to federal law enforcement officers do racial profiling. Even expensively dressed (or because they are expensively dressed) men of color get regularly stopped by the police, as they also do if they drive expensive cars. In fact, especially in urban areas, OUTRAGEOUS PERCENTAGES of African American and Hispanic American men, sometimes nearing 50%, are involved in some way with the legal justice system — arrested and in jail, in prisons or on parole.

Regularly the newspaper stories indicate that your chances of Being Convicted after an arrest Increase Considerably if you are an African American or Hispanic American rather than white. If you are convicted as a man of color, you are more likely to *go to jail*. If you go to jail, you will spend more time there. If you commit a death penalty crime, you are **more likely to die** if you are not white. Data and stories on all of this are constantly in the newspaper and other media. It is NOT hidden or difficult data to get, to see, to believe.

Indeed, the extreme racial bias

in who gets the death penalty,
that is, who gets **killed** murdered
through the use of legitimized state power,
is
so hideous hideous hideous
all by itself, it alone
makes you question
the RACIAL SANITY of the U.S.

Racial bias in the entire legal system from racial profiling to who spends time in prison and gets the death penalty is so Extreme So extreme SO Extreme that when you look at it, you would swear there is a RACE war a race WAR a race war GOING ON. Go to a prison. Go to a prison. We are overwhelmingly *imprisoning men of color*. That is almost exclusively what the prison system is about—except for serial killers and race-oriented killers, who are overwhelmingly white.

✗ Another good example of readily available data: A recent newspaper account indicates that for every one dollar ($1) of family wealth the median white family had in 1999, the median African American family held barely 9 cents. While most white researchers, including myself, are likely to be above the median for whites, just think, for every $100 dollars you have, an African American family has $9 dollars, and I doubt that the wealth of Hispanic families is much different than the latter.

$9 for families of color; $100 for white families; the 1100% advantage of white racism. Hip! Hip! Hooray!

> All of these Patterns
> All of these Patterns
> All of these Patterns
>   are either known by whites or are readily available to them in the media—
>   all right *before our eyes*
>   all right before *our eyes*
>   all right before our *eyes*.
>   the white eyes

In addition, there are other patterns that are not so readily available to the public, but we in education, we researchers know them. In fact, the pattern is so overwhelming and systematic that Schooling in the U.S. is White Racism Personified.

Assignment to special education is disproportionately children of color, even though scholars of special education say this is not defensible.

Boys of color receive a disproportionately higher rate and level of discipline.

Zero tolerance discipline policies can easily be argued to be a code for discipline and control of boys of color.

Zero tolerance policies can easily be argued to be a code for discipline and control of boys of color.

Children of color get the worst buildings,
the worst and least supplies,
more outdated technology or none,
the least experienced and least educated teachers,
more teachers assigned outside their areas of expertise.

They typically get the least funded schools.

Schools filled with children of color are overwhelmingly less successful academically than schools filled with white children.

Teachers and administrators, who are overwhelmingly white, typically do not believe children of color can or will do as well academically as white children.

Children of color are disproportionately located in the lowest academic tracks.

They are typically given a dumbed-down, informal curriculum in the classroom (often beyond the apparent conscious awareness of the apparently colorblind teacher).

Children of color are often treated negatively in the classroom.

Teachers and administrators often have low expectations toward them, do not believe in them, do not believe in them, and CERTAINLY CANNOT NON-PATERNALISTICALLY, NON-PITYINGLY LOVE THEM LOVE THEM LOVE THEM.

And then, and then, and then, the dominant discourse in schools is that the children of color are themselves—or their parents, their neighborhood, their race, their culture, their language, their genes—to blame.

Blame them!!! Blame them!!!

It is their fault that they are not succeeding. It is their fault. *But never us whites.* **Never us.** Never OUR system of schooling, never our White Racism.

Never, never, never, never us.

In addition, as we move up the educational hierarchy, where most of us white researchers live, the differences become even more extreme. The Elite, Research Universities in each state, the ones where the most influential researchers live and work, the ones where the faculty think they Are Better, Know More than faculty at lessor universities and know more than lowly "practitioners," the typical path to higher paid, more powerful positions, are thoroughly white, while students of color largely attend the community colleges or don't attend any. We The Most Powerful, Elite White University Professors—we live steeped in whiteness, but who among us respects community college professors, practitioners, and students as our equals, who are much more likely NOT to be white. We look down our white noses at All of them. THIS IS RACIALIZED.

The racialization of the higher education hierarchy is also a racialization of research, epistemology, ontology.

If we could simply look at these various patterns—in employment, housing, economics, and education, they are staggering and unquestionable. They are a HORROR. We take for granted a HORROR. We sleep comfortably within a HORROR.

There is a monumental racial inequality throughout U.S. social life. White racism rules.

Anti-Racist Scholarship

Because white racism is ontological and because I am white, I can never totally escape white racism and white privilege. The very constructions through which I experience my life, including my subjectivity, are deeply interlaced with white racism. The categories I think with are interlaced with and constructed in terms of the shapes and contours of white racism. Every day I experience white privilege through uncountable semiotic circulations and from the treatment I receive from clerks to scrutiny by law enforcement, and the ways this privilege becomes embedded within me, within my subjectivity and my "reality" over time. Thus, I am never and can never be free of white racism, including in the writing of this book (i.e., it is inevitably racist in many ways).

One of the ways this racism works among white scholars who are critical of racism is that they want a way to be in the world so that they can regard themselves as not being a white racist. They also want to create "new" subjectivities and subject positions that are not interfused with white racism. It cannot be done. Even being a race traitor is insufficient. Trying to find or construct these "outs" is an indication of a misunderstanding and an underestimating of the ontological nature of white racism.

What then, in my view, is our choice as whites? That we as whites are at our very core white racists no matter how hard we work against racism must be accepted, said, repeated. We must always carry and speak this explicitly in our understanding, in our publications, and in our actions. This means that everything we do will have white racism in it for the present historical moment.

However, simply turning then to despair is just one more example of white racism. People of color do not get to escape white racism no matter what they do. Why should we whites think we can somehow escape white racism or despair about our lack of escape? Our actions and efforts, our directions, our anti-racist practices must be constructed both within and against the constructions of white racism in which we are embedded and which are embedded throughout our very beings.

Playing off Derrida, you cannot escape a fundamental binary by simply choosing the dominated side (the racial other) over the dominating, privileged side (the white side). Nor can we simply step outside of it. It is too deep and pervasive, embedded, interlaced, interwoven, sewn throughout the whole semiotic schema we know as reality. As Stuart Hall might suggest, we must use the tools from within white racism to work against white racism.

Consequently, we must refuse suggestions that somehow there is a right path for whites that is not woven with white racism. All white paths are thus woven; in fact, all paths period in our society are ladened with white racism. That is just a condition of our contemporary social "reality." We must thus refuse all suggested possibilities, no matter how radical, that we whites can somehow not be sewn within and of white racism; we all are always already within and of white racism.

We also must understand that we cannot displace white racism as advocated by some white scholars (e.g., Frankenburg, 1997). In addition, claims that white racism is interrupted and complexed by sexism, classism, heterosexism, while true to a certain extent, are also easily used to dilute white racism and its effects. Certainly, it is true that our positionality is a complex intersection of multiple axes of power patterned in various ways, as by gender, for one. Nonetheless, it is also dangerous if we use this "complexing" to dilute or undermine the pervasiveness of white racism. What we can do, instead, is to remain strongly focused on white racism and to disrupt and interrupt current arrangements, current assumptions, and current practices in a thousand different ways. The same is true of sexism, heterosexism, etc. Complexing them can dilute them. Not complexing can distort them. We must do both complexing and not complexing at the same time in each and every area. It is not an either/or choice; it is both/and.

Consequently, the first step for we whites who want to do anti-racist scholarship is that we must always keep in the forefront that we are white racists and we are continuously priviledged by white racism. We must include this understanding as central to our scholarship, our teaching, and our service. An example of this in this book is "Toward a White Discourse on White Racism." In this, my first published anti-racist piece, I tried to make clear my own white racism, my white skin privilege, and my inevitable historical and positional connection to all whites through white racism. In fact, the purpose of this piece when it appeared as an article in 1993 in *Educational Researcher* was to promote a discourse among white scholars on our own white racism.

Second, we must be profoundly open to criticisms of our white racism from scholars of color and other white anti-racist scholars. Being defensive and closed to criticisms of our anti-racist work is destructive. Given our historical location and positionality, no white anti-racist scholar can claim the true or right or best position, and no white anti-racist scholar can claim that by their words or their actions that they can somehow escape white racism and are thus the true and perfect anti-racist. We are all corrupted by white racism and intermeshed in its contradictions and ambiguities as we try to do anti-racist work.

An example of this in this book is the rejoinder, "In the United States of America, in Both Our Souls and Our Sciences, We Are Avoiding White Racism," of Michelle D. Young and I to Cynthia A. Tyson's critique of our "Coloring Epistemology," which itself is in chapter 2 of this book. Michelle and I tried to respond to Cynthia's criticisms in a positive, nondefensive way. Cynthia said that our article and its publication were in several ways another example of white racism at work, and we agreed with her. She was right, and her critique was helpful to us in strengthening our own understanding.

Another example in this book is the reprinting of perspectives that are highly critical of mine. W. B. Allen, an African American, is deeply critical of "Toward a White Discourse." Steven Miller is strongly critical of "Coloring Epistemology," though in different ways than Allen. While I do not agree with their critiques, it is singularly important to anti-racism work that we always leave ourselves open to any critique whatsoever from anyone, no matter what their perspective. It is just extremely important that no one assume they have THE answer to white racism.

Third, we white anti-racist scholars must understand that all scholars of color will not agree with our view of white racism. In my view, we must make no judgment of this. We whites do not have to live as people of color within white racist society. We cannot know what this is like nor judge what directions a person of color might take to survive within or to understand this environment. In my view, as white anti-racists, it is none of our business to judge or evaluate the position of persons of color on white racism. An example of this approach in this book is in my rejoinder to W. B. Allen's critique of "Toward a White Discourse." He is what would be considered a conservative African American, but that he advocates this position should not be a focus of critique for me. My acceptance of his criticism and my effort to respond positively to his critique is my attempt to respect him and his perspective.

Fourth, we white anti-racist scholars need to be deeply steeped in the critique of white racism by scholars of color. Furthermore, it is particularly critical that we use our white positionality to help communicate this critique to other whites, scholars and students. To a certain extent, this was one of the purposes of "Coloring Epistemology." Michelle and I wanted to show in this piece that we understood what scholars of color were saying about the white racism embedded in the dominant research epistemologies, and then we wanted to stand up and loudly express this understanding to other whites.

Fifth, we white anti-racist scholars need to critique the work of whites in ways that continuously highlight the ways that white racism is embedded in white scholarship. One example of this in this book is Michelle Young's and my rejoinder to Steven Miller's response to "Coloring Epistemology" in the first section of this book. Michelle and I critiqued how Miller's response to "Coloring" was itself an example of white racism. Another example is Julie Laible's and my response to the knowledge-base project in educational administration. In this example, Julie and I were critiquing the white racism of the knowledge-base project itself. A third example is my critique of Carl Glickman's promotion of democracy as the underlying value for schools. In this example, I discuss how the white majority often uses its numerical majority to support white racism and thus use "democracy" as a cover behind which to hide white racism. A fourth example is my criticisms of the new *Handbook of Educational Administration* (1999). My critique in this case is but one part of a dialogue among several colleagues about the *Handbook*. A fifth example here is my criticism of Harry Wolcott's seemingly "apolitical" approach to research methodology.

Sixth, we white anti-racist scholars must address and devise ways to provide scholarship on students of color in our educational system, but this scholarship needs to work against white racism. For me, I do not trust that I can do this alone as a white person. I do not trust that I will not inevitably embed my white racism in the research, no matter how strong my conscious anti-racism is. In fact, I do not trust *any* white scholar in this regard. I, somewhat similarly to Julie Laible (2000), think that white scholars should *not by themselves* or *just with other white scholars* do research on people of color.

The history of such research is so hideous, so destructive, beyond whites' almost always good intentions, that I think we should have at least a temporary ban or lockout, a quarantine, on such research for the present historical moment. Richard Valencia's work (1997) with others on "deficit thinking" and Angela Valenzuela's work (1999) on "subtractive schooling" show how we whites continue to embed white racism in our research and scholarship on students of color and the ways we educators continue to embed white racism in schooling at all levels.

What I have currently worked out, rather than doing research and scholarship on students and adults of color on my own or just with other whites, is always, at a minimum, to work *equally as colleagues* with persons of color to do this kind of research. I have not always done this, though. I wrote chapter 7 by myself—"Highly Successful and Loving. . . ." This chapter is highly appreciative and respectful of school leaders of color. Please look at it; few would judge it as racist, and many would judge it as anti-racist. Nonetheless, it is highly dangerous. It is a white person, me, working alone, working inevitably out of my own positionality and privilege, to define the work of administrators of color.

This was a mistake. Colleagues had told me that my tenure file would be much stronger if I had one more research-based article, which was what this was. I did not have the understanding of white racism that I do today, but, regardless, this is an example of the use of research on people of color, no matter how respectful, for the benefit of a white person by a white person, me. That I did not have the understanding of white racism that I have today is not a legitimate or sufficient excuse. It remains simultaneously an example of white racism and an example of an article that may be judged to be useful and valuable to anti-racist struggles. This, though, is the nature of white anti-racist scholarship—both within and against.

My subsequent response to this problem is, as I suggested above, to work with colleagues of color as equals from the beginning to the ending of such research. Two examples and a description of this approach are provided in chapters 8, 9, and 10. All of these examples are based on a research project, led by my colleagues Pedro Reyes, Lonnie Wagstaff, and Jay Scribner, on education for children of migrant agricultural workers. In the first example, chapter 8, Gerardo López (previously one of our students and now a professor at the University of Missouri at Columbia), Miguel Guajardo (a community activist and one of our students), and I did research on students who were the children of migrant parents, and together we wrote an article for a special postmodern issue of *Educational Administration Quarterly*. A second example, in chapter 9, is a script that the same three of us used for a presentation at several conferences, including the American Educational Research Association (AERA) Annual Meeting (1998). Key to me in both of these examples was the leadership of Gerardo and Miguel as Latinos and the participation of Miguel, who himself grew up as a child in a family of migrant agricultural workers.

Miguel is also central to the third example, in chapter 10. This example is a video documentary, so while I provide a description here, I do not provide the documentary. However, anyone can obtain a copy of this documentary by mailing a blank 90-minute or 120-minute video to me, Educational Administration, Sanchez 310, The University of Texas at Austin, Austin, Texas 78712 and $10 for handling and mailing costs. Its title is *Labores de la Vida/The Labors of Life*, and it was produced in 1998–1999.

This documentary was made in its entirety by four people, and all four participated fairly equally in all decisions. When I was given this project, I set out to find an activist who had grown up in a family that had been migrant agricultural workers. I was highly pleased to find Miguel Guajardo, who agreed to participate as a colleague on this project. I also found Elissa Fineman, a doctoral student who had some film experience (none of the rest of us had any). Finally, Miguel found Patricia Sanchez, who did not migrate with her family to do agricultural work, though her father migrated as an adult to do this kind of work. The four of us, with the help of Carlos Colon on technical editing issues, constructed this documentary. Together, we decided the focus, developed the questions we used to interview our participants, did the interviewing and the filming, and edited the film. However, Miguel, his experiences, his history, and his connections to many of our participants, were central to the documentary. Thus, this was not primarily my documentary; it was a truly collective effort. And, Miguel, for me, sits at the center of it. To me, he makes it a documentary that largely belongs to those who have worked as migrant agricultural workers, a documentary that, to a great extent, is for and by them, and it is certainly one that is all in their words.

Nonetheless, and this is critically important, Francisco, who was one of the participants in the documentary, was critical of the project in personal communication with me. He said that in his view we brought this equipment and expertise into his community; got his friends, students, and his colleagues on the documentary; left the community with our expertise and equipment; and completed the documentary. While he and the other participants thought the documentary was well done and did "represent" the participants in a way they approved, when we left, no member of his community had learned new expertise that they could then use to support and empower their own community. He thought we should have done it in such a way that members of his community, particularly the students in his community, could have had new expertise that they could then use for the benefit of their community. In this way, he thought we had been exploitive.

In saying this criticism, I believe he was talking exclusively to me. He was criticizing me for my racism in my conceptualization of the project. This goes to exactly what I have been trying to explain above. White racism is always embedded in my thinking, and so I must always be open to criticisms of it from people of color or from other anti-racist scholars. I will continually make racist "mistakes" (though this can never be used as some kind of excuse), but if I am continuously also open to critique, I can grow in my understanding and my actions. I am not claiming, though, that this approach that I am arguing for removes or totally prevents my white racism from being somehow embedded in the research project; it doesn't. However, the participation of people of color as co-authors, as equals (though because of white racism we can never be totally equal in this society) is a much better choice than proceeding alone or just with other whites. To repeat, though, nothing—no action, no procedure, no arrangement, can give a guarantee of no white racism.

A second aspect of working with scholars of color in doing research on students and people of color is a deviation from traditional ways of representing scholarship. Due to the interests of those scholars of color whom I have worked with and due to my own interest in questioning traditional modes of representing research, in my recent anti-racist work I have attempted to find ways both to transgress traditional research presentations because of their history of racism and to make the way the research is presented fit better with the ways of the people being represented. In these regards, in this volume, "Windows/Venturas" is one such attempt, with Gerardo Lopéz and Miguel Guajardo, to represent the lives of migrant agricultural workers, their children, and the schooling of their children in a way that disrupted our typical ways of "seeing" and representation and that connected in a less distanced way to the lives of those being represented. The video documentary briefly discussed here, *Labores de la Vida/The Labors of Life,* is another example of this approach to research representations. It too deviates from traditional research in several ways, not the least of which is that it is totally in the voices of those who were migrant agricultural workers as children. Finally, there is a "script" of a multimedia presentation at a session at an annual meeting of the American Educational Research Association (AERA) that involves the audience in speaking themselves the words about and by migrant agricultural workers, their children, and the schooling of their children. In all of these examples, my colleagues and I were struggling to find and create some representational forms that were disruptive to the status quo, transgressive of traditional research representations, and more emotionally connected to those being represented.

These recommendations then are my advice to white scholars about being a white scholar doing anti-racist scholarship. As I mentioned at the beginning, though, my way is only one of many, and anyone wanting to do anti-racist work should investigate several. Neither I nor anyone else has the correct or best way for white scholars to do anti-racist scholarship. What follows is a further explanation of the examples provided in the three parts of this book.

Reading This Book, Writing Anti-Racism

Each of the three parts provides examples of my own anti-racist scholarship, along with, where possible, the published reaction of others, scholars of color and whites, to the scholarship I have co-authored with others and to ones I did alone. The chapters within the parts can be used as a collection of anti-racist scholarship, read through by choosing one's own path or read sequentially as the chapters are ordered. This book is meant to be a resource for anti-racist scholarship and used in any way that will serve that purpose.

Part I is called "Anti-Racist Critique and Dialogue." It is composed of two chapters, each with four sections. The first section in each chapter is the original work that either I did alone or with Michelle Young. The second and third sections are two responses to this original work. The fourth section in each chapter is the rejoinder to these responses.

For chapter 1, the first section is "Toward a White Discourse on White Racism," which I published in *Educational Researcher* in 1993. The two subsequent sections of chapter 1 that follow "Toward a White Discourse on White Racism" are responses to it by W. B. Allen and Christine E. Sleeter. The fourth section, following the two responses, is my rejoinder to the responses to "White Discourse." I am fairly certain that "White Discourse" was the earliest article published in an AERA journal that was focused on whites addressing white racism or, what has been called, critical white studies. It is certainly my first attempt to do explicitly anti-racist scholarship and my first opportunity to respond to the criticisms of others of this effort. Particularly important in this piece is my assertion that I too am racist and privileged by white racism and that because of the way white racism works, no white can argue that she or he is outside white racism and its privileges.

For chapter 2, which is probably the most well known piece I have published, the first part is "Coloring Epistemology: Are Our Research Epistemologies Racially Biased?," which Michelle Young and I published in 1997, also in *Educational Researcher*. The second and third sections are by Cynthia A. Tyson and Steven I. Miller, respectively. These latter two are responses to "Coloring Epistemology." The fourth section of chapter 2 is the rejoinder that Michelle and I wrote in reaction to the two responses. "Coloring," with its focus on epistemology, tries to do anti-racist scholarship at the very heart of university-based research. It is our attempt, as whites, to take seriously the criticisms of scholars of color that the white-dominated educational and social science research communities is racist, even in its epistemologies. We agree with much of this criticism, and Michelle and I, as whites, were trying to explain to other whites why we agreed.

Consequently, both "White Discourse" and "Coloring Epistemology" (chapters 1 and 2, respectively) are critiques of white racism in education and research. The second and third sections of these two chapters are critical responses to my work or my work with Michelle. The fourth sections in these two chapters are my or my and Michelle's responses to these critiques. Thus, these two chapters provide two examples of taking a public anti-racist stance and of conducting a respectful, hopefully self-critical, dialogue with others on the issues raised. My hope is that these are exemplars of anti-racist scholarship and of respectful ways to dialogue in response to others who are criticizing or supporting my work.

Part II is called "Anti-Racist Responses to the Scholarship of Others" and is composed of four chapters. Each of these chapters is either my work or my work with my colleagues and students that begins as a response to the work of other white scholars. Chapter 3, "The Buck Stops Here," was done with Julie Laible, an anti-racist scholar who died last year, who was my former student, and to whom I have dedicated this book. She and I were asked by the editors of the *Educational Administration Quarterly* to respond to what was called the "knowledge-base project" in educational administration. In the early 1990s there were efforts to establish a legitimized "knowledge base" for each area of education. I was a critic of this project in educational administration almost from the beginning, both because of its limited epistemological range and because of its lack of address of issues of inequity in schooling. As a result of my disagreements with this knowledge project, I was the co-author of an edited book that provided a wide range of views either that critiqued the proposed knowledge base in educational administration or that offered alternative views (Donmoyer, Imber, & Scheurich, 1995).

After the project was completed, the journal, *Educational Administration Quarterly*, decided to publish dialogue on each of its seven domains: societal and cultural influences on schooling, teaching and learning processes, organizational studies, leadership and management processes, policy and political studies, legal and ethical dimensions of schooling, and economic and financial dimensions of schooling. (See http://tiger.coe.missouri.edu/~ucea, click on "Publications," and then click on "Educational Administration: The UCEA Document Base" to see the seven domains and illustrative readings in each.) Although the journal did not follow through on this for all domains, they did, for example, address the "learning and teaching" domain in volume 31, number 1. Then, in volume 31, number 2, they addressed "social and cultural influences on schooling." As often occurs in education, and it is a racist practice, issues of race are segregated to one area, like this domain area or like a multiculture course. Consequently, while the coverage of race was good in this area, having much to do with the leadership in this domain of Kofi Lomotey, who is an Afrocentric-oriented scholar with strong scholarship on racism, issues of race were virtually nonexistent in other areas, like "learning and teaching." Given the widely available work of Luis Moll, Gloria Ladson-Billings, Etta Hollins, and Henry Trueba, all scholars whose work directly addresses the intersections of race and teaching/learning, this segregation of race to one domain was typical of white racism. Consequently, in this article, which is chapter 3 here, Julie Laible and I used this opportunity to critique the racism of the knowledge project as a whole.

Chapter 4 has three sections. In the first issue of the then new journal *International Journal of Leadership in Education*, edited by Duncan Waite, Carl Glickman was asked to contribute an article for that opening issue. His article was entitled "Educational leadership for democratic purpose: What do we mean," and it is the first section of this chapter. I was then asked to respond to Carl's piece, which I did in "The Grave Dangers in the Discourse on Democracy," which is the second section of this chapter. Carl is a friend, and in my critique of his work, I tried to be respectful, as I have argued for earlier and as I have tried to be even with those who in my view are defending racism, because I do not believe, as I have also argued earlier, that any of us can claim the correct answer or the right stance in anti-racist work. Nonetheless, even though Carl has worked for years to improve schooling for all children, I think he seriously misunderstood how "democracy," for all of its critical importance and value to anti-racist struggles, has been used by the majority white population to maintain and provide a rationale for white racism. The third section of this chapter, then, is Carl's rejoinder to my response.

Chapter 5 is a somewhat similar situation as was the context for chapter 3. Recently, a *Handbook of Research in Educational Administration* (1999) has been published. This was largely done by the same group of scholars who did the earlier knowledge-base project in educational administration. It, also like the knowledge-base project, is a kind of current survey of knowledge in educational administration. Again, the Editors of the journal *Educational Administration Quarterly* asked various scholars to respond to different chapters in this new *Handbook.* Jay Scribner, one of my colleagues, was asked to respond to the first three chapters of the *Handbook.* He talked to me about working with him on this. We decided to have a "conversation" among ourselves and some of our doctoral students, Gerardo López, Jim Koschoreck, and Kanya Mahitivanichcha, which is this response. This chapter, then, is that conversation.

Again, similar to the knowledge project, the three chapters of the *Handbook* we responded to and the rest of the chapters in the book, except for one chapter in another part of the book, largely ignored race as it intersects with education and educational administration. Also, other than for the one chapter exception, all the authors were white. This was again the segregation of issues of race to a small, defined territory. Consequently, in my part of the conversation in the response, I tried to address the racism in the book in a way that could be heard by those being criticized. It is thus another example of me as white scholar trying to address white racism with other whites.

Chapter 6 is based on a request from Henry Trueba to respond to a paper by Harry Wolcott. However, what I did was to respond to Wolcott's work more generally. For those familiar with his extensive work on ethnographic methodology, though he has no problems with the intersection of personal or subjective issues and methodology, he is generally avowedly apolitical in his approach to methodology. As can be seen in "Coloring Epistemology" in chapter 2 of this book or in a prior book of mine, *Research Method in the Postmodern* (1997), I do not believe that it is possible for any researcher or any methodology in the social sciences to be apolitical. In my critique of Wolcott's work published here, I argue that his neutrality toward the severe white racism in society is itself an example of that racism. This, then, is a third example of my anti-racist critique of the scholarship of other white scholars.

Part III is called "Anti-Racist Representations of the Racial 'Other.'" Here I provide exemplars of my evolving research on and with people of color. The first of these is chapter 7. As I mentioned earlier, while many scholars of color have valued this article and while I continue to think it is a valuable contribution, at the same time, I now consider it an example of white racism. By myself—as a white scholar— I assumed that I could represent well the racial "other." Given the deadly history of the representations of people of color by white scholars and given the fact that I too continue to embody white racism, acting alone as a white scholar like this is much too dangerous.

Chapters 8, 9, and 10 are examples of my *move away* from any assumption that I can rely on myself as a white researcher or rely on working with other white researchers to represent fairly people of color *and* of my *move toward* collaboration with people of color in doing research on people of color. In chapter 8, Gerardo R. Lopéz, Miguel A. Guajardo, and I developed "A postmodern re-presentation of children in migrancy" for a special postmodern issue, edited by Bill Foster, of the *Educational Administration Quarterly*. In this piece we tried to provide readers with a radically different approach to presenting academic work. It is a pastiche or collage from many different sources, from government documents to migrant children's poetry, bounded by an introduction and a conclusion. The reason we chose this form was that we hoped this radically different form disrupted traditional responses of white readers to the typical representations of migrant children. Thus, our shift in representational forms was directly connected to both our political commitments (axiology) and our epistemological commitments.

Chapter 9 is drawn from the same material and was similarly developed by Gerardo, Miguel, and myself. Although there is a repeat in chapter 9 of some of the material in chapter 8, I include it because it is an example of how we used the material in an entirely different context, and in different ways. This was a 20-minute multimedia "presentation" at a session at the AERA conference (Maricela Oliva, a former student and now a professor at the University of Texas at Pan American took my place at the presentation because I had been scheduled to present a paper at another session at the same time). We had music playing that is popular among Mexican-American migrant agricultural workers. We had a video about migrant workers playing on a television set; it was *The Wrath of Grapes,* United Farm Workers of America, AFL-CIO, 1986, Keene, California, narrated by Cesar Chavez (15 minutes). We also had a slide projector moving through a carousel full of extraordinary black-and-white photos of migrant agricultural workers shot by Allan Pogue, an ethnographic photographer who lives in Austin, Texas. What I have provided in chapter 9 is the script we handed out to various audience members. Each of those who received a copy was assigned a number as a reader, and then when we came to that point in the script, that audience member read her or his assigned part. This is a kind of audience-based readers' theater. Thus, we had three different kinds of "media" going at the same time that the audience participated with us in reading through the script. We were trying to break out of conventional epistemological strictures and to disrupt the typical academic session experience of data and research. We wanted to provide an experience for the audience that was disruptive of common white knowledge, attitudes, and be-liefs about migrant workers, their children, and the education of their children.

Chapter 10 is a brief description of a research-based video documentary, called *Labores de la Vida/The Labors of Life*. Miguel Guajardo, Patricia Sánchez, Elissa Fineman, and myself collaboratively produced a video documentary of a group of adults who had been children, recently or decades ago, in migrant agri-cultural worker families. The four of us did everything together, from designing the research and developing the interview questions to deciding which footage to use in the final documentary and editing the footage. We worked very carefully to produce a representation that was appreciative and respectful of the people being represented and of their culture and historical experiences. We worked carefully to produce a documentary that would be valued by those represented. We worked carefully for the video to show both the destructive conditions they face, on the one hand, and the dignity and strengths they use to endure and overcome these conditions, on the other. As was mentioned before, anyone can obtain a copy of this documentary by mailing a blank 90-minute or 120-minute video to me, Ed-ucational Administration, Sanchez 310, The University of Texas at Austin, Aus-tin, Texas 78712. Please include $10 for handling and mailing costs. Once again, I was doing research on people of color in collaboration with people of color, rather than trying to do it alone or just with other whites. Also, once again, the way we represented the research data, as a documentary, was designed to disrupt racist conceptions of children who had grown up in migrant worker families. What is provided here, though, as chapter 10, is a brief description of the video documen-tary. However, following the description is a reflective commentary by Miguel Guajardo, one of the four who did the documentary and the one, whom I describe above, was for me the heart of the project.

Conclusion

✳White racism steals lives of color, destroys people, and convinces many that they are not intelligent, capable, important, valuable. At best, it constantly places bar-riers in the paths of people of color. At worst, it literally kills. In between, it hurts, damages, stunts, limits, contorts. Even for us whites, it corrupts our soul and de-values our lives.

White racism is complex and wily, constantly reappearing in new ways and means. It is not just where it is obvious or apparent. It is interlaced throughout vir-tually all of social life.

We white people hide from and ostensibly ignore white racism, act as if it doesn't exist or has little meaning or effects, and are highly defensive when it is raised directly.

We white people are deeply dependent on white racism, dependent on its privilege, dependent on the existence of the rejected racial other, dependent on being able to push our cold cold cruelty off on the racial other and then stigmatize them as violent, inadequate, uncultured, unmannered, uneducated.

We whites are deeply cruel in our "turning away" from white racism and its effects. We reveal a frightening inhumanity in our heart of hearts.

I am white. I too am a white racist. I cannot escape this. I can, though, struggle and act into the hope of a transformed future. I can be an anti-racist in my personal life, in my community, and in my work.

It is not surprising, then, that his book has no conclusion. As argued earlier in this introduction, any conclusion that I might offer would be inappropriate and incorrect. Indeed, I deeply believe that no one has the right answer or solution to white racism, and I know that I do not. No one, in my view, should attempt closure on this deadly issue. Instead, as Miguel Guajardo says at the very end of chapter 10, the last chapter, "The answer is . . . in the critical discourse that must take place for change to happen." Given his role in important aspects of this book and given his influence on me and my thinking, it is altogether fitting that it is Miguel who has the last word in this moment and for this book.

Part I
ANTI-RACIST CRITIQUE AND DIALOGUE

Part I is composed of two chapters, and each of the two chapters has four sections. The first section in each chapter is the original work that either I did alone or with Michelle Young. The second and third sections in each chapter are two responses to this original work. The fourth section in each chapter is the rejoinder to these responses. Each chapter with its four sections is an example of an anti-racist critique followed by a resulting dialogue in the same journal.

Chapter 1

Preface

The first piece in chapter 1 is "Toward a White Discourse on White Racism," which was published in *Educational Researcher* (1993). The two subsequent pieces in chapter 1 that follow "Toward a White Discourse" are responses to "White Discourse" by W. B. Allen and Christine E. Sleeter, respectively. The fourth section, following their responses, is my rejoinder to their responses to "White Discourse." "White Discourse" was arguably the first article published in an AERA journal that has directly come from the recent effort of whites to take on white racism, in what has been called critical white studies. Whether or not it was the first one, it was certainly my first attempt to do explicitly anti-racist scholarship and my first opportunity to respond to the criticisms of others. Particularly important in this piece is my assertion that I too am racist and privileged by white racism and that because of the way white racism works, no white, no matter what her or his politics or actions, can argue that she or he is outside white racism and its privileges.

Section 1

Toward a White Discourse on White Racism

James Joseph Scheurich

We are deeply concerned about the increasing incidence of racial and ethnic tensions in our country and the lack of focused attention being paid to this issue (U.S. Civil Rights Commission, quoted in "Civil Rights," 1991).

My intention in this essay is to "talk" as a white academic with other white academics about racism. In my opinion, this is an unusual kind of effort. There is a considerable amount of work by people by color[1] that addresses racism and its numerous collateral topics, such as equity, multiculturalism, and affirmative action policies. There is also work by whites that addresses these same issues. I have read extensively in both of these domains, but what I have *not* found are efforts by white academics to talk among ourselves about our own racism, even though prominent academics of color, such as hooks (1990) and Spivak (1988), have repeatedly said that one of the most important efforts white people could undertake to address racism would be to examine self-reflectively how white racism works.

Few educators will disagree that racism is one of the major social problems in this country. DuBois, perhaps the most widely and deeply respected African-American intellectual (West, 1989, p. 138), in his seminal work *The Souls of the Black Folks* (1903/1989), concluded that "the problem of the Twentieth Century is the problem of the color-line" (p. 29) and that "the white man, as well as the Negro, is bound and barred by the color-line" (p. 129). Unfortunately, Dubois's conclusion continues to be as accurate at the end of the twentieth century as it was at the beginning. For example, Pine and Hilliard (1990) recently wrote:

Every time we are almost convinced that the nation is *rising* above the muck of racism, there are reminders of how little headway we have made — even at eliminating the most vulgar and conspicuous manifestations of the disease. Blatant, crude, egregious, and overt racism has come out of the closet again and into our schools. (Pine & Hilliard, 1990, p. 593).

The recent candidacy of David Duke for governor in Louisiana, the Clarence

Thomas hearings, and the numerous episodes of racism on university campuses and in our neighborhoods and schools are but a few examples of the continuing hold that racism has on our society.

The Issue of Racism in the Academy

In over 20 years of experience with the academy, I have known very few white professors in education who would disagree that racism continues to be a deep and serious social problem. All of those with whom I have become familiar were against racism. Many of them even became visibly saddened when the topic was raised, as if they had just been reminded of an ongoing tragedy they had temporarily forgotten.

This picture of the white professorate, though, is not meant to dispute contentions by people of color and by some whites that the academy is racially biased. In fact, I have had African-American friends who provided specifics of racist behavior by the very same white faculty who had expressed anti-racist sentiments to me. Even more importantly, I have had African-American friends point out my own racist thoughts and behaviors. So I do not mean to give the impression that white faculty's opposition to racism means that they are not racist or that my own opposition to racism means that I am not racist. In fact, it is this contradiction between the conscious anti-racism of white faculty, on the one hand, and the judgment of some people of color, on the other, that the academy is racist that is the central issue of this essay.[2]

This contradiction creates a confusing and difficult dilemma. One side of this dilemma, the conscious anti-racism of white faculty, is founded solely on my own experience and my judgments of that experience. It is not based on a random sample of respondents to a survey, nor is it based on conclusions drawn from an experiment. It is founded only on my interactions with my own colleagues. Yet I feel reasonably confident that a high percentage of white faculty, even under conditions that would erase social desirability response effects, would judge that they themselves do not support racism and are, for the most part, not racist. I would even go so far as to say that white faculty, in education at least, would say that they themselves strongly oppose racism in any form.

The other side of the dilemma is the contention by many people of color (and by a few whites) that the academy is racist. For example, Frierson (1990) asserts that "the presence of racism in the institution[s of higher education] should be acknowledged as a reality" (p. 16). Reyes and Halcon (1988) claim:

Discriminatory policies and manifestations of racism in educational institutions have changed little over the years. . . . Chicano academics today are generally experiencing many of the same kinds of racial prejudices experienced by those who preceded them into the academy a generation ago. (pp. 310-311).

While I could cite numerous authors with similar viewpoints who are widely respected and write extensively about complexities of racism,[3] it would also be possible to find individual people of color who have had prolonged interactions with institutions of higher learning and who think that white faculty as individuals or as a group are not racist. For instance, I am a somewhat more than casual friend with one African-American student who has said to me that he never experienced racism from white faculty. So I do not want to give the impression that people of color monolithically think the academy is racist.

The question embedded, however, in the contradiction between academic whites who think they are not racist and others who think the white academy is racist is, how can we determine whether a person or group is racist or not? There is, of course, an extensive body of legislation and case law that confronts this problem from many different angles, most of which are based upon following overt effects, such as the percentage of African-Americans hired in relation to African-American applicants, back to overt and covert causes.[4] While this approach has been anywhere from fruitful to fruitless, depending on the commentator, I would like to explore a different approach here.

How People of Color and Whites Define Racism

In my estimation, people of color, and those whites who have concluded that white academics are racially biased, are correct, but this does not primarily mean what white academics may think it means. Highly educated whites usually think of racism in terms of the overt behaviors of individuals that can be readily identified and labeled.[5] A person who does not behave in these identified ways is not considered to be a racist. Within this perspective, racism is a label for individuals but not for social groups, except for what are seen as extremist groups. In fact, Kluegel and Smith (1986) found that educated whites see racism as an individual issue, not a racial group issue.

People of color, on the other hand, usually experience racism differently. DuBois (1989) speaks of the "double consciousness" of African-Americans. Because of this double consciousness, which evolves as a coping response to racism, people of color grow up learning to look at themselves not through their own eyes or through the eyes of their own race but through the eyes of whites:

> The Negro is a sort of seventh son, born with a veil, and gifted with second-sight in this American world,—a world which yields him no true self-consciousness, but only lets him see himself through the revelation of the other [white] world. It is a peculiar sensation, this double-consciousness, this

sense of always looking at one's self through the eyes of others, of measuring one's soul by the tape of a world that looks on in amused contempt and pity. One ever feels his twoness, — an American, a Negro; two souls, two thoughts, two unreconciled strivings; two wanting ideals in one dark body, whose dogged strength alone keeps it from being torn asunder. (DuBois, 1989, p. 3)

Dubois's self-concept is not rooted in his individual self, nor is it solely rooted in his own race; his self-concept is rooted in a "double," composed of both Black and white. But in this double, the white view is privileged over the black view: "This American world . . . yields him no true self-consciousness, but only lets him [the African-American] see himself through the revelation of the other [white] world" (DuBois, 1903/1989, p. 3).[6]

While many things have changed in this country regarding racial issues since Dubois's statement was published nearly 90 years ago, he has captured a feature of the lives of people of color in this society that is still relevant.[7] Because of racism, because "they are constantly reminded by words, deeds, and unconscious gestures that they are out-group members" (Stanfield, 1985, p. 400), because they experience themselves collectively and historically as being treated differently based on their skin color, people of color learn to see themselves as a racialized people, as a social group defined by skin color.

Because of racism, people of color are not only treated as a social group; they also come to see themselves as defined by that group. As Kramer (1970) says, "Members of minority groups have no choice about the status that is imposed upon them" (p. vii). In addition, because racism is imposed by whites upon people of color, the racialized group sense that people of color have does not originate in their own group. It originates in the actions and attitudes of the white race, that is, "through the revelation of the other [white] world." (DuBois, 1989, p. 3)

We whites, however, experience ourselves as nonracialized individuals (Kluegel & Smith, 1986; Ogbu, 1978). We do not experience ourselves as defined by our skin color. We especially do not experience ourselves as defined by another race's actions and attitudes toward us because of our skin color. As Stanfield (1985) asserts, whites do "not even . . . notice they are white" (p. 400).

This difference in how whites and people of color experience themselves is, I think, crucial to understanding why whites misunderstand judgments that they are racist. When people of color assert that the academy is racist, individual whites in the academy, who do not see themselves as racist, are offended or think the judgment does not apply to them. People of color see this unwillingness of whites to acknowledge their racism as one way that white academics protect their position of privilege. Neither whites nor people of color seem to understand that there is a clash here between a social group perspective, learned by people of color through the social experience of racism, and an individualized perspective, learned by whites through their racial socialization.

Individualism and Social Positionality

Among whites, the idea that each person is largely the source or origin of herself or himself, that is, individualism, is considered a natural facet of life.[8] Within the frame of this belief, individualism is seen as a naturally occurring, transhistorical, transcultural condition to which all humans naturally aspire. This belief, then, is deeply infused in white judgments about the way life works. For example, if a person does "well" in life, it is seen as being largely due to her or his own individual choices; if she or he does "badly" in life, it is also largely due to her or his choices. While it is thought that people have different capabilities, what a person does with her or his capabilities is considered to be more important than the capabilities themselves (Schuman, 1971), especially among more educated whites (Kluegel & Smith, 1986).

The problem with individualism, though, is that it hides the inequities in our social structures, especially racial inequities.[9] It also hides the fact that "prejudice, discrimination, and racism do not require [individual] intention" (Pine & Hilliard, 1990, p. 595). People of all races are social beings, that is, "human behavior is largely shaped by social/cultural experiences" (Gordon, Miller, & Rollock, 1990, p. 16). Boden, Giddens, and Molotch (1990) make the same point in an article addressing the lack of sociological understanding in the academy: "All too easily . . . academics define human actions as 'psychologically' driven when they are, deeply and significantly, social in origin and orientation" (p. B2).

In different times and in different places, people have acted, thought, and believed differently about virtually everything. Even in our own time, middle-class Cuban-Americans, to name just one group, have different codes of conduct than upper-class whites or lower-class Hispanics. For instance, Stanfield (1985) contends:

> It is simply wrong to assume that everyone in the United States has the same cognitive style. . . . The cognitive styles of classes, races, and ethnic groups differ; each of these social categories has different experiences, priorities, and ideas of what is relevant. (pp. 399–400).

In fact, each of us is socially positioned or located by major sociological categories, such as race, class, and gender. Those in different positional intersections, like white lower-class women or Asian middle-class men, are socialized in different ways.

These positional intersections, however, are not equal in our society. There is a hierarchy of positions, with upper-class white men at the top and lower-class men and women of color at the bottom. Resources and power—economic, intellectual, and emotional—are largely distributed according to this hierarchy (hooks, 1990; Ogbu, 1990; Ransford, 1977; Spivak, 1988; Stanfield, 1985; Waller, 1988; Yetman & Steele, 1971, pp. 3–15; among many others). Whites as a group get more resources and power than people of color. The upper class as a group gets more resources and power than the middle class as a group, which gets more resources and power than the lower class. Men as a group get more resources and power than women.[10]

This inequitable distribution of resources and power by social group, however, is concealed by middle- and upper-income white people's investment in the idea of individualism. In contrast, because of racism's grouping effect and the double consciousness it produces, people of color are not as seduced by the idea of individualism. People of color, through their socially positioned experience, know that they are a racialized group rather than simply separate individuals.

Although we live in a culture that distributes its resources most disproportionately to middle- and upper-class white men, this does not mean that there are not exceptions to this arrangement or that other groups do not persistently resist the inequitable distribution. Middle- and upper-class white men, nonetheless, consistently reap the most benefits and have done so for a very long time within Western culture. The result of this historical dominance is that the styles of thinking, acting, speaking, and behaving of the dominant group have become the socially correct or privileged ways of thinking, acting, speaking, and behaving (Kovel, 1970 [cited in Pettigrew & Martin, 1987]; Kramer, 1970; Stanfield, 1985; Waller, 1988).

One of the main ways this happens is that the ways of the dominant group become universalized as measures of merit, hiring criteria, grading standards, predictors of success, correct grammar, appropriate behavior, and so forth, all of which are said to be distributed as differences in individual effort, ability, or intelligence. Membership in a social group and the group-related, inequitable distribution of resources and power thus disappear under the guise of individualism.

Social Success and Social Awards

The best way, then, to succeed—that is, to receive rewards, recognition, promotions, salary increases, material resources, and so forth—is to learn and reproduce the ways of the dominant group. This learning and reproduction is easiest for those who grow up socialized into these dominant ways. Thus, the children of middle- and upper-class whites are the ones most likely to succeed because they have been raised (socialized) in the ways of the dominant group. Some children of the dominant group, of course, fail, and some children from lower social groups succeed, but on average, the chances of success are substantially better for a person raised within a dominant group family.

Members of nondominant groups and their children have a chance to succeed if they learn the ways of the dominant groups and if they are socially or economically closer to the top of the hierarchy. But, contrary to the popular idea that anyone can succeed, there are limits no matter how well one learns the ways of the dominant group. A person low enough in the social hierarchy of groups—no matter how well she or he learns to internalize the ways of the dominant group—will never attain the level of success that comes much more easily to one who grows up within a dominant group family.[11]

Although each individual is to some extent different, and thus there is some contribution that is due to an individual's particular constellation of skills and abilities, the rewards each person receives are to a considerable extent an effect of the inequitable distribution of resources and power by race, class, and gender. However, the socially reinforced belief in individualism allows those at the higher reaches of the social hierarchy (which, in my opinion, includes white academics) to believe that they receive more rewards because they are special individually, because they have more skills, more talents, more intelligence, and so forth. They do not see how these rewards are related to their group position within the social hierarchy.

In a very real sense the cream is skimmed off the social milk and fed to those in the higher groups as if they are individual rather than social rewards, while those at the very bottom of the hierarchy drink a milk so diluted as to be hardly distinguishable from water. Those in the upper levels of the social hierarchy become addicted to the seductive connection of various rewards with the idea that they receive these rewards because of their uniqueness as an individual.

Individualism Is Addictive

This process occurs within the academy as well as virtually everywhere else within our society. I have experienced it myself. While I grew up within a working-class family and have had to train myself to behave like an upper middle-class person, I did grow up a white male. Although my working-class origins placed some hurdles along the way, I was aided by the fact that I am a white male and that I have been able and willing to learn upper middle-class ways. Such accommodations (or compromises, if you will) have allowed me to be fairly successful in terms of garnering social rewards, mostly within the academy.

I can personally say that this process is highly addictive and very difficult to resist. All of the rewards are offered in terms of the idea that I am receiving them because of my special, individual talents, abilities, and efforts. It is very easy, then, to convince myself that this individual specialness is true and to become deeply committed to a kind of personal egotism or arrogance. While it is surely true that individual differences play some significant role in the distribution of social rewards, it is very easy to forget, even in the face of the kind of commitment I have tried to express in this essay, that the rewards I receive are deeply connected to my race, class, and gender, that is, to my membership in a highly favored social group.

According to Bledstein (1978), this cult of the individual is an integral part of academic life. There is a special emphasis on the freedom of professors, once they are tenured, to be highly individualistic and thus not defined by any social group categories. Bledstein (1978), in his book on higher education in this country, has said:

The culture of professionalism [Bledstein's referent for the academy] emancipated the active ego of a sovereign person as he performed organized activities within comprehensive spaces. The culture of professionalism incarnated the radical idea of the independent democrat, a liberated person seeking to free the power of nature within every worldly sphere, a self-governing individual exercising his trained judgment in an open society. . . . [This professional person strove to achieve a level of autonomous individualism, a position of unchallenged authority heretofore unknown in American life. (pp. 87–88)

The culture of the academy not only emphasizes the individual standing of each professor but also inculcates a rationalization of individualism as a positive virtue.

The price we white academics pay for this orientation is that we lose sight of the multiple effects of our membership in a favored social group. We lose sight of how much we and, more importantly, our intellectual productions (books, articles, presentations, symposia) are, at least to a significant extent, enacted by our race, gender, and class. Our intellectual products, which play an important part in how our society knows and reproduces itself, are marketed as if they are individual products, unrelated to or reproductive of social group membership. Our social positionality simply disappears from the conscious surface of our products. For example, a book I might write would be seen solely as the work of my individual self; it would not be seen as a white upper middle-class male production.

This perspective returns us to the earlier point that white academics tend to misunderstand judgments that white professors are racist. As I said before, we white academics tend to see this as a judgment of our individual behaviors rather than as a judgment of our membership in a social group. People of color, on the other hand, because of the "double consciousness" forced upon them by racism, see both themselves and whites as enacted by their racial categories. When people of color contend that we white academics are racist, they are not primarily judging our individual behavior (though certainly they sometimes are); they are, most importantly, judging our membership in a racial group that has produced and maintained skin color as a socially enforced category of difference within a hierarchy of social groups.

In addition, people of color are saying, correctly I think, that we whites operate as if we are oblivious of our racial positionality and its effects in terms of the inequitable distribution of resources and power within our society. Because of this lack of awareness, we white academics learn to act as if our social rewards—salary, position, recognitions, and so on—are solely the product of our special, idiosyncratic individuality. We thus ignore the inequitable distribution of such awards by social group and the impact of this inequitable distribution on ourselves and our intellectual products. More critically, we ignore the fact that the inequitable distribution of resources and power is, in a very important sense, constitutive of whom we are as upper middle-class academic whites.

We Whites Are in This Problem Together

Recognizing our social group position raises another important point for us whites. Virtually all academic whites occupy, as whites, the same general social position no matter what each individual's opinions about racism may be. Even if a white academic strongly opposes racism in her or his intellectual work, she or he still benefits as a white from the inequitable social distribution of power and resources. There is no individual escape from one's racial group. We whites, because of our social group membership, are socially bound together, just as people of color are, in terms of addressing racism. This social group membership orientation is particularly relevant to efforts by whites to confront white racism. Unfortunately, many whites who have made a commitment to addressing racism also consider themselves superior to those whites who have not made the same commitment. This division into "good" whites who address racism and "bad" whites who do not is implicit in the writings of many anti-racist whites. It is also implicit, albeit in a much more complex fashion, in such philosophical orientations as those versions of Marxism that locate racism as a phenomenon secondary to the class hierarchy (McCarthy, 1988; Young, 1990).

A full recognition of the advantages we gain as a result of our racial positionality means that all whites are in the struggle against white racism together. None of us gets an individual dispensation that releases us from our racial position, from its inequitably derived rewards, or from white racism. Our positionality requires that we whites must work together to address this situation; otherwise, we are assuming we can escape our social group membership and its effects through claims for special status for individual anti-racist whites.

I do not make this last point lightly. I know from my own personal experience that it is very easy to divide those who are "politically correct" from those who are not. I often fall into this myself. The indirect claim of superiority, because I am focusing on white racism when others are not, is highly seductive. It is very easy for me to think that I have done my part because I am on the "politically correct" side.

What arises out of this is a way of talking or writing (through tone or word choice, for instance) that implicitly communicates my ideological or political superiority. Not only does this approach alienate those I need to communicate with, but it also falsely represents me as being less affected by my racial group membership than those whites who do not address white racism. In my opinion, no matter how much I individually confront the issue of white racism, I cannot escape being white. I cannot escape the inequitable distribution by race and its effects on me. As West (1990) says of those in my position, I am both "progressive and coopted" (p. 94). Since I cannot individually escape my racial group and its position within the inequitable social hierarchy, no matter how much I individually detest racism, I am compelled to work inclusively with other members of my racial group to address white racism.

Two Suggestions

I would thus make two suggestions to facilitate a white discourse on white racism within the academy. We white academics need, first, to begin to understand and make conscious, especially within our intellectual work, the fact that in our society all people are racialized persons, that is, all people are socially influenced in significant ways by their membership in a racial group. We whites need to study and report how being white affects our thinking, our behaviors, our attitudes, and our decisions from the micro, personal level to the macro, social level. We need to make white racism a central, self-reflective topic of inquiry within the academy. We need to become aware of our racial positionality as it affects our intellectual products and then infuse this reflexivity into those products.

Second, we need to undertake this effort in a way that does not attempt to separate "good" whites, willing to confront white racism, from "bad" whites, unwilling to confront white racism. While this nondivisive approach makes good, practical, political sense, it is even more important to understand that as long as the discourse on white racism divides "good" whites from "bad" whites, it misses the central argument advanced in this essay. That is, in our society everyone is racially located and experiences the inequitable distribution of resources and power by racial group, even though a belief in individualism conceals this inequitable distribution. It does not matter whether we are a "good" or a "bad" white; all whites are socially positioned as whites and receive social advantages because of this positionality. No individual white gets to be an exception because of his or her anti-racism.

Virtually no one would dispute that racism is one of the chief social problems in this society and in many other societies. It is certainly not surprising that no consensus exists on how to solve the problem. In this essay, following the advice of the victims of racism, I have tried to start from where I am. Since I am a white male academic, I have tried to start from there. I have attempted to consider how we white academics participate in the reproduction of racial inequity. I have attempted, at least to some extent, to be candid about my own participation in that reproductive process, to talk, for instance, about my own experience of the seductions of individualism. I have made suggestions about what we white academics need to do and how we need to do it. It is not my intention, however, that this essay be a definitive consideration of white racism in the academy. It is neither the first word nor the last. It is only an attempt to discuss my thoughts about white racism in the academy and to provoke additional conversation, in agreement or disagreement (both are helpful, useful, and important). While none of us can escape the innumerable, intricate, large and small ways that our society daily advantages or disadvantages each of us racially, I do not believe we are fatally condemned to continue the present inequities. The key question is how do we end this tragedy? I suggest that we white academics begin with a white discourse on white racism. I hope this essay facilitates that conversation.

Notes for Chapter 1, Section 1

1. I will use the phrase "people of color" to denote the collective of all nonwhite races in the United States. I do not wish, though, to imply in some totalized fashion, that the different nonwhite races are all somehow the same either in general or in regard to racism. Each race has had a different historical experience in this country that is constitutive of its racial culture. Ogbu (1978, 1990) for instance, has written that because of the historical effects of slavery, the contemporary position of African-Americans is different from that of other races, such as those that freely immigrated to this country. In addition, throughout this article, I do not mean to imply that each race is monolithic in its viewpoint about anything, especially racism; there are, as West (1990) says, "differences (class, gender, region, sexual orientation)" among all peoples of color (p. 103). In addition, McCarthy (1988) asserts that "the characterization of minority groups in monolithic terms leads to unwarranted generalizations about the social, political, and cultural behavior of racially oppressed groups" (p. 272). (See also Ransford, 1977, on this issue.) Nonetheless, since the focus of this article is on whites and white racism, and not primarily on the experiences of people of color, I need a single, collective term for the other-than-white races. Other possible terms that have frequently been used are more problematic for various reasons. The term "nonwhite" is deficient because it derives its meaning from whites rather than from people of color themselves, thus reinscribing a hegemonic relationship of whites over people of color. Sometimes, though, it is the only term that works grammatically; for example, the term "people of color" cannot be used as an adjective. The term "minorities" is also inadequate because people of color are minorities only at the national level and within some other specific contexts: In the world as a whole and in many contexts, people of color are the majority. For example, "California is already a 'majority' of 'minorities' insofar as its schools are concerned" (Gutherie & Reed, 1991, p. 7). Finally, although the term "people of color" is also deficient because everyone is, strictly speaking, a person of (skin) color, this term is the one that is currently most frequently used by people of color that I read.

2. That a person of color in an institutional setting with whites is the only one to recognize that there is racism in the setting is a common point made in the literature on racism. For example, Feagin (1991) says that it is typical for "a black employee to perceive the subtle undercurrent of prejudice not perceived by white employees" (p. 86). Pettigrew and Martin (1987) contend that "often the black is the only person in a position to draw the conclusion that prejudice is operating in the work situations" (p. 50).

3. See, for example, Baratz & Baratz, 1970; Feagin, 1991; Higham, 1971; Pine & Hilliard, 1990; and Reyes & Halcon, 1988. For more philosophical treatments of the racism of the Western knowledge project, see Gordon, Miller, & Rollock, 1990; hooks, 1990; Minh-ha, 1989; Said, 1979; Spivak, 1988; Stanfield, 1985; and Young, 1990.

4. See, for example, Pettigrew and Martin (1987) in the *Journal of Social Issues*, which devoted one complete issue to the topic of racism and employment (43:1, 1987).

5. I would suggest that what many academic and other middle-class whites see as racism is the style of racism historically common to working-class whites. Indeed, in much

of the public, popular discourse on racism in the media (newspapers, television, radio, movies), racism is characterized almost solely in terms of white working-class racism. Pettigrew and Martin (1987) call this style of racism "raw, overt bigotry" (p. 46), while Kovel (1970) calls it "dominative racism" (quoted in Pettigrew to Martin, 1987, p. 46). While many middle-class whites find "raw, overt bigotry" or "dominative" examples of racism to be repugnant, they tend not to be aware of their own, more subtle styles of middle-class racism.

6. Pine and Hilliard (1990, p. 596) make the same point about students of color: "Students of color . . . experience conceptual separation from their roots: they are compelled to examine their own experiences and history through the assumptions, paradigms, constructs, and language of other people."

7. The determination of which racial groups in the United States experience Dubois's "double consciousness" would initiate a lively debate. I do not think, however, that the central purpose of this essay requires that I take some stand on this issue. My unwillingness to engage this here does not mean that I think this debate is unimportant; it is very important. Neither does my unwillingness mean that I do not have a sense of where I would stand in such a debate; I simply think that to attempt to discuss this issue here would not only take too much additional space, but, more importantly, would also detract from the central point I am trying to make.

8. I do not mean to imply that people of color do not also value individualism. What I am saying is that people of color are much more aware of their racialized group status than whites are of their racial group status and that thus the influence of the idea of individualism, especially as this awareness relates to racism, on people of color is significantly less than on whites.

9. The idea of individualism as hindering white attention to racism does not originate with me. For example, Ogbu made this same point in his *Minority Education and Caste: The American System in Cross-Cultural Perspective* (1978). I do, however, think that raising this issue within the context of white academics talking to other white academics is an important addition.

10. Although I appear here to treat the social categories of race, class, and gender as if they operate independently from each other, I do this only to simplify the larger argument that I am trying to develop. Actually each category intersects with the other categories in very complicated ways.

11. DuBois (1903/1989) expressed awareness of this difference in life chances in 1903 when in speaking of a young African-American man, he said, "I had feared for him. With a cultured parentage and a social caste to uphold him, he might have made a venturesome merchant or a West Point cadet" (p. 49).

Section 2

Response to a "White Discourse on White Racism"

W. B. Allen

I would prefer not to respond to the "White Discourse on White Racism," but I am constrained to do so. I do not wish to address the question because Scheurich's essay confirms my opinion that America does not need a discourse on race. Rather, America needs to transcend the discourse on race. Nevertheless, I am constrained by a circumstance that imposes on my conscience. For the (or at least an) apparent source of the reflections in this essay is a statement that originated with me. As a member of the U. S. Commission on Civil Rights from 1987 through 1992, I initiated and ultimately participated in authoring the statement from which the epigraph to Scheurich's essay was drawn. Insofar as the author takes that epigraph to announce the theme of the essay, he largely, if not completely, misunderstood the point.

"Focusing attention" on rising tensions ought to eventuate in a renewed resolve to remove race and ethnicity as points of moral reference in our society. Many, however, believe that race/ethnicity constitutes the unique point of moral reference, even on the side of the "angels." This has occurred, I believe, on account of profound and gradual reorientations in our understanding of education. The theme of this response, accordingly, is that every effort to root education in the confirmation or elaboration of fundamental racial or ethnic beginnings directly contradicts the true purpose and character of education. In a word, we have lost touch with the true etymological bearing of our usage, *education,* and tacitly substituted the etymological meaning of the French usage, *formation.* Where the former seeks a "leading forth" toward thoughts unthought, the latter treats the soul as filled with blank place holders waiting to receive constructivist projects (the model of which remains Rousseau's *Emile*).

The thought that education ought to liberate folk from their former prejudices does not spring newly to our minds. It is an old conception, prefigured in Socrates' notion of the *periagoge* or "conversion" that real learning brings. The foundation of this conception arises precisely from the understanding that education is not the filling up of an emptiness but the correcting of systemic errors or prejudices imbibed effortlessly and on faith. Thus, our "upbringing" is the *precondition* of our education. As we begin to discover the shortcomings of our upbringing, in the light of genuine or natural human possibility, we turn toward those efforts that are designed to supply a more accurate foundation for judging courses of action and relationship. We arrive in this manner to the insight of the Declaration of Independence, for example—namely, that no one is by nature the ruler/ master of another, no one by nature superior or inferior—and we consequently abandon all such prejudices derived from our upbringing.

I believe that this healthy approach to education was heedlessly abandoned under the pressure of a cultural relativism that gained its greatest accession of strength in the context of a multiculturalism movement that seeks to attribute human potential, and therefore value, to social groups in direct contradistinction to individuals. On the theory that groups "have something to say to us," we find ourselves evaluating individuals in light of the "message" that we expect groups to deliver. Thus, American blacks speak to us not as humans but as American blacks or, still more perversely currently, as African-Americans. Whatever they may say must be heard through this lens (which the term *political correctness* seems all too mild to describe). Because the message of any individual American black is framed thus, so too is the auditor's hearing framed; that is, the auditor does not need to think himself or herself addressed in his or her humanity by another human being. Rather, the auditor receives the message of any given American black as testimony about African-Americanism, testimony that may have nothing to do with the auditor's human potential to the precise extent the auditor is not himself or herself an African-American.

Putting aside this awkward and rather stupid usage, let us come to the point. The idea of a "white discourse on white racism" is just another version of a "white discourse on white superiority." For it matters little what the specific claim of racial purity/difference is. The claimant ultimately seeks to privilege his or her individual concerns through group identity. In that light, the understanding he or she offers is by definition superior to any other. It cannot be simply one of an infinite number of equivalent understandings, for in that case there would be no moral or rational basis for inculcating one view in preference to another. That is, our burdened white male could just as easily find grace by participating in a "black discourse on black racism," or any of the other infinite range of possible turns of the expression, if his situation did not impose upon him this particular "white discourse" as the *only* effective mode of expression. What is the "only" effective mode of expression that is necessarily the "best" in the context.

·   While it is easy to discern a logical fallacy in this approach, one may still see that it arises naturally from the present state of the discourse. For if all social discourse is a form of power relationship, and only those subject to oppressive power can correctly express the nature of the oppression, so, too, must it be the case that those locked with the oppressed in a fatal and reciprocal embrace of oppression must have a unique and characteristic voice. Since the oppressor by definition cannot speak with the voice of the other, then it must follow that the oppressor must speak with *(and for)* an oppressor's voice.

The evolution of bilingual education in the United States provides unique testimony to the process I have described. Without entering into details and avoiding contested points, it may readily be asserted that the development of bilingual education has progressed from a program aimed at facilitating competence in English to a program aimed at cultural preservation. Now, the ideas that led to the notion that specific efforts of cultural preservation were required were precisely such ideas as those I have adduced above. Furthermore, it is clear that such ideas ultimately call forth responses on behalf of other cultures (including so-called majority culture), insofar as the ideas themselves admit of no principle by which to distinguish according this treatment to some cultures but not to others.

In this light, it is fair to say that a "white discourse on white racism" can eventuate in no positive results for nonwhites in the United States, apart from the putative advantages associated with any regime of noblesse oblige. For the record, it must also be insisted that the essay is curiously nonhistorical in its assertion of the total absence of works by whites discussing the phenomenon of racism in the United States. To avoid descending into a war of footnotes, I would submit that the extensive work of historian Eugene Genovese is sufficient testimony of the converse. There are many more.

I am concerned about another aspect of this work, one that is much more impressionistic. It is very difficult to avoid the conclusion that one who publicly declares himself a "white racist" acts effectively to declare himself important, powerful, and highly respected. Since the entire discussion of this essay is predicated on the claim of the pervasiveness and powerfulness of white racism (the standard setters and decision makers), I do not think that I exaggerate the character of the personal claim the author seeks to make. Let's consider one passage:

> We whites, however, experience ourselves as nonracialized individuals. . . .
> We do not experience ourselves as defined by our skin color. We especially
> do not experience ourselves as defined by another race's actions and atti-
> tudes toward us because of our skin color. As Stanfield . . . asserts, whites do
> not "even . . . notice they are white."

Now this is patently incorrect, historically speaking. Benjamin Franklin testifies most eloquently to that fact when, in 1789, writing for the Society of Political Inquiry in the *American Magazine,* he proposed policies of immigration with specific reference to the propriety of preserving a fair complexion among the people. But this is still more importantly a revealing self-portrait of the author. The "we whites" phrase speaks volumes about the very claim that is being made. There is more.

The claim that "we whites" hardly notice our race is further belied in the overgeneralization that "people of color" can hardly think of themselves in any terms but of race: "They come to *see* [italics added] themselves as defined by that group." Note, then, that "we whites" are nonracialized, while *those* "people of color" lack such intellectual facility! The citation of DuBois at this point will hardly sustain the incredible claim being made, besides the fact that DuBois's personal testimony does not constitute a scientific principle. What the author really means by *seeing* is *accepting*. But it is false to insist that nonwhites "accept" being defined by others. If the author contests this reading, if he insists that *seeing* and *accepting* are not synonyms, then surely it must follow that nonwhites, American blacks in particular, arrive at their separate self-consciousnesses in a far more complicated manner than is suited to a "white discourse on white racism." Indeed, it is altogether likely that they see themselves as human!

One may think that I have pinioned the author on what should be charitably treated as a merely polemical exaggeration. I insist, however, that the orientation revealed in these passages is precisely the ground upon which the elaborate attack on individualism stands. There, too, the author maintains that whites have the advantage—namely, the capacity to be individuals—while nonwhites have the hind end—the inability to be individuals. But notice, yet again, that this fabled inability requires "conceding" total "white dominance" in everything. Grant the author's case about whites; grant the author a socialist critique of capitalism; grant all of his explicit argument. How, now, shall you also grant the absolutely necessary tacit argument that within the groups of nonwhites, the outsider white dominance remains so powerful that none of the dynamics of group interaction can arise? Individualism, remember, arises only in the context of the opposed interests of groups and persons. Is there no within-group socialization among nonwhites? Do not some persons experience socialization as constraint, thus giving rise to all the motive that individualism as a human phenomenon requires? I believe the answers are dear and that it equally clearly follows that the argument of Scheurich's essay can be sustained only by means of denying fundamental human qualities in nonwhites. I take this very seriously.

Let's return to the beginning. Does it really matter that some—or, for that matter, even all—whites are racists? Judging on foundations that admit differences of human potential into the calculation, surely one must reason not only about the "victim's" power to resist racism but also about the "tyrant's" power to impose it. For certainly persons of, at best, modest powers and only limited resources may blow their racist souls up as large as the fabled frog only to shatter themselves by their efforts. They who have real talents, real claims to be able to impose on others may seriously challenge others to think what a menace they might pose. The contemporary academic world, on the other hand, is simply filled with people with talents too modest to pose a serious challenge to anyone.

The rising racial and ethnic tensions in our society constitute a great moral dilemma, one that shall be well considered and responded to only to the extent that it attracts the concerted attentions of people who can recognize in their co-citizenship the determinative ground of an effective response to the dilemma. This was the point of my and the commission's lament in 1991. It is a mystery to me how something so simple and clear can be made so completely nonsensical. The facts were apparent: Not only had we experienced an alarming rise in racial incidents since the mid-1980s, but also the most palpable evidence appeared first on university campuses. As I indicated in 1988 and afterwards, the campuses that were most embroiled were not the "Redneck Us" of a retrograde region of the country but rather our elite institutions, those from which so much had been hoped a scant 20 years earlier.

Something was wrong in our expectations of racial progress, in our approach to the goal of racial harmony, or in both. The commission continues its inquiry into this vexing question. Accordingly, there is no result to report at this writing. Nevertheless, early hearings, much reading, and wide travel do confirm me in certain hunches. The most important of these is that our campuses are not at war because of intransigent white racism; rather, they are at war because we have succeeded in communicating to our young that they have nothing in common that approaches in importance and value the differences they have. What we witness today is their acting out the emotional consequences of the conviction that their differences constitute the *sum* of their humanity. When they demand that we teach them "who they are," they only repeat what we have told them they most need. When they assume that such lessons will focus on the superficialities of color and ethnicity, they reflect faith that our conduct in policy and in sermon is well founded. In short, we have undermined the erstwhile truth of the dignity of the person and substituted the solidarity of the group as the determinative moral code for our time.

There are other elements of our present conduct that contribute to rising racial and ethnic tensions in the country. But the important fact to emphasize—the fact the Commission on Civil Rights meant to emphasize—was that it is our *present conduct* and not our ancient practices that is most in question.

Section 3

Advancing a White Discourse: A Response to Scheurich

Christine E. Sleeter

The difficulty I experienced writing a response to Scheurich illustrates the accuracy with which he has named a problem: There is very little discourse among whites about white racism, although some very helpful works do exist (e.g., Avis, 1988; Dyer, 1988; McIntosh, 1992; Terry, 1992; Van Dijk, 1993; Wellman, 1977). Rather than taking issue with Scheurich—I believe his argument is correct and very well stated—I will attempt to add to a white discourse about white racism. First, I will identify several initial reactions I had to Scheurich's article that sidestep his challenge, which other white readers may experience.

One reaction I had was to shake my head in agreement: Scheurich said it all; there is nothing I can add. In addition, some readers may also experience self-righteousness for being moved by the article, or guilt for being white. But to applaud his article and experience emotion while reading it, but then to add nothing (and return to what one was doing before reading it), is to avoid the development of a discourse among whites about racism. Scheurich wants us to dialogue, not simply nod our heads.

Another reaction I had was to intellectualize. After all, this is a research journal, and response articles are usually critiques, so I should pick apart Scheurich's argument, question his references, or ask for his data. By "intellectualize," I mean to distance myself from my own participation in a racist system, using scholarly words, quotations, and citations to assert my authority as an "objective," detached expert in an area of study. I could also intellectualize by instructing white readers what to do about racism, again assuming the role of detached expert (and "good" white). Intellectual work that critiques our own racism and informs anti-racist action is helpful; displays of intellectual prowess are not.

Still another reaction was to reflect on the fact that I was probably invited to write this essay (as well as others I have written, I suspect) because of my whiteness, and to consider declining the opportunity to prepare this response, suggesting that it should be given to a person *of* color. It is true that my own successes have been due partially to privileges connected with my race and social class membership. White privilege in accessing the academic spotlight is no more glaringly revealed than in an essay about white racism in a prestigious journal. Indeed, learning to share the spotlight or step aside altogether is one of the things whites need to work on. But whites are not spectators of racism; we are participants, and I cannot help to reconstruct white racism if I do not participate. There definitely are times to step aside, but this is not one of them.

Why Evade a White Discourse on White Racism?

Whites evade a discourse on white racism to protect our own interests. For at least 500 years, Europeans and their descendants have taken huge amounts of land, wealth, labor, and other resources from peoples of color around the world. With the exceptions of small, sporadic attempts at restitution, such as that offered belatedly to Japanese-American concentration camp survivors, white Americans have never returned or repaid what we have taken. Historically, Europeans and Euro-Americans openly justified appropriation of other people's land and labor in terms of presumed European cultural, intellectual, and moral superiority. Today, many of our policies and everyday actions continue the pattern of taking from others, but instead of openly justifying, we evade discussion altogether.

We do so because we do not want to give up the lifestyle, privileges, and resources that we control and that are built on those our ancestors took from others. The very locations on which our homes rest should rightfully belong to Indian nations; very few white people want to admit that, because to do so suggests that perhaps we should return the land we now occupy. Some of us are from families whose wealth was generated partly by slave labor; even if our own familial ancestors did not own slaves or exploit Mexican or Asian laborers, they still did have access to jobs, education, and other opportunities from which whites barred people of color. To open up a discussion of white racism challenges the legitimacy of white peoples' very lives. But I believe that doing so may have the potential of developing among us the willingness to share and give back, and to learn to live with the rest of the world at eye level rather than from above.

Strategies for Evading a Discourse

White people tend to retreat from identifying racism with ourselves; we have strategies that enable us to talk about racial issues, but at the same time remove our own responsibility from scrutiny. One of these strategies is to equate racism with individual prejudice, thus allowing us to assume that every group is racist and to avoid acknowledging the power differential between whites and groups of color. Scheurich noted that whites tend to adhere to individualism and to think of racism as an individual belief rather than a collective act. Consider the following passage from a children's book about racism: "Racism is the mistaken belief by some people that their group, or race, is better than others" (Grunsell, 1991, p. 7). While I applaud the book's effort to help children understand racism, the book barely hints at the power differential between whites and groups of color and the subsequent control whites maintain over most resources in the United States and the world.

At least, however, discussing racism is less evasive than discussing diversity. Cultural differences do exist, of course, and ought to be discussed and expressed. However, whites transmute many issues that are rooted in racism into depoliticized questions of difference, which often take on a "tourist" frame of thinking. For example, a line of action whites could take vis-à-vis Indians, Mexicans, Puerto Ricans, or Hawaiians, is to return good land and control over that land. But few of us take such action seriously. Instead, we tend to show interest in such groups by learning about certain cultural artifacts and practices (and then sometimes appropriating them), and paying homage to Indian, Latino, and Hawaiian heroes and contributions to white culture. Unfortunately, that is too often the form multicultural education takes. Multicultural education is sometimes criticized for failing to address racism directly (Mattai, 1992). To the extent that this criticism is valid, I believe it is largely a result of the low tolerance whites have for acknowledging racism.

Equating ethnicity with race is a related strategy for evading racism. When whites conceptualize cultural diversity within the United States, we usually subdivide white groups by ethnic origins, placing groups such as Germans, Poles, and Scots within the same conceptual plane as African-Americans and Native Americans. This conceptual plane highlights cultural heritage; it denies whiteness as a phenomenon worth scrutiny and, with it, white racism (Dyer, 1988).

We semantically evade our own role in perpetuating white racism by constructing sentences that allow us to talk about racism while removing ourselves from discussion. One such semantic evasion is to personify racism, making it (rather than ourselves) the subject of sentences. This allows us to say, for example, "Racism forced urban housing to deteriorate" (I heard variations of this phrase permeating a student report recently). Who was responsible for the deterioration of urban housing? Naming responsibility moves us toward a critique of institutionalized white supremacy and our own role in that institution, and toward actions *we* can take to make changes.

We also evade our role semantically by avoiding use of a subject altogether; passive sentence constructions allow us to talk about racism without ever naming our own complicity. For example, consider the following sentence: "Africans were brought to the colonies and forced to labor a lifetime for no wages" (McKissack & McKissack, 1990, p. 16). *Who* brought them and forced them? The sentence does not say. Nor does this passage: "If LD-labeled children are considered to be at risk, language minority LD children are considered to be doubly so. Not because of conditions inherent in such children, but because of the institutional cultures that surround them" (Richardson, Casanova, Placier, & Guilfoyle, 1989, p. 116). I agree with the critique offered here and have undoubtedly written many such sentences myself, but the construction, which is very common in our discourse, removes the necessity of specifying that *white people* (English-speaking, in this case) are the ones who consider language minority children to be at risk.

If we find it difficult to discuss white racism or even to specify the subjects of our sentences related to race, we may identify that difficulty as rooted in fear and ignorance. The fear could be of offending other white people or of having to change our own lives in order to confront racism. The ignorance might be based on our lack of critical reflection on how white racism works, our lack of practice in talking about it, or our habit of not taking seriously what people of color say.

From Discourse to Action

My discussion here has focused largely on discursive evasions of white racism (for a detailed discussion of discursive evasions of racism, see Van Dijk, 1993). Ultimately, a discourse among whites about racism must lead to action. Academicians can learn to talk proficiently about almost anything, but the point is what we plan to do to reduce or eliminate white supremacy. Our own role as whites is rather different from that of people of color, because of the power that accompanies our color.

A helpful analogy of white women is to consider how men should be involved in eliminating sexism. Eliminating sexism requires changing male behavior; men cannot simply opt out and leave sexism to women to address. Changes in male behavior would include learning to be quiet and not dominate conversations; not to speak for women; recognizing that male privileges nurture a sense of self-assurance that men tend to take for granted and do not see, even when they are trying to help. Changes in men would also include learning to share with us in a reciprocal fashion that respects what women can do; learning to step aside; learning to listen as nondefensively as possible when women try to tell them what bothers us; and generally taking us seriously. Men's roles would also include actively supporting anti-sexist policies and programs, even (and especially) when they are unpopular with one's male friends and associates, and educating other men in order to win their support for anti-sexist policies and behaviors.

Now replace the term *sexism* with *white racism*, and the appropriate gender groups with racial groups. (I do not mean to imply here that challenging sexism helps to address racism. It does not; white women are as racist as white men. But I find the analogy helpful.) This begins to provide an agenda for work white people need to do on ourselves.

Section 4

A Difficult, Confusing, Painful Problem That Requires Many Voices, Many Perspectives

James Joseph Scheurich

Racism is without question a most confusing, difficult, and painful issue. It goes to the very heart of how we are to live together in what Toni Morrison (1992) has recently called "the wholly racialized society that is the United States" (p. xii). It goes to the very heart of that resurgent dream of both a truly democratic community that respects, appreciates, and cares equally for all of its individual members and an educational system that does the same for all of its students.

Unfortunately, the distance between the confusion, difficulty, and pain, on the one hand, and the dream, on the other, is considerable. How to map the journey of a large, complicated, multiracial society or educational system from one side to the other is, in my opinion, beyond the capabilities of any one person, group, perspective, or political position. I would suggest, therefore, that this particular journey requires an openness that includes all voices.

My chief response, consequently, to both W. B. Allen and Christine Sleeter is appreciation. We need multiple perspectives, no matter how much those perspectives might differ or conflict. This does not mean that I do not have disagreements or agreements with the respondents; it does mean that my rejoinder is meant to continue the conversation rather than to privilege my "voice" over others. In other words, Allen's strong disagreements with my point of view are just as important for all of us as Sleeter's agreements are.

Christine Sleeter's Response

As she indicates, Sleeter is largely in agreement with my article, and, thus, she chooses to advance the white discourse on white racism. Her chief topics are how and why we whites avoid confronting our racism. The question that her response raises for me is the same one that I struggled with during the writing of my original article: How can I discuss or critique white racism so that the critique will be heard by white professors who are anti-racist but who have not tended to actively consider whether their professorial practices might unintentionally or unknowingly reproduce racial inequalities?

Increasingly, my conclusion in this regard is that critique is not enough, even though this is the strongest feature, in my opinion, of both my original article and Sleeter's response. For most of us to hear something about ourselves that is difficult or painful or embarrassing usually requires that we feel that the critic is also supportive and caring. If what I hear from someone I do not personally know, as in a journal article, is heavy on criticism and light on compassion, I will tend to find it more difficult to be receptive to the message. If this is true, one problem for me, and I think for Sleeter also, is that our critiques are not sufficiently balanced with care and compassion. This is not to say, however, that the critiques of white racism should be diminished; rather, they should be deeply intertwined with a caring regard for our white colleagues that is strongly communicated within our writing. Otherwise, we may end up speaking only to the choir.

While I was thinking about my rejoinder to Sleeter's response, two serendipitous events helped me to become clearer on this balance of critique and compassion. The first occurred when one of my students stopped by my office to tell me about a course on racism that she had taken during this past summer. In the midst of the conversation she recommended an article to me, Beverly Daniel Tatum's "Talking About Race, Learning About Racism: The Application of Racial Identity Development Theory in the Classroom" (1992). On the same day the most recent edition of the *Phi Delta Kappan* arrived in the mail. As I was leafing through it, I noticed an article by Gary R. Howard, entitled "Whites in Multicultural Education: Rethinking Our Role" (1993).

While neither of these articles directly addresses racism among white professors, they both discuss how whites can learn to understand our own racism. What struck me most about these two articles, though, was the remarkable balance of critique and compassion. Both Beverly Daniel Tatum, a black woman who teaches university classes on racism, primarily for white students, and Gary R. Howard, a white man who directs a national K–12 curriculum and staff development program focusing on multicultural education, were able to critique white racism in an unflinching way while communicating a strong sense of care and compassion for whites who undertake the difficult process of confronting their own racism. I think Tatum and Howard have shown Sleeter and me a better way, though the onus of that judgment should certainly weigh much heavier on my own article than on Sleeter's response.

W. B. Allen's Response

W. B. Allen's response was obviously much different from Sleeter's. He is in almost total disagreement with my point of view.[1] My first response is to say to myself and to others who agree with me that it is extremely important, a necessity, that we truly hear what Allen has to say. The crucial significance of all viewpoints, especially conflicting ones, cannot be underestimated. My second response is to feel pressed against a wall by the strength of his passionate disagreement. I am literally accused of reproducing that which I intended to oppose, that is, white racism. While I do not agree with his judgment, I cannot say with full certainty that Allen is wrong on this. One of my fears when I began this enterprise was that I would do exactly what Allen claims I did—that I would hurt more than I would help, that I would expand white racism rather than decrease it.

I am also concerned about his judgment that, out of an assumption of white superiority, I denied individuality to all races in addition to whites, a point of view that, if true, would be as heinous as Allen contends. This was certainly not my intention. The original impetus for my article was to follow the advice of scholars of color that we whites ought to begin talking about our own racism (e.g., hooks, 1990). But one of the most significant barriers, according to several scholars (e.g., Ogbu, 1978), that prevents whites from seeing our own racism is an overemphasis on individuality and an underawareness of our racial group status. People of color, on the other hand, because this "wholly racialized" society persistently treats them as racialized rather than as individuals, experience whites as equally racialized.

I do not mean by these points to imply that anyone is less individual than anyone else, no matter what a person's race is. Each one of us is an idiosyncratic and shifting intersection of many influences, including race, gender, class, and sexual orientation. But this idiosyncrasy does not, unfortunately, cancel the substantial and persistent effects of the highly inequitable distribution of power, resources, and wealth by race in this country, nor does it cancel the overt or the unintended ways that we maintain and reinforce that inequitable distribution.

I have other disagreements with W. B. Allen: I disagree with his negative portraits of constructivism, bilingualism, and multiculturalism, and I disagree that recent examples of overt racism are more related to perspectives like mine than to powerful structural barriers to racial equality. But, and I cannot overemphasize this point, I do not want my view to be seen as more important than Allen's, Sleeter's, or others. The best result of this three-person exchange would be for it to provoke many other individuals to join the conversation.

Note for Chapter 1, Section 4

1. In my opinion, the general orientation of my original article, contrary to Allen's characterization of it, would be within what Banks (1993) has recently labeled as "transformative academic knowledge" or what West (1990) has called "a cultural politics of difference."

Chapter 2

Preface

Chapter 2, which is probably the most cited piece I have published, is also composed of four sections. The first section is "Coloring Epistemology," which Michelle D. Young and I published in 1997 in *Educational Researcher*. The second and third sections are by Cynthia A. Tyson and Steven I. Miller, respectively. These latter two are responses to "Coloring Epistemology." The fourth section of chapter 2 is the rejoinder that Michelle and I wrote in reaction to the two responses. "Coloring," with its focus on epistemology, takes anti-racist scholarship to the very heart of research. It is our attempt, as whites, to take seriously the contention of scholars of color that the white-dominated educational and social science research communities are much more racist than is commonly accepted, even in their epistemologies. We agree with much of this criticism, and Michelle and I, explicitly positioning ourselves as whites, were trying to explain to other whites how this criticism could be an accurate one. Thus, both this chapter and the prior one provide examples of taking a public anti-racist stance and of conducting a respectful, hopefully self-critical, dialogue with others on white racism.

Section 1

Coloring Epistemology: Are Our Research Epistemologies Racially Biased?

James Joseph Scheurich and Michelle D. Young

Respected scholars of color have suggested (e.g., Stanfield, 1985, 1993, 1994), even within the pages of *Educational Researcher* (J.A. Banks, 1993, 1995; Gordon, Miller, & Rollock, 1990), that the epistemologies we typically use in educational research may be racially biased. They have argued that our epistemologies,[1] not our use of them, but the epistemologies themselves, are racially biased ways of knowing, implicitly proposing, thus, a new category of racism that could be labeled *epistemological racism*. There has been, however, a provocative lack of response—pro or con—to this race-oriented argument by leading educational methodologists in journals of education.[2] But this lack of response is in curious contrast to the lively and contentious debates on other epistemological issues, such as quantitative versus qualitative (e.g., Cizek, 1995), objectivity versus subjectivity (e.g., Heshusius, 1994), validity (e.g., Lenzo, 1995; Moss, 1994), or paradigmatic issues in general (e.g., Bereiter, 1994; Delandshere & Petrosky, 1994; Gage, 1989).

If we were among those raising this race-oriented issue, we would wonder why our efforts to argue that the epistemologies of educational research were racially biased provoked virtually no response, particularly among those who author the quantitative and qualitative research methods textbooks we all typically use. We would certainly wonder whether our argument was ignored because it raised the disquieting issue of race, because it was thought to be a weak or irrelevant argument, or because the argument was simply not understood. Unfortunately, we might also wonder whether this was just one more incidence of Ellison's (1972) "invisible man" syndrome, of whites ignoring racial issues and people of color.

As researchers whose race is white and who have written and presented on both epistemological and racial issues (Scheurich, 1993, 1994b; Young 1995a, 1995b), we want to offer a substantive response to the argument of the scholars of color who have contended that our research epistemologies are racially biased. It will be our claim that the lack of response to date to the racial bias argument is not primarily a function of overt or covert racism, as some might argue, or of institutional or societal racism, as others might suggest. Instead, we will contend that this silence is a function of a different lack—a lack of understanding among researchers as to how race is a critically significant epistemological problem in educational research.

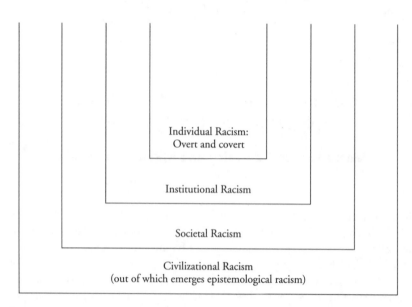

Figure 1

X Our purpose then is to discuss how our range of research epistemologies — including positivism, postpositivisms, neorealisms, interpretivisms, constructivisms, the critical tradition, and postmodernisms/poststructuralisms[3] — can be understood as racially biased in a way that will (a) facilitate an understanding of just what *epistemological racism*[4] is; (b) ignite the kind of spirited debate that has occurred around other, arguably lesser, research issues; (c) draw some of the prominent research epistemologists, especially those who author methods textbooks, into this debate; and (d) provoke additional efforts among scholars of all races to address this problem. We will pursue this purpose by discussing five categories of racism and their linkages to research, and we will conclude with some suggestions about what initially needs to be done to address *epistemological racism.*

The first two categories of racism we shall discuss— overt and covert racism — are typically defined as operating at the individual level; the next two are organizational and social categories — institutional and societal racism — and, in effect, create the social context for the prior two categories. The final one is a civilizational category, and it, we will contend, creates or constitutes the possibility for all of the prior four categories.[5] Further, it is the latter category that is the salient one for discussions regarding the racial bias of research epistemologies. Figure 1 illustrates and positions these categories; it also graphically depicts the structure of this essay. The individual level, which includes both overt and covert racism, sits within the institutional level, which sits within the societal level. All of these four sit, in a hierarchy of smaller to larger and broader, inside the largest and broadest category, the civilizational level.[6]

Two Categories of Individual Racism — Overt and Covert Racism

⚹ Racial bias or racism is typically understood in popular culture and in academia in terms of individual acts of overt prejudice that are racially based, i.e., *overt racism* (see, for example, Kluegel & Smith, 1986; Ogbu, 1978; Reyes & Halcon, 1988; Rizvi, 1993; Scheurich, 1993; Tatum, 1992). For example, if a college professor makes a racial slur during a class lecture, this is seen as overt racism. Overt racism, then, is a public, conscious, and intended act by a person or persons from one race with the intent of doing damage to a person or persons of another race chiefly because of the race of the second person or persons.[7] While there are many in the United States who are overt racists, there is a general social consensus, at least at the public level,[8] that these behaviors are socially unacceptable (though verbalizations of overt racism are constitutionally protected in most cases).

A second kind of individual racism is covert racism. The only real difference between overt and covert racism is that the latter is not explicitly public. For example, a superintendent may consciously not promote a Hispanic-American to the principalship in a majority white geographical area even though the Hispanic-American applicant may be the most qualified. While this superintendent may be consciously acting in a racist manner, she or he will publicly provide a socially acceptable reason for her or his decision. Persons making covert, racially biased decisions do not explicitly broadcast their intentions; instead, they veil them or provide reasons that society will find more palatable. A public consensus, though perhaps not as strong as the one for overt racism, also exists regarding covert acts of racism, and, in fact, many laws prohibit such acts, particularly in the area of employment practices.

Whether covert or overt, however, racism in the United States is overwhelmingly seen as an individual phenomenon (Kluegel & Smith, 1986; Ogbu, 1978). And this is as much true in academia as in popular culture (Scheurich, 1993). If a person answers "no" to the question of whether she or he is racist, the respondent typically means that she or he does not, as an individual, engage in conscious, intended racism or that she or he is not, as an individual, consciously racist. Researchers, just like other members of this society, typically judge their own lack of racism based on personal evaluations that they do not, as an individual, have a negative judgment of another person just because that person is a member of a particular race. While this individualized, conscious, moral, or ethical commitment to anti-racism is a significant and meaningful individual and historical accomplishment, the fact that it restricts our understanding of racism to an individualized ethical arena is a barrier to a broader, more comprehensive understanding of racism — for society and for researchers.

Understanding that we need to get beyond issues of individual racism, whether overt or covert, is critical to initiating a consideration of whether our research epistemologies are racially biased. For example, if we, as researchers, were to read an article that argued that our research epistemologies were racially biased and if we disagreed with this argument because we did not consider ourselves, as individuals, to be consciously or intentionally racist, this judgment would indicate that we did not understand epistemological racism. The error here is that racial critiques of research epistemologies have virtually nothing to do with whether an individual researcher is overtly or covertly racist. A researcher could be adamantly anti-racist in thought and deed and still be using a research epistemology that, given our later discussion of epistemological racism, could be judged to be racially biased. Consequently, researchers considering the issue of epistemological racism need to get beyond the question of whether personally they are racists because this latter judgment is not related to judgments about epistemological racism.

Institutional Racism

Institutional racism exists when institutions or organizations, including educational ones, have standard operating procedures (intended or unintended) that hurt members of one or more races in relation to members of the dominant race (for further discussions of institutional racism, see Feagin & Vera, 1995; Hacker, 1992; Reyes & Halcon, 1988). Institutional racism also exists when institutional or organizational cultures, rules, habits, or symbols have the same biasing effect. For example, if an institution's procedures or culture favor whites for promotion, such as promotion to a full professorship or to a principalship, over persons *of* color, this is institutional racism. If a school's standard pedagogical method is culturally congruent with the culture of white students but not with the cultures of students of color (a widespread problem — see, for example, Cummins, 1986; Hilliard, 1992; J. E. King, 1991; Ladson-Billings, 1994; Lee, Lomotey, & Shujaa, 1990; among many others), this is institutional racism.

One particularly important type of institutional racism that occurs in research communities arises when racially biased beliefs or assumptions are embedded within a research discipline or a particular community of researchers or within the variables, labels, or concepts of a discipline or community (Paredes, 1977; Stanfield, 1985; 1993a, 1993b). For example, if educational researchers commonly use, as they once typically did, a phrase like "culturally disadvantaged" or "cultural deprivation" to indicate why some students of color did not succeed in school, this is institutional racism (McCarthy, 1993). While not using this particular phrase ("institutional racism"), Gordon et al. (1990) have argued, that this kind of racism is endemic to the social sciences: *"Much of the social science knowledge* [italics added] referable to Blacks, Latinos, and Native Americans ignores or demeans [members of these races] and . . . often presents distorted interpretations of minority conditions and potentials" (p. 14).

But Gordon et al. (1990) are not the only ones who have made this point about the endemic institutional racism of social science research. James Banks (1995), Barakan (1992), and Shuey (1958), among many others spread across the different social science disciplines, have asserted that "scientific" knowledge has commonly been based on racially biased assumptions, labels, perspectives, etc. From Linneaus' 1735 categorization that related race to psychological attributes and positioned the white race as having superior psychological attributes (Webster, 1992) and Caldwell's similar contentions in 1830 to *The Bell Curve* (Herrnstein & Murray, 1994) and the works of Shockley (1992) in the present era, scientists and social scientists have used racist ideas regarding inherited characteristics of different racial groups (J. A. Banks, 1995).

Unfortunately, educational researchers have been and continue to be essential participants in this reproduction and elaboration of institutional racism. Examples of such racism by educational researchers in the past are the mental and intellectual measures taken from "cranium estimates," "theories of racial difference" taken from anthropology and biology, "theories of race and intelligence" taken from genetics, and "curriculum theories" that argued that "Black families and Black communities . . . were 'defective' and 'dysfunctional'" (McCarthy, 1993, p. 332; see, also, Gould, 1981). While the use of these racially oriented "cranium estimates" or other such categories would now be considered unacceptable, label-based institutional racism continues to exist. For example, higher percentages of students of color are currently more likely to be labeled "at risk," "learning disabled," or "emotionally disturbed" (see, for example, Cuban, 1989; Mercer, 1988; Ortiz, García, Wheeler, & Maldonado-Colon, 1986).

But, while institutional racism is more widespread than commonly realized (see Feagin & Vera, 1995; Hacker, 1992) and while expanding our understanding of it is critically important, institutional racism is not epistemological racism. For instance, one could use either racist or anti-racist concepts or labels within a positivist or a constructivist epistemology, but research epistemologies themselves are not necessarily a function of the concepts or labels with which they are used. (This could be argued to be incorrect for the critical tradition; many of its advocates would consider racist assumptions to be incongruent with its epistemology, but this will be addressed later.) Our point, similar to the point we have made about individual racism, is that researchers who think that epistemological racism is equal to institutional racism misunderstand the former.

Societal Racism

The second type of social racism is *societal racism*. Societal racism is similar to institutional racism, but it exists on a broader, society-wide scale, though societal racism has received even less attention than institutional racism. In fact, it usually takes major social conflicts, like those of the mid and late 1960s, or major social events, like the O. J. Simpson trial, for societal racism to receive broad social attention, as, for example, in the "Report of the National Advisory Commission on Civil

Disorder" (National Advisory Commission on Civil Disorder, 1968). This report is, of course, the one that used the often-quoted statement that "Our Nation is moving toward two societies, one—black, one white—separate and unequal" (p. 1). This report also argued that the "most fundamental" (p. 5) cause of the inequitable bifurcation was a long-term national history of "White racism" (p. 5) and that this racism deeply pervaded numerous facets of national life, from employment and housing to education and political representation.

Societal racism, then, can be said to exist when prevailing societal or cultural assumptions, norms, concepts, habits, expectations, etc. favor one race over one or more other races (Feagin & Vera, 1995; Hacker, 1992). For example, while it is certainly true that there is a complex range of definitions of what good leadership is within the mainstream of public life in the United States, that range is actually relatively limited when compared with definitions of good leadership in other cultures, inside or outside the United States. The widely respected anthropologist James Clifford (1988) has demonstrated how mainstream definitions of leadership served as a disadvantage to a Native American tribe known as the Mashpee. In a United States trial held to determine the validity of the Mashpee's status as a tribe, the mainstream culture's definition of leadership was used to weaken the testimony of the Mashpee chief, especially in terms of proving whether the chief was a "true" or "real" leader. This "proof" of a leadership deficiency was then used to undermine the legitimacy of the Mashpee's claim to be a tribe.

Similarly, if the socially promoted idea—through the media, through legal practices, through governmental programs—of what a good family is, is primarily drawn from the dominant culture's social, historical experience, that is societal racism. The privileging of one view over others, like the favoring of a white middle-class view of families over an African-American[9] view of families, results in social practices that have direct negative effects on families that deviate from the dominant norm (Billingsley, 1968; Hill, 1972; Littlejohn-Blake & Darling, 1993; Stanfield, 1985, p. 408; Willie, 1993). The idea that a Mashpee definition of leadership or an African-American definition of a family might be considered equal to mainstream definitions is typically not seen as reasonable or warranted in formal or informal social practices.

However, societal racism is, also, not epistemological racism. The latter is drawn from a more fundamental level than societal racism. Epistemological racism comes from or emerges out of what we have labeled the civilizational level—the deepest, most primary level of a culture of people. The civilization level is the level that encompasses the deepest, most primary assumptions about the nature of reality (ontology), the ways of knowing that reality (epistemology), and the disputational contours of right and wrong or morality and values (axiology)—in short, presumptions about the real, the true, and the good. But these presumptions emerge from a broader terrain than just the United States; the presumptions to which we refer are fundamental to Euro-American modernism, the historical period within which the ontologies, epistemologies, and axiologies of contemporary western civilization have arisen (see, for example, Bernstein, 1992, or Lyotard, 1984). Our argument, then, is that epistemological racism is drawn from the civilizational level, and, thus, it is to the civilizational level that we must turn to engage directly the question of whether our research epistemologies are racially biased or not.

Civilizational Racism

The civilizational level is the level of broad civilizational assumptions, assumptions that, though they constrict the nature of our world and our experience of it, are not typically conscious to most members of a civilization (Foucault, 1979, 1988). These assumptions are deeply embedded in how those members think and in what they name "the world" or "the Real" through various categories or concepts (Said, 1979; Stanfield, 1985, 1994). But these assumptions are different for different civilizations, such as the Hopi civilization (Loftin, 1991) or the Zuni civilization (Roscoe, 1991), and, thus, each civilization constructs the world differently for its inhabitants; not all people [i.e., civilizations, in this case] 'know' in the same way" (Stanfield, 1985, p. 396). In addition, large, complex civilizations often include a dominant culture and one or more subordinate cultures. In this context, subordinate cultures, races, and other groups often have different civilizational assumptions: "Just as the material realities of the powerful and the dominated produce separate [social, historical experiences] . . . each [racial or social group] may also have distinctive epistemologies or theories of knowledge" (Collins, 1991, p. 204). One consequence is that "[d]ominant racial group members and subordinate racial group members do not think and interpret realities in the same way because of their divergent structural positions, histories, and cultures" (Stanfield, 1985, p. 400).[10] For instance, "What is considered theory in the dominant academic community is not necessarily what counts as theory for women-of-color" (Anzaldúa, 1990, p. xxv; see, also, J. A. Banks, 1993, pp. 7-8; 1995, p. 16; Cose, 1993; Collins, 1991).

The name for the Euro-American culture's construction of "the world" or "the Real," as was noted above, is modernism. Modernism is an epistemological, ontological, and axiological network or grid that "makes" the world as the dominant western culture knows and sees it (Foucault, 1970, 1972, 1979, 1988; Frankenberg, 1993; Goldberg, 1993; Stanfield, 1985; West, 1993a, 1993b). Though this grid has evolved and changed somewhat, it has, nonetheless, maintained a kind of coherence and consistency, particularly in terms of some of its primary assumptions (that is, its civilizational level assumptions). One of these primary assumptions, the one we are addressing here, is civilizational racism.

Beginning with the modernist period, European colonial and territorial expansion was typically undertaken under the rationale of the supremacy of white civilization, along with other rationales, such as those about economics and religion. For instance, Hacker (1992) asserts that "For at least half a dozen centuries . . . 'white' has implied a higher civilization based on superior inheritance" (p. 7; see also, Takaki, 1993). To the English attending the Globe Theatre to see Shakespeare's *The Tempest*, "Caliban [the character who epitomizes the native people of the 'new' world] represented what Europeans had been when they were *lower* [italics added] on the scale of development" (Takaki, 1993, p. 32), while Prospero (the character who depicts the English conqueror) declares that he came to the new world "to be the lord on't" (Shakespeare, quoted in Takaki, 1993, p. 35; see also, Feagin & Vera, 1995; Frankenberg, 1993; Goldberg, 1993; Harris, 1993; Stanfield, 1985; Webster, 1992; West, 1993a, pp. 3–32). Widely circulated racial hierarchies and exclusions such as these became, then, a central feature in the emergence of western modernism and modernist thought, and, consequently, white racism or white supremacy became interlaced or interwoven into the founding fabric of modernist western civilization (for an extended discussion of this point, see Goldberg, 1993; see also, Stanfield, 1985).[11]

These racial rationales were central, along with other rationales, to the founding of the United States. Taking land from and killing Native Americans was justified by the whites' definition of property as well as the supposed supremacy of white civilization, like that depicted in Thomas More's *Utopia* (Takaki, 1993, p. 35; see, also, Feagin & Vera, 1995; Hacker, 1992; Harris, 1993). Similar rationales were used in taking the Southwest from the Mexicans, whom Stephen F. Austin, one of the prominent political leaders of the "Texas revolution," disparagingly called "a mongrel Spanish-Indian and negro race" (De Leon, 1983, p. 12; see, also, Takaki, 1993). The enslavement of African-Americans and the "subsequent decades of Jim Crow laws, peonage, tenancy, lynchings and second class citizenship" (West, 1993a, p. 256) were also justified in the same racially exclusionary terms (Feagin & Vera, 1995; Hacker, 1992; Harris, 1993; Takaki, 1993), though, of course, these justifications were not the only justifications driving slavery or the appropriation of Native American and Mexican-American land.

While this is an extremely brief summary of a complex argument about white racial supremacy and the fact that it was interlaced within the founding assumptions of western civilization, our point can be made in a simpler way. The white race, what Stanfield (1985) has called "a privileged subset of the population" (p. 389), has unquestionably dominated western civilization during all of the modernist period (hundreds of years). When any group — within a large, complex civilization — significantly dominates other groups for hundreds of years, the ways of the dominant group (its epistemologies, its ontologies, its axiologies) not only become the dominant ways of that civilization, but these ways also become so deeply embedded that they typically are seen as "natural" or appropriate norms rather than as historically evolved social constructions (Stanfield, 1985). To a large degree, the dominant group, whatever its composition, makes its own "community the center of the universe and the conceptual frame that constrains all thought" (Gordon et al., 1990, p. 15). Thus, the dominant group creates or constructs "the world" or "the Real" and does so in its own image, in terms of its ways and its social-historical experiences (J. A. Banks, 1993a; Collins, 1991; Minh-ha, 1989; Morrison, 1992; Stanfield, 1985, 1994; West, 1993a; see, especially, Said, 1979, for an entire volume that discusses how the West gave "reality" to its construct of "the Orient").

In this view, ontologies, epistemologies, and axiologies are not outside history or sociology; they are deeply interwoven within the social histories of particular civilizations and within particular groups within those civilizations. As Gordon et al. (1990) assert, "Knowledge, technology, and the production of knowledge are cultural products . . . . Knowledge production operates within communicentric [ontological and epistemological] frames of reference, which dominate and enable it" (p. 14). Similarly, Stanfield (1994) has said

> The experiences that construct paradigms in sciences and humanities are derivatives of cultural baggage imported into intellectual enterprises by privileged residents of historically specific societies and world systems. This is important to point out, because it is common for scholars to lapse into internal analyses while discussing paradigms and thus to ignore the rather common sense fact that sciences and humanities are products of specific cultural and historical contexts that shape the character of intellectual word. (pp. 181–182)

Or, as James Banks (1993) more simply states, "All knowledge reflects the values and interests of its creators" (p. 4).

Consider whom the major, influential philosophers, writers, politicians, corporate leaders, social scientists, educational leaders (e.g., Kant, Flaubert, Churchill, Henry Ford, Weber, Dewey) have been over the course of western modernism. They have virtually all been white. And it is they who have constructed the world we live in — named it, discussed it, explained it. It is they who have developed the ontological and axiological categories or concepts like individuality, truth, education, free enterprise, good conduct, social welfare, etc., that we use to think (that thinks us?) and that we use to socialize and educate children. This racially exclusive group has also developed the epistemologies, the legitimated ways of knowing (e.g., positivism, neorealisms, postpositivisms, interpretivisms, constructivisms, the critical tradition, and postmodernisms/poststructuralisms) that we use. And it is these epistemologies and their allied ontologies and axiologies, taken together as a lived web or fabric of social constructions, that make or construct "the world" or "the Real" (and that relegate other socially constructed "worlds," like that of African-Americans or the Cherokee, to the "margins" of our social life and to the margins in terms of legitimated research epistemologies).

These influential whites and their "world-making" or "reality-making" activities or practices, however, are not separate from the social history within which they live: "all knowledge is relative to the context in which it is generated" (Gordon et al., 1990, p. 15). And, thus, "when academics and public opinion leaders construct knowledge[,] . . . they are influenced by the ideas, assumptions, and norms of the cultures and subsocieties in which they are socialized" (J. A. Banks, 1995, p. 16). Just as Julius Caesar was "constructed" by the social history of his particular group, saw and understood the world in terms of the social constructions of his people in their time and place, the influential authors of modernism have been constructed by their position, place, and time. Just as Caesar did not see the world from the point of view of other cultures that Rome dominated, these influential western modernists did not see the world from within the epistemologies and ontologies of other races and cultures inside or outside of western modernism. "How we create, define, and validate social knowledge [and, thus, reality] is determined largely through our cultural context" (Stanfield, 1985, p. 388).[12]

Our argument, however, is not that these influential white individuals were involved in a racial conspiracy or moral bad faith, but that these individuals can only name and know from within the social context available to them, from within the social history in which they live. While we seem to have little trouble understanding that those far away in time existed in terms of their social contexts—i.e., Julius Caesar—we seem to resist understanding this about ourselves. We, as our predecessors did, live, understand, work, think, and act within a particular social history, within a particular social construction. We do not live, in some universal sense, above culture or history; we live inside a culture, inside a civilizational social construction; we live in the terms and ways of a particular social history.[13]

This, then, is our central argument about epistemological racism. Epistemologies, along with their related ontologies and epistemologies, arise out of the social history of a particular social group. Different social groups, races, cultures, societies, or civilizations evolve different epistemologies, each of which reflects the social history of that group, race, culture, society, or civilization; that is, no epistemology is context-free. Yet, all of the epistemologies currently legitimated in education arise exclusively out of the social history of the dominant white race. They do not arise out of the social history of African-Americans, Hispanic-Americans, Native Americans, Asian-Americans, or other racial/cultural groups—social histories that are much different than that of the dominant race (a difference due at least partially to the historical experience of racism itself [see, for example, Collins, 1991]). Cornell West (1993a) validates this judgment when he says "social practices . . . [and research is a social practice] are best understood and explained . . . by situating them within . . . cultural traditions" (p. 267). It is, then, in this sense that scholars of color contend that the dominant research epistemologies are racially biased.[14]

By epistemological racism, then, we do not mean that the researchers using, say, positivism or postmodernism are overtly or covertly racist as individuals. Nor do we mean that epistemological racism is a conscious institutional or societal conspiracy in favor of whites (B. M. Gordon, 1993, p. 267). Epistemological racism means that our current range of research epistemologies—positivism to postmodernisms/poststructuralisms—arise out of the social history and culture of the dominant race, that these epistemologies logically reflect and reinforce that social history and that racial group (while excluding the epistemologies of other races/cultures), and that this has negative results for people of color in general and scholars of color in particular. In other words, our "logics of inquiry" (Stanfield, 1993a) are the social products and practices of the social, historical experiences of whites, and, therefore, these products and practices carry forward the social history of that group and exclude the epistemologies of other social groups. But, again, the critical problem—for any of us, both whites and people of color—is that the resulting epistemological racism, in addition to unnecessarily restricting or excluding the range of possible epistemologies, creates profoundly negative consequences for those of other racial cultures with different epistemologies, ontologies, and axiologies.

Some Negative Consequences of Epistemological Racism

First, epistemologies and research that arise out of other social histories, such as African-American social history or Cherokee social history, are not typically considered legitimate within the mainstream research community (see Anzaldúa, 1990; Collins, 1991; B. M. Gordon 1990, 1993; Minh-ha, 1989; Sarris, 1993; Stanfield, 1993a, 1993b, 1994; among many others). As Reyes and Halcon (1988) suggest, "the traditional Euro-centric perspective used to evaluate their [scholars of color] scholarship disadvantages nontraditional [race-based] research because predominantly white male academics lack the appropriate cultural perspectives from which to judge its real merit" (p. 307). Similarly, Collins (1991) contends that "[w]hile Black women can produce knowledge claims that contest those advanced by the white male community, this community does not grant that Black women scholars have competing knowledge claims based in another [equally warranted] knowledge validation process" (p. 204; see also, Stanfield, 1994, p. 176). Or, as Sarris (1993) asks, "Can Apache stories, songs, and so forth be read (or heard) and thus understood in terms of Euroamerican-specific expectations of language and narrative [i.e., Euro-American epistemologies]" (p. 427)?

Second, there has been a large chorus of scholars of color (including Anderson, 1993; Anzaldúa, 1990; Collins, 1991; Paredes, 1977; Sarris, 1993; Stanfield, 1994; among others) who have contended that dominant group epistemologies and methodologies—the epistemologies and methods themselves and not just "bad" applications of these epistemologies and methodologies—tend to distort the lives of other racial groups. For example, Gordon et al. (1990) have asserted that epistemologies create profoundly negative consequences for those of other racial cultures with different epistemologies, ontologies, and axiologies:

> Examination of the social and educational research knowledge bases relative to Afro-Americans indicated that these sciences have traditionally attempted to understand the life experiences of Afro-Americans from a narrow cultrocentric perspective and against equally narrow cultrocentric standards [i.e., epistemological racism].

Consequently, as Stanfield (1985) has said, mainstream "[s]ocial science knowledge production about racial minorities still dwells on the pathological and on the sensational" (p. 411). A result of this is that these negative distortions pass into the dominant culture as "truth," thus becoming the basis of individual, group, and institutional attitudes, decisions, practices, and policies (i.e., institutional and societal racism). Another result is that these distortions are often enculturated into those who are the victims of the distortions (hooks, 1990; Rebolledo, 1990), especially children, who have less ability to resist (McCarthy, 1993; Stevenson & Ellsworth, 1993; Weinberg, 1993), necessitating "painful struggle[s] of accepting and rejecting internalized negative and disenabling self-conceptions" (West, 1993a, p. 270; see, also, J. A. Banks, 1993). A further result is that frequently, "minority scholar's time is consumed in efforts to refute or neutralize fallacious findings, questionable theories, and inappropriate interpretations" (Gordon et al., 1990, p. 16) of mainstream research and scholarly commentary.

Third, the dominant research epistemologies—from positivism to postmodernisms—implicitly favor white people because they accord most easily with their social history (J. A. Banks, 1993; B. M. Gordon, 1993; Stanfield, 1985). Thus, even though it may be unintended, the "clothes" that an epistemology could be said to be fit better and are more comfortable to white researchers because white researchers themselves are a product of the social history of whites, just as the dominant epistemologies are a product of white social history. That is, the range of epistemologies that have arisen from the social history of whites "fit" whites because they themselves, the nature of the university and of legitimated scholarship and knowledge, and the specifications of different research methodologies are all cultural products of white social history. While scholars of color have had to wear these "white" clothes (be bi-cultural) so that they could succeed in research communities, however sociologically, historically, or culturally ill-fitting those clothes might be, white scholars have virtually never had to think about wearing the epistemological clothes of people of color or even to consider the idea of such "strange" apparel. The negative consequence for scholars of color, however, is that they must learn and become accomplished in epistemologies that arise out of a social history that has been profoundly hostile to their race and that ignores or excludes alternative race-based epistemologies because mainstream research communities have assumed that their epistemologies are not derived from any particular group's social history, i.e., are free of any specific history or culture. That scholars of color have successfully become epistemologically bi-cultural to survive as scholars is a testament to them—their strength, their courage, their perseverance, and their love of scholarship—rather than a testament to the race/culture-free nature of mainstream research epistemologies.

The critical tradition might argue, however, that it has not participated in the production of these negative consequences, that it has consistently opposed racism in all of its many aspects or forms (for examples of critical tradition-based, anti-racist work, see Scheurich & Imber, 1991; Scheurich & Laible, 1995; among many others). And to a significant extent this is true. Many white scholars have literally devoted their careers to anti-racism. In addition, the critical tradition has, for many scholars of color, been the only epistemologically friendly set of "clothes" (West, 1993a, pp. 78–79; Stanfield, 1994). Some scholars of color even contend that, to some extent, the "new" epistemologies (to be discussed shortly) based on the sociocultural histories of people of color are derived from the critical tradition (e.g., Gordon et al., 1990, pp. 18–19). Consequently, it is important that the critical tradition be honored for its anti-racist work and insight and its willingness to question and oppose racism in environments that are often hostile to such efforts.

Nonetheless, the critical tradition, even if more favored by intellectuals of color, is itself almost exclusively drawn from white social history, from what Stanfield (1985) has called "European-derived paradigms" (p. 399). The critical tradition's ontology, epistemology, and axiology are predominantly the creation of white scholars and their social context (e.g., B. M. Gordon, 1993; Stanfield, 1994). Corned West (1993a), one of the eminent scholars of the critical tradition, argues, therefore, that the dependency of intellectuals of color on the critical tradition may be "debilitating for black intellectuals because the cathartic needs it [critical theory] satisfies tend to stifle the further development of black critical consciousness and attitudes" (p. 79). In addition, virtually all of the different critical approaches—including critical theory, feminisms, lesbian/gay orientations, and critical postmodernism—have been repeatedly cited for their racial biases (see, for example, Alarcón, 1990; Bell, 1992; Frankenberg, 1993; hooks, 1990; Huggins, 1991; Minh-ha, 1989; Stanfield, 1994, pp. 179–181; Stevenson & Ellsworth, 1993; West, 1993a). Consequently, as Ellsworth (1989) argued in a different context, while critical theory has been important to anti-racist efforts and perhaps important to the development of new race-based epistemologies, it is not necessarily the appropriate epistemological frame for all race-oriented emancipatory work. Advocates for the critical tradition, therefore, need to support the emergence and acceptance of other epistemologies that are derived from different racial or cultural social histories,[15] to which a brief introduction follows.

"New" Race-Based Epistemologies

One prominent example of an effort to develop, and apply, a "new" race-based epistemology (some of them actually are historically "old") is Patricia Hill Collins' *Black Feminist Thought* (1991). In this important work, she has a chapter entitled, "Toward an Afrocentric Feminist Epistemology," in which she names and discusses the four "contours" (p. 206) or characteristics of her race-based epistemology: "concrete experience as a criterion of meaning" (pp. 208–212), "the use of dialogue in assessing knowledge claims" (pp. 212–215), "the ethic of caring" (pp. 215–217), and "the ethic of personal accountability" (pp. 217–219). To develop this epistemology, she says she "searched my own experience and those of African-American women I know for themes we thought were important," and she relied "on the voices of Black women from all walks of life" (p. 202), many of whom she cites and discusses in her explanation of the four "contours." Accordingly, her Afrocentric feminist epistemology, "like all specialized thought[, such as positivism to postmodernisms], reflects the interests and standpoint of its creators" (p. 201).

That this epistemology is respected by other black women is evidenced by the fact that Gloria Ladson-Billings (1994) recently published, in the *American Educational Research Journal,* results from a three-year research study[16] that uses Collins' Afrocentric feminist epistemology as her "theoretical grounding" (Ladson-Billings, 1995, p. 471).[17] Ladson-Billings, in her study of "successful teachers of African-American children" (p. 471), after stating her choice of Collins' epistemology, briefly discusses each of Collins' four contours and her use of them to provide the epistemological grounding for her study of these successful teachers. Ladson-Billings' appropriate concern is to select an epistemology that reflects "who I am, what I believe, what experiences I have had," given her "membership in a marginalized racial/cultural group" (p. 470). That is, she chooses to use an epistemological frame that "fits" her social history, that emerges out of her race/culture's social history, rather than an epistemological frame that has emerged out of the social history of the dominant race.

But Collins is not the only one who has developed a race-based epistemology, nor is she the first. Molefi Kete Asante has for some time advocated an Afrocentric epistemology that he developed through a relatively large body of work (e.g., 1987, 1988, 1990, 1993), and this work, along with that of other African-American scholars advocating a similar perspective, has inspired or supported a wide range of scholarship, including that of Azibo (1990), Baldwin (1981), W. C. Banks (1992), Beverly Gordon (1990, 1993), Kershaw (1989, 1992), W. M. King (1990), and Taylor (1987), among numerous others (see also, the entire issue of *The Journal of Negro Education,* 61[3], 1992, guest edited by Edmund W. Gordon). From Asante's viewpoint (1993), "Afrocentricity *is a perspective which allows Africans to be subjects of [their own] historical experiences rather than objects* [author's emphasis] on the fringes of Europe" (p. 2). Later in the same book, Asante, in a chapter titled, "On Afrocentric Metatheory," briefly discusses the Cosmological

Issue" (pp. 106-107), the "Epistemological Issue" (pp. 107-108), the "Axiological Issue" (p. 108), and the "Aesthetic Issue" (pp. 108-109—four issues that he sees as central to Afrocentricity. In "Afrocentrism and the Afrocentric Method," Kershaw (1992) discusses the steps of an "Afrocentric emancipatory methodology," a method that includes qualitative methodology, analysis and description of the data collected, critical dialogue with those involved in the research, education, and action, all leading to the generation of Afrocentric knowledge. Kershaw (1992) cites John Gwaltney's *Drylongso: A Self Portrait of Black America* (1980) as "an excellent example of Afrocentric generated practical knowledge" (p. 165).

More recently, another race-based epistemology has begun to gain the attention of "progressive intellectuals of color" (West, 1995, p. xi). This epistemological perspective originated in legal studies. According to Cornel West (1995),

> Critical Race theorists have, for the first time, examined the entire edifice of contemporary legal thought and doctrine from the viewpoint of law's role in the construction and maintenance of social domination and subordination. In the process, they not only challenged the basic assumptions and presuppositions of the prevailing paradigms among mainstream liberals and conservatives in the legal academy, but also confronted the relative silence of legal radicals —namely critical legal studies writers—who "deconstructed" liberalism, yet seldom addressed the role of deep-seated racism in American life. (p. xi)

However, this perspective has just begun to migrate from legal studies into the social sciences generally and into education specifically.[18] That this migration is occurring, though, is evidenced by a "Call for Papers" on critical race theory for the *International Journal of Qualitative Studies in Education,* under the special-issue editorship of Donna Deyhle, Laurence Parker, and Sofia Villenas, all at the time in the Department of Educational Studies at the University of Utah.

Most white scholars are, however, unfamiliar with this race-based range of work because it often appears in explicitly race-oriented academic journals (like *The Journal of Negro Education*) or in books by race-oriented publishers (like Africa World Press) that have typically been started because of the lack of acceptance, in mainstream journals or by mainstream presses, of research on African-Americans by African-Americans using African-American perspectives. For example, Padilla (1994) suggests that the lack of research on African-Americans in six of the leading APA journals may be "because the peer-reviewing process serves the gatekeeping function of excluding research that does not conform to acceptable *paradigms* [italics added] or methodologies" (p. 250). Similarly, Beverly Gordon (1990) says

> The number of Black Studies libraries at universities and at private and public collections around the country bears witness to an enormous body of literature written by African-American scholars, while the academy gives little credence or visibility to this work in preservice and in-service discussions.

This curricular gap says as much about *the theories and paradigms* [italics added] embraced and disseminated by university faculty as do the resulting pedagogical practices and worldviews of teachers, principals, and school districts. (pp. 89–90)

In other words, the very existence of these journals is one of the consequences of the mainstream exclusion of race-based epistemologies and the research resulting from these perspectives; the problem, of course, for scholars of color is that for tenure and promotion these race-oriented journals are not as respected as the mainstream ones.

It is not our intention, however, to privilege some of the race-based epistemologies over others. The ones we have briefly introduced here are those we have become most familiar with and those that we increasingly see being used in educational research. There are other efforts to develop these new race-based epistemologies and extensive arguments among scholars of color about these epistemologies, but a comprehensive survey of these race-based epistemologies and current discussions of them would require an entire article (an article we would certainly like to read). Our point is that these new epistemologies exist and that they need to be understood, respected, and discussed, just as those epistemologies that have been produced by the dominant race are understood, respected, and discussed.

What Is to Be Done?

Research needs to be based on the reality of our [Hopi] existence as we experience it, not just from the narrow and limited view American universities carried over from the German research tradition. (Hopi Tribal Council Chairman, Vernon Masayesva, quoted in Krupat, 1993, p. xix)

While there has been a powerful social tendency among whites and white society to define racism in individual terms or, at best, in limited institutional terms, such as in hiring or promotion, we do not think most white researchers consciously support racism in any terms—individual, institutional, societal, or civilizational. But this intention is not sufficient if our argument here is a persuasive one. In a very important sense, we white researchers are unconsciously promulgating racism on an epistemological level. As we teach and promote epistemologies like positivism to postmodernism, we are, at least implicitly, teaching and promoting the social history of the dominant race at the exclusion of people of color, scholars of color, and the possibility for research based on other race/culture epistemologies. We can, however, use our opposition to racism to consider the question of whether our dominant epistemologies are racially based or not and, if they are, to begin to change this situation.[19]

The single most important effort needed is to initiate a vigorous debate/dialogue among scholars of all races, including particularly those who write the commonly used methods textbooks. Of all the myriad issues crucial to educational research, surely this ought to be a hotly debated one. For instance, we know there are many scholars who would oppose our contention that epistemologies arise out of the social history of specific groups. Many traditional researchers or social scientists, for instance, argue that their epistemology reaches above history toward a context-free kind of truth. Let these scholars join the discussion. Let them lay out their arguments in public debate. Let us have a fierce row over this. If the possibility that our typical epistemologies are racially biased is not genuinely worth the price of a spirited intellectual conflict, what is?

Second, those of us who teach methods courses must begin to study, teach, and thus, legitimate the research epistemologies that arise out of the social histories of people of color. Often "students get the message either directly or indirectly that ethnic-related research is not something that they should engage in as part of their training or for their dissertation research" (Padilla, 1994, p. 24). As professors, we need to support an informed understanding and skillful use of these race-based epistemologies by interested students of color. (But we ought not to try to force them in this direction, as most students of color typically know that race-oriented scholarship is more risky than mainstream-oriented scholarship.) As scholars, we need to add race-oriented journals to our own reading lists, and we need to increase our valuation of those journals during tenure and promotion proceedings. As dissertation chairs, we must support doctoral studies drawn from these new race-based epistemologies. As journal editors, editorial board members, and journal reviewers, we must study and support the publication both of discussions of these epistemologies and of studies based on them, like that of Ladson-Billings (1994). Even better, we need to solicit this kind of work, including doing special editions of our journals. As editors and reviewers for publishing companies, we must insist on the inclusion of race-based perspectives in methods textbooks.

We know that efforts of these sorts are possible. We have taught research methods courses in which we cover other race/culture-based epistemologies (African-American, Hispanic-American, Native American, Asian-American, among other racial designations), along with positivism to poststructuralisms. We have class members help find new materials, and the students of color are continuously educating us through their class discussions of the materials and through their written work. In addition, other professors at our university have become interested in this approach, and there is now serious discussion of a collegewide course of this sort. Furthermore, we know of professors at other universities who have been doing the same. In addition, we, the new editor and managing editor of a respected academic journal, promote the publication of scholarship discussing race-based epistemologies and research based on those perspectives.[20]

Obviously these suggestions are insufficient, but they are only intended as initial steps toward a crucially needed conversation that to date, unfortunately, has largely been attended to only by scholars of color. But our hope is that other white researchers will join this conversation because we have been able, hopefully, to provide a useful discussion of just what *epistemological racism* is. We especially hope that those who write, or are considering writing, research methods textbooks will join this conversation.

Racism of any sort is heinous, most terribly for its victims but also for its perpetrators.[21] One of the worst racisms, though, for any generation or group is the one that we do not see, that is invisible to our lens—the one we participate in without consciously knowing or intending it. Are we not seeing the biases of our time, just like those 100 years ago did not see the biases of their time? Will those who look back at us in time wonder why we resisted seeing our racism? The unfortunate truth is that we can be strongly anti-racist in our own minds but be promulgating racism in profound ways we do not understand (Pine & Hilliard, 1990, p. 595). As Cose (1993) says in *The Rage of a Privileged Class,* "people do not have to be racist—or have any malicious intent—in order to make decisions that unfairly harm members of another race" (p. 4). It is our contention here, based on the seminal, groundbreaking work of scholars of color, that we educational researchers are unintentionally involved, at the epistemological heart of our research enterprises, in a racism—*epistemological racism*—that we generally do not see or understand. Once we see and understand it, though, we cannot continue in our old ways. To do so would be to betray our fundamental commitment as educators and as educational researchers.

Notes for Chapter 2, Section 1

1. Although the scholars of color who address the issue of whether our epistemologies are racially biased do not name all of the specific epistemologies to which they are applying this question, we argue that this judgment can justifiably be applied to a broad range of currently "popular" epistemologies, including positivism, postpositivisms, neorealisms, interpretivisms, constructivisms, the critical tradition, and postmodernisms/poststructuralisms (all of which are briefly defined in note 3).

2. Race, undeniably, is a tricky social construction: to use it is to reinforce it as really "real," to naturalize it (Webster, 1992); to not use it is to act as if race were no longer a significant differentiating variable in social life (Wright, 1994) or in education and research (Webster, 1992). In some southern states in the past, to have but one drop of African-American blood was, according to law, to be an African-American, while today the race of a child of parents of two different races is problematic or even a personal choice on some official forms. Race, then, has always been a mobile construct. As Rizvi (1993) says, race as a construct "is continually changing, being challenged, interrupted, and reconstructed, in the actual practices in which people engage" (p. 129) and in the discourses that they employ (See also Toni

Morrison's *Playing in the Dark Whiteness and the Literary Imagination* [1992] for one discussion of this issue). By race, we mean historically and socially situated race-based cultures that are tied both positively (i.e., cultural pride) and negatively (i.e., racism) to skin color (see for instance Lee, 1995). We understand, however, both that skin color within "one" race can vary considerably and that the experience of a race-based culture by its members can also vary considerably. We also understand that the growing, though still relatively small, number of biracial or even tri-racial individuals significantly complicates what a particular race-based culture is and who is a member. We would, nonetheless, argue that there is a range of "positive" consistencies or features within a race-based culture that makes it a culture, such as the Mexican-American one (though we would not say that all of those consistencies or features apply equally to all members). We would also argue that the "negative" external force of persistent racism, past and present, against these race-based cultures is a significant factor in maintaining these cultures as more or less consistent entities that could be called a "culture." (For a provocative discussion of these issues, see Appiah, 1992.)

3. We define "positivism" as the traditional application of the scientific method within the social sciences. We are aware, nonetheless, of the debates about whether this is the appropriate label or not and agree that, strictly speaking, it is not (Phillips, 1987), but language, as usual, is at least partway uncontrollable, and thus it seems that the meaning we give it is the one that has passed into common academic parlance. With "postpositivisms," we concur with Guba and Lincoln (1994) that they represent "efforts of the past few decades to respond in a limited way (that is, while remaining within essentially the same set of basic beliefs) to the most problematic criticisms of positivism" (p. 109). By "neo-realisms," we mean that range of realisms, including scientific realism (e.g., Bhaskar, 1986, 1989) and coherentist realism (e.g., Evers & Lakomski, 1991), that has sought, similarly to postpositivism, to address the strong criticisms of the scientific method that have emerged over the past few decades, while maintaining the basic validity of the scientific method. By "interpretivisms" and "constructivisms," we agree with Schwandt (1994) that they are "a loosely coupled family of methodological and philosophical persuasions . . . that share the goal of understanding the complex world of lived experience from the point of view of those who live it" (p. 118). Within the "critical tradition," we include critical theory, feminism, and lesbian/gay perspectives, all of which start from the experiences of a social group that has been excluded, marginalized, or oppressed over lengthy historical periods; which typically include a critique of social inequities related to those experiences; and which work toward, directly or indirectly, some sort of emancipatory social change for those groups. By postmodernisms/poststructuralisms, we include the work of the French theorists like Foucault, Irigaray, and Derrida that subjects the fundamental, civilizational assumptions of modernism itself to critique. But we also include in this category the work of many others, like that of Patti Lather (1991) or Judith Butler (1993), who have extensively appropriated this philosophy to their own interests.

4. While our focus is on "epistemological racism," a similar argument to the one that we have made here could be made about "ontological racism" or "axiological racism," all three of which, we say later, are aspects of the "civilizational level." Of course, none of these

three can really be separated from each other; an epistemological position, an ontological position, and an axiological position are "strongly" interdependent. However, we focus here on "epistemological racism" because we are researchers and because research itself is the technique or process for "producing knowledge" within a particular epistemology. In a certain sense, then, research as technique or process is "housed" within epistemology rather than within ontology or axiology, though as we said above, any particular epistemology is interdependent with a particular ontology or axiology. This is not to say, though, that ontological or axiological positrons are not fundamental to research; in fact, we would hope someone would provide a discussion of axiological racism for researchers.

5. We do not mean to imply that these categories exhaust all types of racism, though we believe they are reasonably comprehensive. We also do not mean to imply that our category schema is better than others, such as those of Dube (1985); virtually all category schema in the social sciences are heuristic devices, the utility of which must be evaluated within the discourse in which they are used. As James Banks (1993) says of his knowledge categories, "The . . . categories approximate, but do not describe, reality in its total complexity. The categories are useful conceptual tools . . . but the relationship between the categories of knowledge is dynamic and interactive rather than static" (p. 6).

6. For those familiar with the poststructuralist work of Foucault, we would argue that what we are here calling the "civilizational" level is somewhat similar to an "archaeological" level, the level, that is, at which the "real" is constituted. In his genealogical period, however, Foucault would oppose the structuralist metaphor of levels (though his archaeological works have been argued to be structuralist [see Gutting, 1989]); he would argue in this later work that "levels" occur at the level of human activity (Gutting, 1989). While we agree with his latter or genealogical positron, our diagram of the "levels" of racism and our argument are based on a structuralist metaphor, one in which each subsequent level is deeper and broader than the prior one. We have done it this way because the structuralist bias is so deeply embedded in all of us that it is remarkably difficult to draw a readily understandable graphic that can portray multiple influences, some of which are more fundamental or more primary or more constitutional than others, while drawing them at the same "level." We have, consequently, adopted a structuralist metaphor (graphic) in the interest of making our larger point about the racial bias of research epistemologies more accessible. However, our focus on the "civilizational" level actually grows out of a larger project in which one of us (Scheurich) has drawn from the archaeological work of Foucault (1970, 1972, 1979, 1988) to formulate a poststructuralist approach to social theory and research methodology. For those interested in seeing the initial efforts to sketch the outlines of that project, see "Policy Archaeology: A New Policy Studies Methodology." (Scheurich, 1994a).

7. The difference between white racism and the racism of people of color is a highly contentious issue. We strongly agree with Tatum (1992) who, in the context of an article about her personal experiences as teacher of a course entitled, "Group Exploration of Racism," and attended primarily by white students (who typically evaluate the course as one of their best college educational experiences) says, "a distinction must be made between the negative racial attitudes held by individuals of color and White individuals, because it is

only the attitudes of Whites that routinely carry with them the social power inherent in the systematic cultural reinforcement and institutionalization of those racial prejudices. To distinguish the prejudices of students of color from the racism of White students is *not* [her emphasis] to say the former is acceptable and the latter is not; both are clearly problematic. The distinction is important, however, to identify the power differential between members of the dominant and subordinate groups" (p. 3). Similarly, Hacker (1992) says that "individuals who do not have power may hold racist views, but they seldom cause much harm" (p. 29; see also Feagin & Vera, 1995, pp. ix-x). Consequently, for individual racism, we have stated our definitions in race-neutral terms, though the tendency to define racism solely as individual is chiefly done by whites; for all of the other types of racism we discuss, our definitions are constructed in terms of the racism of the dominant group.

8. Numerous scholars of race argue that this social consensus is "lip service" opposition to racism and not a real commitment (see for example Howitt & Owusu-Bempa, 1990, for a discussion of this). Unhappily, our classroom experience with white students validates this. These students will readily support racial equality, but the distance between that initial verbal support and a strong commitment to change racial inequalities is very large.

9. We are not suggesting that either of the two mentioned groups—Hopi or African-American—are completely homogeneous or would totally agree on what good leadership is. Nonetheless, if U. S. society were seriously drawing on ideas of what good leadership is from these two or from the many other race/culture groups within this society, there is little doubt that the presidential campaign would be significantly altered. For instance, Hopi ideas of leadership are much different, because for the traditional Hopi acts are sacred acts (Loftin, 1991), an approach very foreign to US. presidential campaigns. See Stanfield (1993a, pp. 19-25) for an insightful discussion of this issue.

10. This assumption that dominant culture and a nondominant culture, both within the same society, can "see" the same event in entirely different ways—through different cultural "lenses"—is recently apparent with the O. J. Simpson criminal trial. Near the end of the trial but prior to the verdict, over 70% of those in the dominant white culture believed Simpson was guilty, while over 60% of those in the African-American culture believed Simpson was not guilty. Each group was seeing differently, in our opinion, because each was looking through the lens of a different social history.

11. Premodernist Europe typically was biased against "barbarians," not races; at that time, "race" tended not to be a primary category of exclusion (Goldberg, 1993a). West (1993a) verifies this when he asserts that "the first substantial racial division of humankind is found in the influential *Natural System* (1735) of the preeminent naturalist of the eighteenth century, Carolus Linnaeus" (p. 262). Foucault (1980a) also substantiates this view that race emerges as a critical exclusionary category in the modernist period when he says, in reference to the beginning of modernity, that "the new concept of race tended to obliterate the aristocratic particularizing of blood" (p. 148).

12. To argue that these people were influential because they, at least in part, saw beyond or were superior to their social circumstances does not work. W. E. B. DuBois was easily one of the greatest intellectuals of his era or of any era. If anyone can be said to rise

above or be superior to her or his time and place, DuBois was that person, but he had only limited influence on the social mainstream during his life and continues to be largely underappreciated by intellectuals in general. The anti-racist discourse, which itself arose out of the cultural experience of African-Americans, that he "spoke" was not significantly legitimated in his time and still is not in this one.

13. It is a modernist assumption, one that we disagree with, that subjectivities and discourses or individuals (agents) and their contexts can be separated. That is, modernism posits that an individual (an agent, a subjectivity) can act or think outside of the epistemological, ontological, and axiological web (context, discourses) within which the individual exists. However, we would suggest, following the French poststructualists, that individualism (agency) or subjectivity itself is a production of the web, context, discourses. Consequently, when we cite influential philosophers, writers, etc., we do not intend to imply that epistemological racism is an individual production. It is not; it is a production of the western modernist web, and these influential individuals are "spoken" by that web. Of course, alternative webs, discourses, contexts do exist. For example, anti-racist discourses do exist, even among a small proportion of whites (though we would argue that this white anti-racism is deeply dependent, for its existence and survival on cultures of color and their anti-racist efforts). However, these anti-racist discourses, whether asserted by people of color or whites, have been marginalized within western modernism because the anti-racist discourses do not fit the white culture's deeply embedded civilizational assumptions. Whether we are now at an historical moment when anti-racist discourses might be more significantly influential in the modernist west (which would require a shift in civilizational level assumptions to something that might be called postmodernism), we do not know. We are equally hopeful and skeptical. That this essay was published in a major outlet is hopeful; nonetheless, the central initiating point of this essay is that prior discussions of race-based epistemologies authored by scholars of color have largely been ignored by white research epistemologists and methodologists, a not-hopeful fact.

14. A major implication of our argument is a new, and more fundamental, definition of what racism is; it is epistemological and ontological. It is woven at the deepest level into the construction of "the real." That is, racism is primarily located in the founding civilizational categories — the ontology — and the epistemologies that dominate western civilization. Remedies for racism, then, that focus only on the individual level or even only on the institutional or societal level will be insufficient. What is required is the "real" — its dominant ontology and epistemologies — be co-constructed in a relatively equal way by all races/cultures.

15. Race-based discussions of research epistemologies and methodologies by scholars of color in the United States, like the many cited here, can provocatively be seen, by critical theorists, as a significant contribution to global postcolonial studies. In fact, this U.S. discussion can be seen as an "internal" or "domestic" postcolonial literature. A theme-oriented comparison between the literature cited here and that contained in collections, like *The Post-Colonial Studies Reader* (Asheroft, Griffiths, & Tiffin, 1995), will make our point readily apparent.

16. See Ladson-Billings' book The *Dreamkeepers: Successful Teachers of African American Children (1994)* for a more comprehensive treatment of her study.

17. This is the first time that we know of that a specific race-based epistemology has been used in a study published in an AERA journal.

18. In our opinion, the best text to date on critical race theory is *Critical Race Theory: The Key Writings That Formed the Movement* (1995), edited by Crenshaw, Gotanda, and Thomas.

19. John Hope Franklin, in an interview on his 80th birthday, recently said, "I'm not very optimistic [about racism in the United States], I really am not. . . . [J]ust about the time you sit down or sit back and say, 'Oh, yes, we're really moving,' you get slapped back down" (Applebome, 1995, p. 37). Bell (1992) in *Faces at the Bottom of the Well: The Permanence of Racism* argues persuasively that racism is such a necessary part of white U.S. culture that it is, in effect, "a permanent component of American life" (p. 13), but he also argues that this judgment should not stop us from working for racial equality in all aspects of our social life. While we are apprehensive that the first part of what he said is true, the second part is a necessity.

20. One of us, Scheurich, was at the time of the original publication of this essay and still is the editor of *International Journal of Qualitative Studies in Education,* and the other, Young, has been the managing editor of this journal.

21. For those who want to read about the negative effects of white racism on whites — what Wended Berry called "the white misery of white racism" (p. 63) — see Feagin and Vera (1995) for a social account and Wended Berry (1989) for a personal meditation on the effects of racism on whites.

Section 2

A Response to "Coloring Epistemology: Are Our Research Epistemologies Racially Biased?"

Cynthia A. Tyson

This response was originally given at the American Educational Research Association meeting in spring of 1997, at which my colleagues and I were asked to talk about questions of rationale, contributions, resistance toward, and the intersections of race-based qualitative research epistemologies.[1] When I first read and chose to respond to this particular piece, a dissonance propelled me into a backward progression. I began to think of my mother's musings about the historical shifts of nomenclature from "Negro" to "colored" to "black" to "African-American" to "people of color." She repeated the saying, "the more things change, the more things stay the same." Or, put another way, regression is a necessary part of progression. I respond to this piece, then, by regressing as I proceed forward. I cannot begin to discuss race-based research epistemologies without first discussing three prior epistemological issues: an epistemology of dissection and dismantling, one of competing agendas, and one of oppression.

The Epistemology of Dismantling and Dissecting

In their piece, Scheurich and Young (1997) raise the question: What do race-based research epistemologies contribute to the larger conversation on research methods? They also cite Gordon, Miller, and Rollock (1990) in their argument that a dominant group within a complex civilization makes its own "community the center of the universe and the conceptual frame that constrains all thought" (p. 7). This leads me to ask, are these discussions of race-based epistemologies just another exercise in reconstruction of methodologies that will result in a displacement of the center, yet leave the whole—taking apart any troubling pieces only to reconstruct dominant group epistemologies, ontologies, and axiologies? Although the deconstructionist project is not to reconstruct dominant hierarchies, something *is* reconstructed, much like a puzzle that can be taken apart and put together again and again while the picture remains the same. The pieces, though reconstructed, can be reconstructed, creating a privileging of one race-based epistemology over another. For instance, as Stanfield (1994) argues, we then have researchers "who may call for more culturally relevant approaches to Afro-American experiences in the social sciences and humanities, but who do so while embracing and even advocating the most sacred norms" of the dominant paradigm (p. 182). Therefore, as this conversation continues and debates ensue, I question whether race-based methodologies will be dismantled and dissected while racist epistemologies remain intact.

Scheurich and Young (1997) call for (a) "a vigorous debate/dialogue among scholars of all races, including particularly those who write the commonly used methods textbooks" and (b) that "those of us who teach methods courses must begin to study, teach, and thus legitimate the research epistemologies that arise out of the social histories of people of color" (p. 11). Also, in the introduction to the journal, the editor (Donmoyer, 1997) invites readers to "submit examples of studies employing methodologies that have emerged from the various epistemologies of color Scheurich and Young allude to in this article" (p. 2).

Based on these comments, I ask, in the words of Aretha Franklin "who's zoomin' who?" Does such an invitation in itself contribute to the reification of the hierarchy Scheurich and Young demonstrate—that is, is it reconstructing the power relations by placing the burden on marginalized researchers to substantiate the claims that epistemologies and "methodologies of color differ from other qualitative methods" (p. 2) and opening the door once again for white researchers to appropriate and legitimate these methods? Why not ask for examples of racist epistemologies and methodologies as "concrete referents" so that these racist epistemologies and methodologies can truly be dismantled and dissected?

The Epistemology of Competing Agendas

To be black and a scholar in America is to experience competing agendas. The tenor of American race relations demands it. Each racial or ethnic group in America labors under this burden in specific ways. As Scheurich and Young point out, the minority scholar's time is consumed in efforts to "refute or neutralize fallacious findings, questionable theories, and inappropriate interpretations" (Gordon, Miller, & Rollock, 1990, p. 16) of mainstream research. And, in fact, because Scheurich and Young are engaging in academic rigor with issues of epistemological racism at the center, my co-respondents and I began to imagine that at least the first author, James Joseph Scheurich, may be black. After all, he also has two good Baptist names.

However, given that he is white, another very important question is raised yet again: Why now? Why now raise the question about race-based epistemologies and begin debates when a white male calls for it? Race-based epistemologies have been a part of the research discourse for quite some time. Are we now receiving a form of scholarly legitimization, one that comes from the accepted discourse at educational research annual meetings and publications in the journals "that count". When Patricia Hill Collins wrote *Black Feminist Thought: Knowledge, Consciousness, and the Politics of Empowerment* (1991), there was no call at all, let alone a call for debate by the research community. However, her work was a major influence among researchers of color who recognize that the history of race and race relations cannot be ignored in discussions about epistemology.

It reminds me of a story that an elder in my community shared with me. A former member of the Black Panther Party for Defense in the 1960s, he learned a lot about the strategic nature of not only defense but also attack. He shared that a prominent leader of the Party spoke to them as soldiers in preparation for the times ahead by saying that there would be times when they would have to use dynamite to blast a door open. But there was no need to waste dynamite when someone within our midst had the key. Scheurich's writing is a key. And too often in the history of African-Americans, the keys of the master's house have been transferred in the traditional legacy from one white male to another. The transference of the key allows entry only when it is advantageous to the owner. Who has the most to benefit from this call for debate on epistemological racism? Scheurich has used this proverbial key to open a door. But it has already been opened historically by those whose shoulders we all stand on—Carter G. Woodson, E. Franklin Frazier, Charles S. Johnson, W. E. B. DuBois, Zora Neale Hurston, Sadie T. Alexander, Alison Davis, and so on—all of whom used race as a theoretical lens (Ladson-Billings & Tate, 1995).

The Epistemology of Oppression

Nietzsche, in his prose about Zarathustra, commented: "of all that is written I love only what a person has written with his blood. It is no easy task to understand unfamiliar blood."

It seems that the research methodology that Scheurich and Young (1997) are talking about in "Coloring Epistemologies" is an epistemology of blood or oppression. That may explain in part why four African-American female graduate students who responded to their work did not find it hard to resonate with parts of their writing and critically examine other parts. It is the understanding of what has been written in the oppressed blood that allowed us to also understand Scheurich and Young as they work their way through a discussion of racism, highlighting the role of racism in society as endemic to epistemology.

Having accepted this premise, we constantly—throughout many hours of preconference discussions—were brought back to the question: if a race-based epistemology can be African-American or feminist or First Nation, what is it that makes this epistemology different when developing a formalized research methodology that evolves out of that epistemology? My answer is the specificity of oppression, one not based solely on victimization, but also on struggle and survival. As I reflect on the experience of being black in America, I must weave together the African tribal and American familial, community, and religious traditions — folk tales, foods, medicine men, priests and priestesses, black churches — but I must also weave in the threads of racism in the politics, economics, and so-called intellectual thought that allowed for the atrocities perpetuated by the Nazis in the Holocaust, for the Middle Passage and the enslavement of millions of black Africans, for Japanese internment camps, and for the annihilation of indigenous peoples. This epistemology of oppression sets the stage for inquiry from a different plane. The racist ideology that drives hegemony moves the oppressed other into a paradigm of survival so that these intersecting cycles of oppression and survival create a particular epistemological view of the world.

While these stories may resonate with a familiarity to some, the specific way of coming to know in this place of resistance to racial hierarchy and exclusion creates a specific epistemological base out of which our methodology grows. This base connects, as Scheurich and Young suggest, with "ontologies, epistemologies, and axiologies [that] are not outside history or sociology; they are deeply interwoven within the social histories of particular civilizations and within particular groups within those civilizations"(1997, p. 8). These intersections demand that we not only look at theories, methodologies, and epistemologies, but that we also endeavor to uplift as we inquire in an attempt to create an epistemology of emancipation.[2]

Notes for Chapter 2, Section 2

Asante sana to my colleagues — Melanie Carter, Marjorie Davis, Da'aiyah Saleem, Cynthia Dillard, Lawrence Parker, Mary Hermes, and James Joseph Scheurich — to Patti Lather for her support of this work, and to my white critical buddy, Theresa Rogers, for her scholarly critique and editing of the final written version of this piece.

1. We responded from our African-American perspectives, realizing both within and across ethnic groups that there are shared and opposing responses to the issue of race-based epistemologies.

2. For some, this may beg the question: How is this epistemology of emancipation to be created? I purposefully resisted the inclination to prescribe because there are no recipes of epistemology, nor do I want to oversimplify the complexity of the questions and issues at this beginning point of what I hope will be an ongoing conversation.

Section 3

Coloring Within and Outside the Lines:
Some Comments

Steven I. Miller

In their provocative article, Scheurich and Young (1997) are concerned with the lack of response by those in the educational research community. They believe that their argument, contending that our "research epistemologies" may be racially biased, ought to create a forum for debate and reflection. In the remarks that follow, I would like to accept this challenge. I do so not because I disagree with the relevancy of their concerns or its importance for the future of educational research, but because, on my reading, their argument contains a number of serious shortcomings. If these errors are not pointed out, then, indeed, the silence on this issue up until now could be interpreted as agreement by the educational community with Scheurich and Young's thesis.

To begin with, a common practice in engaging in what is taken to be scholarly research is to have knowledge of and to assess the credibility of larger but related domains in relation to what one is studying. Begging the question of whether this type of activity is itself a manifestation of some form of racially biased practice, Scheurich and Young could have cast their intellectual nets beyond the authors they cite as authoritative on the topic. In so doing, they would have discovered that what they take to be a unique problem is really a variety of one that has been around in the philosophy of science and social science for some time now. While the details cannot be examined in this space, the issue was identified early by Quine (1960) and is generally known as the "indeterminacy of translation" thesis. The thesis is basically this: How is it possible for an observer to accurately translate another's culture if it is different from his or her own? Generally, the inscrutability of translation lies in the fact that there is *no* fact of the matter in deciding between alternative translations—that is, the meanings attributed to different claims concerning the world—because they are bound to language and not necessarily to "facts" in the sense of facts in the natural sciences. This can result in an inability to determine which translation is the correct one, and hence, the specter of relativism raises its unwanted head.

This issue of unwanted relativism will, then, serve as a backdrop to investigate a number of assumptions and assertions made by Scheurich and Young. To begin, the authors wonder if the lack of response to their claims is the result of the "disquieting issue of race, the possibility that their arguments are weak or irrelevant or because the argument was not understood." I wish to concentrate on these comments in terms of the second possibility: that their arguments are both weak and irrelevant. What I will try to do, then, is to show where and how their arguments contain serious defects. While such an analysis will deal basically with "philosophical" issues, this choice of critique is simply based on the fact that their position is basically grounded in philosophical concerns — especially, of course, the persistent use of "epistemology." While I will not concentrate on how epistemological theories are identified or debated within philosophy itself, what I intend to do is to show how the basic idea of the term — i.e. how we formulate knowledge or come to "know" — is the level at which Scheurich and Young's arguments must be assessed.

In essence, because their article is so replete with a variety of errors, it may become a central reason why the educational research community has not addressed their concerns. I do not mean this as a disparaging comment to the authors, but what I would like to suggest is that their assumptions actually constitute a large number of errors. I will only focus on some of these errors, but I hope they are salient ones in showing why they are errors and where holding onto such errors will then only produce a cumulative and negative impact on the educational research community. Let us begin.

The most serious general criticism of Scheurich and Young's analysis is simply that it leads to a radical form of relativism, whether of the philosophical or cultural variety. Using only the notion of relativism in its philosophical use, if extended to its logical conclusions, the authors' position must result in a number of racial, ethnic, and gender "epistemologies" that are radically different not only from the "dominant culture's" epistemological heritage but also from one another. From the philosophical framework of relativism, the position is inconsistent and self-defeating because, ultimately, no one outside of a context-dependent epistemology can understand anyone else's "epistemology." Hence, if there are no agreed-on standards of criticism and evaluation across "epistemologies," discourse is not possible. We may, of course, end up with *descriptions* of various epistemologies, but an analysis of their individual worth is impossible. The implications of this for educational research, however, would be disastrous; all descriptions, ex hypothesi, are equally good (valid) interpretations of a given group's actions or behaviors. In other words, if our "race-based" methodologies are just that, whatever they tend to produce or reveal must be "true" — period. I'm not sure that this is what we want to advocate either as scholars or human beings.

This general framework of the negative effects of advocating a position that may result in radical relativism will serve as a backdrop of some of the more specific, but equally egregious, errors advanced by Scheurich and Young. One rather minor but telling error appears in the very first sentence of the article, where the authors are suggesting that "epistemological racism" is a new category of racism. In citing a variety of authors that presumably are sympathetic with this concept, they state: "They have argued that our epistemologies—*not* our *use of them* [italics added], but the epistemologies themselves—are racially biased ways of knowing" (p. 4). Now, one does not "use" an epistemology, but rather one *has* a set of beliefs about how knowledge is found and its claims warranted. What the authors are doing, however, is conflating the issue of having a particular set of beliefs with certain modes or techniques of analysis. If my system of beliefs concerning how knowledge is possible is labeled "coherentist," for example, it does not entail that I am committed to a particular *methodology.* An epistemology and a methodology are related but different things.

But let us assume that epistemologies can be "used" in the sense that the authors are suggesting. If they are "used," then they must be expressed methodologically *in* their use. However, in this case, either the methodology must be an outcome of the epistemology or it is separate from it. If it is the former, the authors would actually have a *stronger* case for "epistemological racism," but if it is the latter, their position is weaker—even though it is exactly *this* position that they are advocating throughout.

Epistemological Racism as Civilizational

By using the example just given, I am suggesting that Scheurich and Young's analysis throughout is weakened by the uncritical assumptions they make. The topic is certainly one that is crucial for all of us in the educational research community, but the importance of the topic is trivialized to the extent that errors in reasoning go unnoticed. I will try to show in this section and another where some of these errors lie. In doing so, I do not wish to sound as if I am creating some type of nit-picking litany, but rather, my intent is to show how these assumptions, if accepted, will eventually lead us to an acceptance of a form of relativism that would be disastrous for the future conduct of educational research. Here is an example.

The authors attempt to construct their case, after a useful presentation (pp. 4–7) of different types of racism—individual, institutional, and societal—by stating:

> Our argument, then, is that epistemological racism is drawn from the civilizational level, and, thus, it is to the civilizational level that we must turn to engage directly the question of whether our research epistemologies are racially biased or not. (p. 7)

First, one may notice that if the "civilizational level" is chosen as the most important or foundational unit of analysis, it is such an all-encompassing (and, admittedly, vague and ambiguous) category that everything can be attributed to it.

Thus, without further detailed analysis, to say that "epistemological racism" can be historically situated within a civilizational level, everything can "fit" into it in one way or another. What is more crucial, of course, is to argue that a given civilization is the *cause* of, in this case, "epistemological racism." This is, I believe, Scheurich and Young's major argument. To it, they append other factors: that any given civilization has a "dominant culture," and in this case, it happens to be white and, by definition, racist. Thus, if the civilizational level is chosen as the principal unit of analysis from which to deduce "epistemological racism," then a very heavy burden of proof is placed on it. That is, if the statement, "civilization, therefore 'epistemological racism' " turns out to be a tautology, both everything and nothing has been said. The real burden of proof is on the authors to show that their major assumption is something more than a truism. Indeed, if they had considered the matter more carefully, they could have made a better case by showing that individual, institutional, and societal racism *does* exist irrespective of the vague notion of "epistemological racism," especially at the civilizational level.

But the more central questions are, how does one show that "epistemological racism" does exist, that it is created by the dominant culture, and that the dominant culture (implicitly or explicitly) shapes and controls a specific version of knowledge formation and verification? These are complex questions, and they can only be touched on here. While the questions are all interconnected, they rest on the foundational issue of whether or not there are at least minimal standards of rationality that direct and verify our epistemological efforts. This issue, in turn, centers on the debates within philosophy and the sociology of science concerning the nature of scientific activity itself (see, for instance, Fuller, 1998; Laudan, 1990). In reality, Scheurich and Young's analysis is a tacit rejection of those norms traditionally associated with the development of scientific rationality and incorporated into research methods in the human sciences—e.g., truth, objectivity, an external reality, generalizability, correctability, intersubjectivity, and so on. Epistemological racism is fundamentally a rejection of the correctness of such norms. The central question, then, becomes, what ought to replace them?

Before we come to this issue, however, it is worth noting what type of case the authors make for their "dominant culture" thesis. The usual one (p. 8) is to drag out a list of dead, white, male figures and claim that if not responsible, they are at least somehow indicative of this cultural "plot" to create and impose a "dominant" ideology. When the "usual suspects" are rounded up in this case (or, perhaps, they are rather *unusual* suspects), they include Kant, Flaubert, Churchill, Henry Ford, Weber, and Dewey. Why these, I have no idea. It is claimed by the authors that "it is they who have constructed the world we live in—named it, discussed it, explained it" (p. 8). They go on to say:

> Our argument, however, is not that these influential White individuals were involved in a racial conspiracy or moral bad faith, but that these individuals

can only name and know from within the social context available to them, from within the social context in which they live. (p. 8)

So, in effect, we have a thesis that says we can simultaneously blame and not blame such individuals for creating "epistemological racism." If they can only "name and know" within their (unique) social context, then any "blame" attributed to them is vacuous.

Other than this, the more important point the authors miss is that, irrespective of how the cultural context shaped these individuals, it does not follow that what they had to say was *necessarily false*. This is Scheurich and Young's primary mistake: They assume that *all* of the ideas evolved by the "dominant culture," by definition, have to be false. Moreover, they fail to realize that even a "dominant culture" need not be devoid of self-adjusting, self-critical mechanisms. That is, even a "dominant culture" may have institutional forms, such as a democratic system of government, public education, and a common law sensitive to principles of equity, which, overall, are intrinsically desirable to have than not to have.

I will only briefly comment on the first two points above because of space limitations. Again, to say that something is the product of the "dominant culture" is not to say that it is necessarily untrue. It may be, but that is something to be *demonstrated*, not assumed. To maintain otherwise, the authors would need to say (and, of course, they do but may not be fully aware of it) that all claims of the "dominant culture" are simply false. For example, everything written by Dewey and Kant was false. If they argue that this is or is not what they mean, then, in either case, they are appealing to a *standard* by which it is possible to judge some claims as true and others as false. But if they claim that this is not possible within the "dominant culture" itself, they must appeal to another standard (i.e., their own). However, making this move blocks them from criticizing the (supposed) falseness of the "dominant culture's" claims because their standard, by definition, must be different. This, again, is relativism with a vengeance.

To the second point: The "dominant culture" that they criticize is the one that has been capable (not perfectly, but to a greater degree than where their position would lead them) of creating and supporting norms of criticism directed at its *own* assumptions and practices. At a very basic level, the very existence of discovering, developing, and using the idea of "logical thought" and "rational argument" argues against their thesis. If it is assumed that even "logic" is not unique to the "dominant culture" but is the result of ancient Greek and (later) Muslim influences, then, of course, this move would argue against the "dominance" of the "dominant culture." More important, however, there *are* norms of criticism that are rather unique to the "dominant culture" and ought not be quickly dismissed. And in an important sense, mentioned previously, these norms are grounded in what can be broadly called the "scientific attitude." For instance, it *is* possible — and one ought to be given the freedom to do so — to subject the ideas of Kant,

Dewey, etc. to some form of critical, rational assessment. In other words, the "dominant culture" is able to subject (and then have the freedom to accept or reject) the ideas, beliefs, and knowledge claims to a "test," as I have been trying to show here, even if such a "test" may only be one of logical consistency. What Scheurich and Young's views about "epistemological racism" show are that they are not only inconsistent, but that they also do not allow for an adequate notion of "testing." This point will be analyzed briefly below.

"Epistemological Racism" and Testability

Epistemological racism claims that the dominant culture's epistemological frameworks are not only racist but also largely irrelevant to understanding the life histories of other groups and subcultures that are nonwhite, nondominant. To show this, Scheurich and Young present a series of examples that illustrate this position. I will only mention some of the more prominent ones. They mention the work of Patricia Hill Collins as an advocate of an Afrocentric-feminist epistemology. This "epistemology" has four "contours": (a) having concrete experience as a criterion of meaning, (b) using dialogue to assess knowledge claims, (c) developing an ethic of caring, and (d) developing an ethic of personal accountability. The authors further quote Collins as saying that she, "searched my own experience and those of African-American women I know for themes we thought were important" relying "on the voices of Black women from all walks of life." And finally, defending her epistemology: "like all specialized thought [such as positivism to postmodernisms], reflects the interests and standpoint of its creators." Because I do not have Collins's work, I will base my comments on the accuracy and representativeness of Scheurich and Young's quotes.

The "contours" mentioned by Collins may be a type of research methodology, but how they are is difficult to say. The difficulty lies in the lack of concrete directives as to how such contours are to be assessed, either within their own context or externally. The quote where Collins attributes her epistemology as being on par with positivism because each reflects "interests" and "standpoints" of its creators is, on one level, accurate but on another, much oversimplified. One principal difference—and one that is important as being characteristic of racial epistemologies not having—is that positivism, for instance, was a well-developed theoretical system open to criticism. It was eventually correctly criticized on such issues as the impossibility of producing a neutral "observation" language, but its potential for criticism as a *general* epistemological system was always there. By contrast, so-called "racial epistemologies" appear to be closed off, by definition, from such criticism. Specifically, they cannot be critiqued externally because any such critiques, being a product of the "dominant culture," are irrelevant, and they cannot be critiqued internally because there are seldom (if ever) clearly articulated standards for assessing their claims. I believe broadly similar considerations could be applied to the analysis of "Afrocentric emancipatory methodology" and others claiming to have a special epistemological status.

Conclusions

The analysis presented by Scheurich and Young has been valuable, I believe, not so much in articulating an alternative methodological position but in (unintentionally) providing support to standard descriptions of what it means to "know." Their major error has been to commit a "category mistake," whereby two different issues are conflated. Here is how it works. Assume a doctoral student, say, from a non-dominant group wants to do her dissertation on a relevant research question emerging from her experience as a member of that group. Now, as her adviser, if I tell her I will not consider her topic because it stems from a particular cultural context, then I could be legitimately accused of exhibiting any or all of the "racisms" described by the authors. If I reject her research question because it is "trivial" from the standpoint of the field, area, or discipline in which she is working, then we are at a standstill. Here, if I am being fair (and I hope I would be), I would state my reasons for my belief and she for hers. Even though the "dialogue" might be imbalanced because she is, after all, the "student" and I am the "professor," if I am behaving ethically, I am under some obligation to give my reasons truthfully and openly, and she hers.

It is here that a true "dialogue" should ensue. If, however, she claims that I cannot say *anything* about the substance of her research questions because I am not a member of her group, then there is certainly no point in going on. Alternatively, if we both agree on the topic, but she argues that my *general* methodological concerns of validity, reliability, sampling, and relevant intersubjective standards of assessment do not apply because, again, such methods simply are irrelevant to "knowing" her group-based reality, then, once more, there is an impasse. If her methodological claims can be articulated and open to critique, then there is a possibility that she can persuade me to her methodological commitment, or I can reject it for the reasons I give. But here, there is at least the possibility for real dialogue and assessment of what it means to be "rational"; such concerns are at the heart of what "epistemology" means. Of course, if I am accused of "epistemological racism" to begin with, then there is nowhere to go other than name-calling.

Scheurich and Young's position is undesirable and, worse, self-defeating because carried out to its logical conclusion, it must lead to a radical form of relativism, both philosophical and cultural. We do not need this as members of the educational research community. Finally, to once more illustrate where such a position leads, consider the following: By their own admission, the authors belong to the dominant culture. As such, they are those who, by definition, engage in "epistemological racism." But if this is so, then they cannot even comment on the possibility of other "epistemologies"—let alone their appropriateness. Hence, they must either reject their own analysis or declare that they were lying about being a part of the dominant culture! And given my analysis here, I would also like the readership of *Educational Researcher* to guess my particular group membership—given the possibility that I may have been adopted.

Section 4

Rejoinder: In the United States of America, in Both Our Souls and Our Sciences, We Are Avoiding White Racism

James Joseph Scheurich and Michelle D. Young

[T]he time has passed when the so-called race question can be relegated to secondary or tertiary theoretical significance. In fact, to take seriously the multi-leveled oppression of peoples of color is to raise fundamental questions regarding the very conditions for the possibility of the modern West, the diverse forms and styles of European rationality and the character of the prevailing modern secular mythologies of nationalism, professionalism, scientism, consumerism and sexual hedonism that guide everyday practices around the world. (West, 1993a, p. 251)

White racism is the real specter that haunts us. Its massively destructive effects continue to be readily apparent in who fails in school—who gets the lowest tracks, the least experienced teachers, the worst hidden curriculum, disproportionate assignment to special education, culturally biased pedagogies, excessive disciplinary actions, underrepresentation in textbooks, the least money spent on them, and the worst buildings (see, e.g., Scheurich & Laible, 1995, p. 314; see also Banks, 1993, 1995; Berliner & Biddle, 1995; Cuban, 1989; Cummins, 1986; King, 1991; Valencia, 1991, among many, many others)—and in who disproportionately goes to prison, gets "legally" executed, is relegated to low-paying jobs and poverty, is the object of racially oriented violence, is discriminated against in employment and banking, and is pushed into racially segregated neighborhoods with the worst housing (see Coramae Richey Mann's *Unequal Justice: A Question of Color* [1993] for but one of literally hundreds of discussions of the effects of white racism in the United States).[1]

In the United States of America, then, our socially constructed reality is itself "wholly racialized"—deeply, subtly, and pervasively (Toni Morrison, 1992, p. xii). However, even in education, where the destructive effects are so obvious and so persistent, we are avoiding white racism in both our souls and our sciences. And one of the principal ways we researchers in education avoid white racism is by be-lieving or presuming that somehow it does not infect our research assumptions, questions, epistemologies, and methodologies, that somehow we in the university have a special immunity that protects us from reproducing white racism, even though education and education research continue to be replete with racist con-cepts like the "deficit model" (see, e.g., Valencia, 1997), which is the assumption that the reason children of color do not do well academically is because of their at-titudes, their parents, their neighborhoods, their cultures, their socioeconomic sta-tus their genetics, or their race. In short, we blame the effects, not the source (see Derman-Sparks & Phillips, 1997, for an insightful and educative discussion of victim-blaming).

In "Coloring Epistemology" (Scheurich & Young, 1997), we concluded that "[t]he single most important effort needed [among education scholars for the purpose of addressing white racism in our research was] to initiate a vigorous de-bate/dialogue among scholars of all races" (p. 11). In this vein, we truly appreciate the two respondents who have joined this "debate/dialogue." We also are aware that others have sent responses to *Educational Researcher*, and while the work of these others has not been accepted for publication, we appreciate their efforts as well. Furthermore, we know that there has been ample commentary and debate about "Coloring" within internet user groups, and we appreciate these interac-tions. Even if we disagree with many of the viewpoints—some of them blatantly racist, expressed within various venues—we believe it is much better to explicitly toil and trouble over the problem of white racism than it is to ignore it. In many ways, white racism is like a monster standing amid us, affecting so much of what we do—or do not do—while we, particularly we white people, appear to hope that if we avoid it, ignore it, or don't look at it, it will quietly go away. It won't.

It is not surprising, then, that there are radically and even vehemently differ-ent disagreements with our perspective. Because we cannot, however, address the entire range of disagreements, what we will do here is reply just to the two re-sponses *ER* has decided to publish, even though we are hopeful that this is not the end of this discussion. Of these two responses, Cynthia Tyson's is, in our view, considerably superior to the other. She offers a more provocative and more funda-mental critique and an insightful one of "Coloring," even suggesting we are repro-ducing the white racism we were ourselves critiquing. She is committed in her approach, in the humane and sensitive way she offers her critique, to dialoguing and moving the conversation forward in meaningful and productive ways.

Cynthia Tyson, an African-American scholar, according to her response, agreed with our critique of the white racial dominance of research epistemologies (see her third section on "Epistemology of Oppression," along with other com-ments throughout her response), but she also turned our argument back on us in her second section, "Epistemology of Competing Agendas." One question she asks is why do the debates "begin" when white scholars raise the issue of racial bias in research epistemologies when scholars of color have been making these points for years? We agree with her critique. We started "Coloring" by asking why didn't the 1990 Gordon, Miller, and Rollock (all of whom are African-American scholars) *Educational Researcher* piece cause a range of responses? We agree with Tyson: Why is an issue ignored when scholars of color raise it, but is not ignored when white scholars, like us, raise it? Why do we get to be the center of attention when we were saying much the same thing, though in a somewhat different way, as Gordon, Miller, and Rollock did? The answer, we think, as does Tyson, is that this is an example of how white racism works among researchers. When white scholars say something about racism, it is "heard" differently than when scholars of color say similar things, even if the scholars of color say it first.

One of the reasons we think "talk" about racism is heard differently by whites when whites are authoring the talk is that when whites discuss racism, it is seen, mainly by other whites, as more legitimate, more important, more objective. It is as if when scholars of color talk about racism, they are seen as just making a self-serving point, as if they cannot be trusted to be "objectively" insightful about race or racism. However, the peculiar flip side of this is that when whites avoid or ignore racism, as often happens, no one accuses them of being self-serving, of not being objective. This is similar to the fact that when white researchers study just white students, few question the racial imbalance in the sample. But when scholars of color want to study only students of color, the racially imbalanced sample issue is often raised (we have frequently seen this in dissertation proposal defenses). We agree, then, with this criticism by Tyson: Because of white racism, the words of white scholars on racism, including ours, are often heard as more legitimate, more objective—particularly by whites—though this, of course, is the essence of hypocrisy.

Another issue that Tyson focuses on is whether our critique, what Tyson calls our "reconstruction," was indirectly racist. She argues that we may have inadvertently—through our own white racism—placed the onus on scholars of color to legitimate their "alternative" race/culture-based research epistemologies. Instead, she suggests, we could have better served our anti-racist goals if we had placed the onus of critical pressure on ourselves and other white professors to identify and root out the white racism in research. Her suggestion is that we have merely tried to add race/culture-based research epistemologies to the expanding array of possible research epistemologies, rather than to critique the dominant research epistemologies for their embedded racism. In effect, we have just said move over and make room for more research epistemologies, rather than doing the more difficult, more politically dangerous task of showing how existing research (and the epistemologies on which this research is based) is racist or reproduces white racism. Her apt concern, then, is that our approach has little chance of changing anything.

We think this is a substantive and insightful criticism of "Coloring." Tyson wants us to make our point in "Coloring" that "reality" itself is "wholly racialized" within the United States, but then she wants us to discuss "examples of racist epistemologies and methodologies as 'concrete referents' so that these racist epistemologies and methodologies can truly be dismantled and dissected" (Tyson, p. 75). She is correct that we did not try to do this. In "Coloring," we were arguing that "reality" itself is, because of the dominant white racism, racialized at the deepest and most fundamental levels, including the level of primary or "civilizational" assumptions, which would logically encompass the research epistemologies that arise out of these civilizational assumptions. In opposition, then, to the dominant research epistemologies, many scholars of color have responded by discussing and developing research epistemologies (or philosophies) that could be argued to arise out of the specificity of the historical experience of people and cultures of color. We contended, then, that ignoring these research epistemologies drawn from the historical experience of people of color was white racism at work.

However, what we did not do, but what Tyson wants us to do, is to discuss "examples of racist epistemologies and methodologies" (p. 75). We did not consider this possibility, so she may be correct that because of our own racism, this was not an option we considered (i.e., it did not exist in our "reality"). We think her suggestion is a profound one, a compelling challenge. In undertaking this challenge, though, it needs to be understood what she is asking for and what she is not. She is not asking for us to examine the ways that racist assumptions, values, and beliefs have shaped research questions, designs, findings, and interpretations as well as the ways these findings and interpretations have been presented as truth and incorporated into educational practices. This kind of work does exist (see, e.g., Valencia's 1997 edited collection on the deficit model or Marks, 1993, on the racist assumptions that underline much demographic work), although there is certainly not enough of it. What Tyson is asking for, we think, is for us to show how the dominant epistemologies and methodologies themselves are racist. The latter is a much more difficult, more complex task, a call to thoughtfully and vigilantly analyze how the dominant epistemologies and methodologies are racist, a task that has received much less attention, although some work of this nature does exist. Cornell West has done some of this (e.g., West, 1993a, 1993c), although from a philosophical perspective rather than from the perspective of research epistemologies, as has Lucius Outlaw (1996). To us, some of the best discussions to date on race and epistemology/methodology are those of John Stanfield (e.g., 1985, 1994, Stanfield & Dennis, 1993).

Because we agree with Tyson's critique of our work and we agree with Tyson that there is a lack of work in this particular area, we will offer one specific example in response. With our example, we argue that one of the principal and most powerful ways white racism works is through invisibility, what we would suggest calling, drawing from Ellison (1972), *the invisibility factor* of white racism. We mean that although the effects of white racism are multifariously present, they are not "seen," mentioned, or named by whites, and thus no action is required. In fact, white racism and its effects are made invisible by and for whites by whites ignoring them—when it is not spoken, ipso facto, it does not exist—the invisibility factor. (This is part of what we meant in "Coloring" when we argued that whites to a significant extent live within a different "reality" than people of color; in white "reality," the existence and effects of white racism are ignored—made invisible—by whites.)

Accordingly, we could argue that, given the deep and pervasive racism in U.S. society and the historical record of incorporation of that racism into research and research processes, education research, in an effort to be perennially vigilant about destructive racial biases (in an effort to avoid validity threats, you might say), ought to have long ago developed a kind of validity that could be called *race-equity validity* as a common research practice applicable to social science research. Like other validity criteria, race-equity validity would be used to evaluate whether we can depend on the research findings to be free of racial biases in all aspects of research. It would be used to identify biases such as the use of deficit models to blame school failure on students of color. Researchers would, if this were widely accepted, commonly expect that each research report would include a discussion of how the researcher addressed race-equity validity.

That these kinds of validity practices are *not* in place—given this society's history of white racism inside and outside of research—could therefore be argued to be strong evidence of the invisibility factor, of the racially biased avoidance of the persistence and depth of white racism. That this avoidance may not be conscious or intended does not undermine the point; we, in fact, would argue that in present conditions it takes tenacious anti-racist practices, like a race-equity validity, to counter the pervasiveness of white racism in research. We think discussions of this sort, that focus on how dominant research epistemologies and practices have avoided the discussion of white racism, are one example of what Tyson is calling for and criticizing us for avoiding. We agree with both her criticism and her call.

In contrast to Tyson's response, Stephen Miller provides a response that was highly disappointing and highly upsetting to us. We were not upset with his philosophical points; his points are not new, nothing that has not been seen several times in other variations in many journals. They are part of a larger philosophical debate about the nature of truth and the standards for judging it (see, e.g., Banks, 1993, 1995; Cherryholmes, 1994; Donmoyer, 1985; Eisner, 1988; Gordon, Miller, & Rollock, 1990; House, 1994; Popkewitz, 1997; Smith, 1997 to name but a few in only *Educational Researcher*). In contrast, two other issues were highly disappointing and even, we believe, destructive. One of these was his tone, his ridicule, and sarcasm; that is, the way that he offered his critique is destructive of any sort of educational conversation. His intent seemed to be to establish some kind of intellectual or philosophical domination. One instance of this was the way he accuses us of philosophical and logical "defects" and "errors," rather than saying he has disagreements with us. Another was his sarcastic use of phrases like "to drag out a list of dead, white, male figures" (p. 24). It does not seem too demanding to us for anyone entering a conversation about racism, a conversation that has a difficult, raw history, to be aware that certain kinds of word choices inhibit conversation and certain other kinds facilitate it.

Worst of all, though, was that *given* how difficult, painful, and conflictual racism is in the United States and *given* the deep and thoughtful commitment of many scholars of color to a point of view close to the one we argued in "Coloring," his virtually total avoidance of the racism issue is horrifyingly insensitive and even injurious. That he focused exclusively on the underlying so-called "relativist" logic of our piece without any substantive discussion of the racism issue easily left the impression, whether he intended to or not, that he was trying to undermine any inconvenient or burdensome discussion of white racism within higher education and research without being caught with dirty hands, no matter what the color of his hands is. Then, to add insult to injury, the trivializing and denigrating nature of his ending—guessing his race with the condition he may have been adopted—left us with both anger and deep, deep disappointment that a point this destructive and this worthless would not be questioned by *Educational Researcher*'s reviewers.

Part of what is so disappointing about Miller's response is that it could easily have been well done. His philosophical critique of our philosophical assumptions is important and relevant in philosophical arguments about the social sciences (see, e.g., Phillips, 1987, who espouses well a perspective somewhat similar to Miller's). We could imagine that someone holding his view could have actually contributed in a positive way to the ongoing conversation about the issues raised in "Coloring." Our imagined author could have sensitively and directly addressed the issues of racism in research, including the recognition that research has an atrocious history of reproducing white racism. She could have, then, developed philosophical arguments in a careful and logical way so that readers could have clearly understood the points within a context of candidness about racism in research, and she could have done all of this in terms of a felt commitment to facilitating conversation within a context in which misunderstanding is all too easy.

It is, thus, puzzling to us that this particular response was chosen as the "best" representative of the disagreements with "Coloring." Part of our puzzlement is why those scholars who are well known and respected for their discussions of research epistemologies and methodologies, in *ER* and elsewhere, and those who are well known for publishing widely used research textbooks have not joined this discussion. As we asked in "Coloring," why the massive silence? Why do prominent white scholars, in agreement or disagreement, keep silent when white racism is publicly discussed? Where are our prominent scholars on this issue? Is this part of how the invisibility factor works? Nonetheless, just as we believe this author was not well served—in a communicative or an educational sense—to simply dismiss our obvious stupidity, we will not simply dismiss the points he tries to make.

First, what virtually everyone else knows, at least since Lincoln and Guba's groundbreaking work, *Naturalistic Inquiry* (1985), but what Miller does not say, is that he represents but one family of philosophical thought about the nature of social science "truth" and the appropriate criteria for judging that "truth." There are, in fact, well-respected philosophers—from race-oriented critical theorists like Cornell West and bell hooks and new pragmatists like Richard Rorty to feminists like Sandra Harding and Judith Butler and poststructuralists like Jacques Derrida and Michel Foucault—who would disagree with Miller's position. For example, Foucault in much of his earlier work argues that the social or human sciences are not "sciences" in the same sense that the natural sciences are: "It is useless, then, to say that the 'human sciences' are false sciences; they are not sciences at all; the configuration that defines their positivity . . . at the same time makes it impossible for them to be sciences" (Foucault, 1970, p. 366).

Within, then, the broad breadth of philosophy and the social sciences, there currently is consensus about very little. Each school or perspective has its own assumptions, beliefs, and conclusions. To argue, then, as if the nature of "truth" is obviously settled is *to* grossly distort the current philosophical debates about the social sciences. To say we were guilty of philosophical errors rather than to say we had philosophical disagreements is not logic but rhetoric, a rhetorical maneuver designed to establish philosophical superiority (see Lynch & Woolgar, 1990; Nelson, Megill, & McCloskey, 1987; Simon, 1989, for critical examinations of the rhetoric used by advocates of Miller's perspective). What Miller needs is less rhetoric and more of a good philosophical argument.

Second, Miller was concerned that we have, through our philosophical ignorance, enthroned relativism (see Rorty, 1982, pp. 166–169, for a brief, useful, and humorous critique of Miller's specter of relativism). Miller contended that our argument that different races in the United States live within significantly different "realities" leads to no possibility for communication ("discourse is not possible" (p. 24). To support this latter conclusion, Miller used Quine's (1960) "indeterminacy of translation" thesis in which it is argued that totally separate realities or cultures mean that no translation or communication is possible between the realities or cultures and, therefore, that no meta-level evaluation criteria (i.e., criteria by which all claims can be adjudicated) is possible.[2] However, nowhere in "Coloring" did we develop any argument that there was this kind of totalized and complete separation of the races in the United States. Instead, we made the argument that because of past and present white racism and because of positive cultural differences maintained over time by many people of color, whites and people of color live within significantly different "realities"—not totally different realities, but significantly different, nonetheless.

An example: As middle-class white people, we academics are rarely concerned that the police are going to stop us just because there has been a crime in the area or we are driving around in, say, a predominantly black area. In contrast, take the all-too-frequent experience of African-American men, even upper middle-class African-American men. They may drive a nice car and live in an upscale section of a city, but they are all too often stopped or followed by police because they are driving a nice car in a "good" white area of the city.

Another example: A Mexican-American woman goes into a middle-class department store, browses around, only to discover she is being "monitored" by a clerk, who assumes she is there only to shoplift. It does not take many of these kinds of experiences before "reality" becomes substantially (though not totally) different. It would surely not be surprising, then, given repeated personal and institutional experiences of white racism, numerous stories told by friends of color, and the historical oppression of cultures of color that scholars of color would attend to different issues or attend differently to the same issues when they carried out research or discussed research epistemologies from the issues to which white scholars would attend. It would surely not be surprising if scholars of color were to argue, as they have, that research epistemologies, as social productions, are affected by white racism. In fact, would it not be even more startling, a kind of Disney-like fantasy, if somehow social science research epistemologies were truly pure creations, totally unaffected by their historical context?

Therefore, contra Miller, none of what we said in "Coloring" means that all of "reality" or that all aspects of research epistemologies and methodologies are different for whites and people of color. Nor does it mean that just because you are, say, African-American, you must be an Afrocentric or a critical race theorist. Again, Miller is ironically—given his philosophical commitments—using a rhetorical maneuver rather than close, careful logic. He was literally leaping to the judgment that arguing any difference leads to a totalized difference. This, we would suggest, could be called committing a *difference fallacy.* Any suggestion that a difference exists automatically is projected to mean a total difference, which means no communication and total separation, which is feared to mean all fall down amidst the chaos of relativism and race war.

Miller's use of the difference fallacy raised for us the question of why any assertion of any amount of difference around issues of race and white racism seems so repeatedly to lead to predictions of cataclysms like "no discourse is possible," relativism, or, as is often suggested in the public media, a Bosnian-like race war. It is as if some difference on race today automatically means a race war tomorrow, or at least relativism. Why is the possibility of opening the door to any difference—or the possibility of directly confronting white racism—so dangerous that it is argued to lead to such terrible consequences? Why is the threat of relativism repeatedly raised in these kinds of contexts? Why is relativism the specter that will haunt us if we address white racism when what is truly haunting us is white racism?

Another aspect of the relativism issue Miller raised is his distress that, given our approach, there would not be any "standards of criticism and evaluation across epistemologies" (p. 24). Our response is: Where do such standards come from historically, and who are in the legitimized positions to decide what these ought to be? We surmise that this author would argue that such standards in the social sciences ought to emerge out of some sort of value-free, ahistorical, logical, rational process. We would argue, in contrast, as a long list of philosophers and social scientists do (like those we cited earlier: hooks, West, Rorty, Harding, Butler, Derrida, Foucault), that "logics" and "standards" of the social sciences are, to a substantial extent, the social productions of different communities of thought (different truth games), communities that are deeply interlaced with the major structural inequities (race, class, gender, sexual orientation, disabilities, etc.) of their historical contexts.

One major problem we have with Miller's stance is that he wants his truth game to be the dominant truth game. This means his "reality" (truth game) gets to dominate all other "realities," that his standards and logic get to dominate all standards and logics. In our view, there are no standards or logic that get to rule all schools of thought in philosophy or the social sciences, nor ought there to be. Instead, in messy, complicated human reality, in the messy human sciences, what we get is negotiation, conflict, education, rhetoric, power, persuasion, oppression, white racism, and anti-racism—the works. Whoever imagined that the social sciences are better than, superior to, elevated above what is going on in the rest of society must be living within the philosophical solipsism of one school of thought talking only to itself because they certainly have not been living within the messy history of the social sciences, encrusted as it has been and continues to be with deep biases of all sorts, ranging from racial to philosophical.

It is not that we have any resistance to discussing standards or logic, but we want to advocate that everyone, all groups, all "realities"—racial in this case—are equally represented at the proverbial discussion table, that all groups are equally influential, and that no group gets to assume it possesses the right standards or the right logic. If any group or perspective approaches the table with the certain assumption that it knows the right way, as Miller argued his perspective does, this group or perspective destroys the table, destroys the conversation. There has to be some assumption of the potential for persuasion, compromise, even education and change for there to be any point to the conversation. Or Miller is right, and he and his tribe have the one and only truly true truth game, and the rest of us have to play his game or shut up.

A third issue Miller raised was whether our perspective eliminates any possibility that whites can be critical of white racism or that critiques of white racism can become embedded in the way scholarship in general is done. We would argue that our perspective does not eliminate any such possibility and that, in fact, our work is part of this critical work. There exists a whole range of scholarly opinion against racism among whites, from even conservative and minimal liberal views to radical left and aggressive anti-racist ones. And, yes, some of this work has made its way into the mainstream of scholarship. Our point, though, is that even with the most aggressive anti-racism, whites live in a social world that is deeply embedded with white racism and thus white privilege. As a result, even the most radical white is to a significant extent influenced by white racism, especially as this works out, often unconsciously, at the institutional, societal, and civilizational level (see e.g., Jensen, 1998, for a highly readable self-account of white privilege by a white journalism professor).

This was one of the valuable points of Tyson's critique of our own work: However seemingly radical or anti-racist "Coloring" might be judged to be, it still, even if unintendedly, reproduces in some ways that which it is intended to work against—i.e., white racism. Our point here, then, is that in the United States, to be white (no matter what your political or moral commitments are), to go through daily life with white skin privilege (a kind of long-term white affirmative action), is, to some degree, to be a white racist. This, though, is not meant to deny the anti-racist work many whites have done or are doing nor to belittle that work. This white anti-racism, including the deaths of some whites for this cause, is supremely important and has played a key role in some anti-racism victories and movements. Instead, our perspective is meant to place that anti-racist work in the broader and deeper, societal and civilizational lived context. The two of us, for example, see ourselves as *both* anti-racist *and* white racists. This, we argue, is the contradictory, ambiguous reality of whites doing anti-racist work. The two of us are *both* inside white racism, deeply and unconsciously affected by it, *and* working against it— both within and against.

We will end by turning to the public schools. We in higher education— overwhelmingly white—have trained the teachers and administrators who educate an extremely high proportion of all U.S. citizens. The beliefs, pedagogies, concepts, and curricula that educators use, like the bell curve or functionalist management approaches or deficit models or monocultural curricular materials, were developed and taught by us whites. We, overwhelmingly white, are, then, to a substantial degree, accountable for the current nature of the public school system. In this system, schools are disproportionately failing huge numbers of children of color. These children are daily experiencing schools as destroying their basic belief in themselves, their talents, and their intelligence. Schools are teaching them that they are failures. We are, then, in the midst of this unbelievable, ongoing national tragedy—the daily destruction of the psychological and intellectual well-being of literally millions of children of color—while we, overwhelmingly white, act as if the problem is not all that bad or as if things are improving or as if this is just one of our many problems along with standards, accountability, site-based management, learning theories, research methodologies, and the like. Children are being destroyed—taught that they are worthless, dumb, bad—while we, overwhelmingly white, avoid the tragedy and our participation in it.

What we are struggling to say is that within the "reality" where we whites live, this wholesale destruction of children of color is not happening or is smaller than some say or is but one of many other relevant issues. Within the lived reality of people of color, this horrible tragedy continues year after year, decade after decade.

We whites, in our souls and our sciences, have been able to ignore this, to not see it, to not believe the tragedy exists. This is similar—and we want to say it carefully but say it nonetheless—to what happened with whites during the times of slavery or Jim Crow or the theft of Mexican-American and Native American lands. In these eras in the United States, white people in general and white scholars in particular were, at best, not aggressively and forcefully addressing racism and, at worst, were legitimizing it. Even though we whites want to focus on the areas of improvement, doing so covers up the fact that we whites, including we white scholars in education, are, at best, avoiding and, at worst, supporting the white racism that is destroying children of color. To think, thus, that our research epistemologies, our scholarship, our logics, and standards are somehow separated from all of this, separated somehow from the deep and pervasive ways that white racism is interwoven throughout U.S. society is, in our view, the essence of white racism itself in action.

Notes for Chapter 2, Section 2

1. We want to thank several people who read this manuscript and made suggestions and comments prior to its submission: Lonnie Wagstaff, Koran Thompson, Gerardo Lopéz, Larry Parker, John Palmer, and Elissa Fineman.

2. One fascinating irony about Miller's response is that the fulcrum of his argument is a 1960 work by W. V. Quine. Setting aside for a moment the existence of other philosophical perspectives, it is almost as if to Miller, analytic/empiricist/realist philosophy ended with or reached an unassailable peak with Quine. However, even within this tradition, this is simply not true. Barry Stroud in *The Significance of Philosophical Scepticism* (1984) provided a substantive critique of some of Quine's positions. Hilary Putnam has significant disagreements with Quine in *Realism and Reason* (1983). Donald Davidson in *Inquiries into Truth and Interpretation* (1984) also has major disagreements with Quine's positions. Of course, Richard Rorty, who emerged from the same general tradition and who draws much of his perspective from Davidson both uses Quine in ways which Quine would likely disapprove of and has substantial disagreements with Quine.

Another fascinating irony is in what Quine says in the last paragraph of the book that Miller cites: "The philosopher's task differs from the others' [he is referring here to scientists and mathematicians] then, in detail: but in no such drastic way *as those who imagine for the philosopher a vantage point outside the conceptual scheme that he takes in charge. There is no such cosmic exile.* He [the philosopher] cannot study and revise the fundamental conceptual scheme of science and common sense without having some conceptual scheme, where the same or another no less in need of philosophical scrutiny, in which to work" (Quine, 1960, pp. 275-276, italics added). This, in a certain sense, is the very point we are trying to make about Miller's philosophical scheme: It is only a philosophical scheme and not cosmic exile or a god's-eye view, as he appears to assume, and it is equally in need of "philosophical scrutiny" as any scheme is.

Part II
ANTI-RACIST RESPONSES TO THE SCHOLARSHIP OF OTHERS

Part II is composed of four chapters. Each of these chapters is either my work or my work with my colleagues and students. Each of these chapters begins as a response to the work of other white scholars. The first one (chapter 3), "The Buck Stops Here," was written with Julie Laible, who is the anti-racist scholar to whom this book is dedicated. Chapter 4 has three parts and starts with an article by Carl Glickman. Chapter 5 is a group response to the *Handbook of Research in Educational Administration* (1999). Chapter 6 was a requested response to the work of Harry Wolcott. Thus, all four of these chapters in Part II are anti-racist responses to the work of other white scholars.

Chapter 3

Preface

In Chapter 3, Julie Laible and I were asked by the editors of the *Educational Administration Quarterly* to respond to what was called the "knowledge-base project" in educational administration. Julie and I were critics of this project in educational administration almost from the beginning. As a result of my disagreements with this knowledge project, I was the co-author of an edited book (Donmoyer, Imber, & Scheurich, 1995) that provided a wide range of views either that critiqued the proposed knowledge-base or that offered alternative views not covered in the official project. This chapter then is our critique of this project.

Chapter 3

The Buck Stops Here in Our Preparation Programs: Educative Leadership for All Children (No Exceptions Allowed)

James Joseph Scheurich and Julie Laible

> We need a bold and radical change in how we [in educational administra-
> tion] do things. . . . We need to practice a leadership that can only be un-
> derstood as part of a broader mission of social responsibility dedicated
> toward improving the community and guaranteeing human dignity for all
> (Reyes, 1993).

Kofi Lomotey's discussion of the "Social and Cultural Influences on Schooling: A Commentary on the UCEA Knowledge-base Project, Domain I" raises troubling, discomforting issues for the educational administration professorate, for our profession, and for the knowledge-base project itself. First, Lomotey (and the domain committee for which he was chair) asserts that "illegitimate forms of exclusion (including racism, sexism, and classism) provide the bedrock of institutions in U.S. society and resultantly offer the foundation of the social and cultural influences on schools" (Lomotey, 1995, p. 297). Second, he argues that these exclusionary influences lead to "the disenfranchisement of large numbers of African-American, Hispanic, American Indian, [Asian],[1] women and poor students in our schools" (p. 297). And, finally, he provides suggestions for a major transformation of both educational administration preparation programs and for schools in general.

His first point about the race, gender, and class biases of our society and our schools is his most important point because, if he is correct on this one, the succeeding two points he makes follow more easily. Many in our profession may readily agree with Lomotey, but others may be more hesitant or more skeptical. Indeed, judgments or conclusions like Lomotey's, about large complex systems, such as our educational system or our society, are difficult to "prove" in a fashion that would convince virtually everyone. Various facts can be cited and arguments mounted from a large range of viewpoints. Furthermore, changing someone's opinion, even those of academics and researchers, about such troubling matters is difficult. Nonetheless, we think Lomotey's first point about "illegitimate forms of exclusion" is correct, and we would like to offer some considerations for those who are reluctant to accept this conclusion.

Our primary point is that success in schools largely, although not completely, corresponds to race, class, and gender inequalities in our society.[2] For instance, if we look at the test results that are used in many states (like in our state, Texas) to compare districts, to a startling extent the hierarchy of district success on those tests mirrors the race/class hierarchy of the districts. That is, the middle and upper middle-class Anglo districts consistently rank the highest, and low-income districts of color consistently rank the lowest. That a few of the latter districts sometimes rank in the middle and upper ranges of the success hierarchy (a point we will briefly return to later) does not abrogate the consistent nature of the hierarchy. Also, we suggest that there is a large body of research across many different areas within education that supports the fact that the race/class hierarchy of our society is similarly reflected in who is disproportionately assigned to higher and lower academic tracks (e.g., Oakes, 1985), who is designated a special education student (e.g., Ortiz, 1986; Williams-Dixon, 1991), who is given the more excessive disciplinary treatments (e.g., Williams, 1989), who receives less or negative attention from teachers (e.g., Wiley & Eskilson, 1978; Winfield, 1986), who has their first language and culture devalued (e.g., Cummins, 1986; Villegas, 1988), who are expected to perform poorly (e.g., Good, 1981; Page, 1987), who drops out or is pushed out of school (e.g., Fine,1991; Rumberger, 1991), who is underrepresented in textbooks (e.g., Apple, 1992, or Bernstein, 1985), and so on.

In addition, the gender hierarchy is typically reflected in whose self-esteem drops throughout middle school and high school (e.g., American Association of University Women [AAUW], 1992), who receives the better math and science tracking—in both formal and informal ways (e.g., Deckard, 1983; Shepardson & Pizinni, 1992), who more typically experiences sexual harassment and harassment in general—from both teachers and other students (e.g., AAUW, 1993; Laible, 1994; Shakeshaft et al., 1994), who receives less or negative attention from teachers (Good & Brophy, 1987), whose acceptance and success is predicated on matching social ideals about appearance (e.g., Mann, 1994; or Minnesota Women's Fund, 1991), who is underrepresented in textbooks (e.g., Sadker & Sadker, 1994), and so on. Of course, it also needs to be recognized that some groups of students simultaneously benefit and are harmed by these unequal treatments and effects. For instance, middle-class Anglo women often benefit from their race and class positionality but are hurt by their gender. Nonetheless, our judgment, like Lomotey's and the Domain I committee's, is that the cumulative evidence from all kinds of research by a wide range of scholars is overwhelming: Societal inequalities are broadly reproduced in schools in a variety of ways, both individual and institutional, and this leads to "the disenfranchisement of large numbers of African-American, Hispanic, American Indian, [Asian,] women and poor students in our schools" (Lomotey, 1995, p. 297). That this conclusion is well within the mainstream of educational scholarship is verified by the fact that John Goodlad and Pamela Keating (1994) have recently published a collection of articles addressing the same point of view argued here. According to the "foreword" of this volume,

> As Professor[s] John Goodlad [and Pamela Keating] . . . and the other contributors have documented, inequities are . . . painfully evident in the level of curriculum, quality of pedagogy, and school environment. Recent research has also revealed some frightening facts . . . about how our schools fail women and girls. (p. vii) [3]

This conclusion, however, requires that we consider the question of why schools reproduce societal inequities. The authors of *The Bell Curve* (Herrnstein & Murray, 1994), two new members of a toxic lineage of others in the past (William Shockley, 1992, would be another member of that lineage; see also Gould's *The Mismeasure of Man*, 1981), offer the explanation that IQ, and thus school success, are significantly related to genetics. The horrendously destructive implication of this is that, because some racial groups and the poor typically do less well in school, these groups have a genetically-based, lower average IQ. We believe, however, that very few in the educational administration professorate accept this explanation, but we often accept an alternative explanation that may be even more problematic.

Many seem to argue that the race, class, and gender biases in schools are a function of the same in society. And, of course, it is inarguable that schools exist within society and thus must to some extent reflect that society, as Dewey (1937, p. 235) has argued. But we would like to suggest, as we think Dewey would, that by the very fact that we consider ourselves educators, we cannot accept this conclusion in a deterministic way. To be an educator, to believe in education, is to believe that education is itself empowering, that education by its very nature can "beat" race, class, and gender inequalities. To reverse our point, could you believe in education and also believe that schools can only reproduce race, class, and gender inequities within society? Would you continue to be an educator if you believed that this reproduction was all that was possible? In fact, we argue, again with Dewey (1937, p. 235), that our public educational system, as well as our personal commitments as educators, is founded on the very idea that education is one of the most important ways that our nation has for ending all of this injustice. Consequently, we advocate that educators, on the basis of their commitment to education, must strongly reject the problematic claim that schools of necessity can only mirror societal inequalities.

If, then, we agree that the evidence is very strong that schools have largely been reproductive of such inequalities and if we agree that as educators we cannot accept this result, our next question is, what can we as professors of educational administration and as educational administrators do? There is, however, no need for

us to repeat the broad range of excellent suggestions made by Lomotey and the Domain I Committee that address what we ought to be doing. Nor is it useful here for
us to repeat the similarly excellent suggestions that Pedro Reyes (1993) offered in his
University Council for Educational Administration (UCEA) presidential address
on these same matters. In fact, we argue that the concrete actions that need to be
taken to decrease substantially the race, gender, and class biases in our schools are already largely known. Scholars such as Banks (1989), Shakeshaft (1986), Grant and
Sleeter (1989), Fine (1991), Edmonds (1979), and Cummins (1986), among many
others, have been making fairly similar suggestions for years in terms of the kinds of
changes that are needed in educational administration preparation programs, in educational administration, and in the schools in general so that all children have a
truly equitable chance to learn without regard to race, gender, or class. For example,
as far back as 1979, Edmonds said, "We can, whenever and wherever we choose,
successfully teach *all children* whose schooling is of interest to us; *we already know
more than we need to do that* [emphases added]" (p. 24). And this is borne out by the
fact that we have good examples all over the country of schools that are successful
with students from each and every race, gender, and class (see, e.g., Comer, 1988;
Levin, 1991; Lucas, Henze, & Donato, 1990).

If race, gender, and class inequalities have such destructively powerful effects on the students in our schools and if we have long had good, concrete suggestions on how to remove, or at least substantially decrease these effects, why have
we not done so? If these effects are so powerful, so influential on which children do
well in school and which do not, why have our educational administration programs not been structured around accomplishing this crucial work? And so, we
have reached the difficult part, the questions that stop at our doorstep, the buck
that stops here. Our intention, however, is not to assign blame or induce guilt; nor
is it our intention to imply that we would or could have done it better—blame,
guilt, and superiority claims are a waste of crucial time and energy. In fact, it is our
opinion, based on knowing personally and reading the publications of many of
our colleagues, that almost all of us have been strongly committed to equality and
inclusion throughout our careers in education. Also, it is this commitment we are
calling upon because any significant change in these matters, even within the limited purview of UCEA and this essay (although this is a purview that could have
enormous impact nationally), will require more than just a few of us. The kind of
change that we are talking about, the kind that Lomotey and the committee suggested, the kind that Reyes discussed in his presidential address, undeniably requires a commitment not just from some of us but from most of us.

Unfortunately, however, the knowledge-base project, taken as a whole and
in 1994 published as *Primis* (an electronic custom publishing system) by
McGraw-Hill, is not the commitment for which Lomotey, the Domain I committee, Reyes, and we are calling. In fact, we argue that a serious acceptance of the
"Social and Cultural Influences on Schooling" committee's work calls into ques-

tion, or even undermines, the entire knowledge-base project itself. As Gail Schneider (1992) said in her 1991 UCEA presidential address, the knowledge-base project's seven domains "look like the major topic areas within our current programs" (p. 5). In other words, the knowledge base's current seven-domain structure reproduces the long-established course structure of educational adminis-tration in UCEA member institutions, the same course structure that trained ed-ucational leaders for the schools that tend to reproduce race, gender, and class differences and that has not been informed by the kind of long-available changes noted above that are needed to stop these reproductive processes.

Ironically, the National Policy Board and UCEA sponsored a 1989 study by Nicolaides and Gaynor that was meant to lay the groundwork for the knowledge-base project but that makes much the same point we are making. They said near the beginning of that report that the "[c]entral challenges [for schools and, thus, for educational administration training programs] are *inequality* [emphasis added] and the rate of poverty" (p. 4) and that "the theoretical approach [functionalism] that has been guiding the knowledge-base preparation programs is inconsistent with the nature of the problems challenging school administrators in the current social context" (p. 4). In the last sentence of their report, they strongly criticize the fact that this "theoretical approach" focuses "on genderless, colorless, and faceless systems of information processing and decision making" (p. 39). They also say in their conclusion that preparation programs are only minimally addressing the kinds of perspectives that would address the "central challenges" that school ad-ministrators daily face. (For a broader discussion of these issues, see Scheurich, 1991; Donmoyer, Imber, & Scheurich, 1995.)

Our point here, however, is not to engage in Gage's (1991) "paradigm wars"; our point is that Nicolaides and Gaynor (1989) confirmed something close to what we have contended are the "central challenges" for schools and, thus, for administra-tors. They also ratify that the present knowledge-base domain structure "is limited to topics and themes shaped by traditional perspectives" (p. i) and that these per-spectives are inconsistent with the nature of our challenges. It could, nonetheless, be argued that the knowledge-base domains, as they are represented in the most recent version of *Primis,* adequately incorporate the new perspectives required to inaugu-rate the programmatic reforms suggested by Nicolaides and Gaynor, by Lomotey and the Domain I committee, by Reyes in his address, and by us here. But our survey of this version of *Primis* does not indicate that this argument is accurate.

Even though multiculturalism is one of the most critical teaching and learn-ing issues (see, e.g., Banks, 1989), Domain II (Teaching and Learning Processes) has no citation focused primarily on race, gender, or class. Domains III (Organi-zational Studies) and IV (Leadership and Management Processes) have only a couple of relevant pieces. Domains V (Policy and Political Studies) and VII (Eco-nomic and Financial Dimensions of Schooling) have only one such citation. Do-main VI (Legal and Ethical Dimensions of Schooling) has a substantial amount on race, gender, and class inequalities because—validating our point about the centrality of such inequalities in schools—many of the most consequential legal cases are about such issues.

Arguing, however, about whether there is sufficient representation from the kind of perspectives that Nicolaides and Gaynor (1989) thought were necessary to the challenges that schools and administrators currently face is insufficient. The direct implications of the conclusions of the Domain I committee, of Reyes's presidential address, and of the research shows that the powerful negative school effects of race, gender, and class will not be addressed by adding several more articles to the present domain structure, representative as it is of the traditional course structure of preparation programs. In short, the knowledge-base project, as presently constituted and structured, moves attention back to the old, inadequate way of doing business and away from the kind of changes and leadership necessary to prepare administrators who are ready and committed to developing—collaboratively with teachers, students, and parents—the kinds of schools that are equally successful for all children. If the current knowledge-base effort helps us realize this, it has been useful; if it does not—if in discussing and reconsidering the work to date, we do not see that we have gone down the wrong road—it is harmful. It is not minor change that we need for our purposes; it is not the traditional course structure and focus that we need. It is a major transformation, a major realignment of our entire way of preparing educational administrators.[4] What we need is a knowledge base, a domain structure, a course structure, focused on leadership committed to all children (no exceptions allowed—by race, gender, class, or any other exclusionary category).

Again, how we need to change or what we need to do to make the necessary changes to our preparation programs is not in question. As we said previously, many astute scholars and practitioners have already addressed this, and, not surprisingly, there is considerable overlap in their various suggestions. The real question, the "buck-stops-here" question, is whether we—not some of us but most of us—are willing to make these changes. As the profession within education that claims to understand and develop leadership, are *we* willing to provide the necessary *educative* leadership? In the end, the most central question is not whether the knowledge-base is the right or wrong one or who has accepted or rejected the knowledge-base project; the question, the really difficult question, is, Are we willing to (a) recognize the enormously destructive effects of race, gender, and class biases on our children; (b) commit to decreasing and eventually eradicating these effects; (c) radically change our preparation programs to accomplish this purpose; and (d) follow through long enough to see real changes in our schools? Our call, like that of Lomotey and the Domain I committee, is to all of us together, to our necessary commitments as educators, to our long-term, deeply held beliefs in equitable schools: If our departments of educational leadership do not lead the way, who will? If not us, who?

Notes for Part II, Chapter 3

1. We suggest that, even though so-called model minorities (like some Asian nationalities) generally do well in school, many from these groups contend that they, too, experience racism of various sorts. In addition, some Asian nationalities, such as the Vietnamese group relocated to western Kansas to work in the meatpacking plants, have severe problems in schools.

2. That there are clearly many exceptions to this does not negate the fact that enormous numbers of children are harmed, and many egregiously, by the innumerable assumptions and practices that—intentionally or, more typically, unintentionally—are race, gender, and class biased. But it is not just the students of color, female students, and students of low-income families who are hurt; the entire educational system that arranges and treats students according to race, gender, and class differences undermines for *everyone* the very possibility of a democratic society, the primary goal of which is the well-being of its citizens and their children. Consequently, there is also real substantive damage from our educational system for middle and upper middle-class Anglo students.

3. This volume also raises the issue of the discriminatory effects on schooling of contextual issues, like district funding levels or segregated neighborhoods. These are also critically important social practices that need to be addressed, but they are not typically accessible directly to educators. We have chosen here to focus primarily on the practices of educators. For an example of research that addresses some of these issues at the interface between educator practices and contextual (community) issues, see Scheurich and Imber (1991).

4. Some will assume that our focus is only toward change in schools that are predominantly schools of color and schools with children of low-income families. Instead, we argue, for instance, that middle-income, suburban Anglo schools are more in need of a radical shift to a multicultural curriculum than are schools of color. Parents and children of color are, to a high degree, already committed to multiculturalism; it is the Anglo parents and children, and their schools, who tend to lack this commitment. In addition, as Shakeshaft et al. (1994), among others, have shown, all schools are mistreating their female students. And, finally, increasingly, Anglo suburban schools have minority students, even if a small number, who suffer various intentional and unintentional forms of racial bias (see also Note 2).

Chapter 4

Preface

Chapter 4 has three sections. In the first issue of the *International Journal of Leadership in Education,* edited by Duncan Waite, Carl Glickman was asked to contribute an article for that opening issue. His article was entitled, "Educational leadership for democratic purpose: What do we mean," and it is section 1 here. I was then asked to respond to Carl's piece, which I did in "The Grave Dangers in the Discourse on Democracy," which is the second section of this chapter. The third section of this chapter, then, is Carl's rejoinder to my response. Like all of the chapters in this part, this provides another example of my anti-racist response to the scholarship of other white scholars.

Section 1

Educational Leadership for Democratic Purpose: What Do We Mean?

Carl D. Glickman

Democracy is a word much used in education in the United States by educational leaders, yet it is rarely defined beyond general statements. The importance of defining democracy and determining compatible educational practice is critical to school success. In this essay, four definitions of democracy are examined. The author then articulates his own definition and makes a case for a participatory, community-oriented democracy achieved through school and classroom structures and activities. The essay concludes with the need for educational leaders to develop their own working definition with others in a school community to provide ongoing guidance to classroom and school renewal. The perennial question of public educators always should focus changes on what public schools should educate for.

Recently I presented a commencement address at a college graduation ceremony on the topic of education and democracy. After concluding with the need to keep education rooted in the spirit of American democracy, the majority of the audience gave a warm round of applause. On the other hand, a Native American woman in the audience came over to the speaker and privately, but adamantly, expressed discomfort with the use of the word democracy. She asserted that American democracy meant to her the systematic exploitation and eradication of her people. She made a most convincing point about the need for educators to carefully articulate what they mean by the word.

I find this issue of definition extremely interesting, complicated, and exciting. I have grappled with others of different racial, cultural, religious, and ethnic experiences over the past two years. For example, the writer, John Oliver Killens (1996, p. 108) explains why many African-Americans do not see the word in the same way as European-Americans:

> . . . the sooner we face up to this social and cultural reality, the sooner the twain shall meet. . . . Your joy is very often our anger and your despair is our fervent hope. Most of us came here in chains and most of you came here to escape your chains. Your freedom was our slavery, and therein lies the bitter difference in the way we look at life.

I wish to make clear to the readers that as I examine the issue of definition, educational leadership, and appropriate practice, I am speaking of the word in the context of the United States of America (USA). I welcome readers of other countries to determine if this examination is of similar value to defining their own purpose of education. I do not assume that it is nor that it should be.

What do I mean by education with a public purpose? How do I define democracy? And what should be the central practice of schools and educational leadership? In this essay, I will examine different conceptions of democracy and what, in my opinion, are essential understandings to the future work of educational leadership and school renewal in the United States.

Definitions of Democracy

There are a number of ways to define democracy. A former student of mine, political theorist Doug Dixon (1997), explains three conceptions of democracy: liberal, participatory, and community.

Liberal democracy is the belief in a republican government of elected representatives, government officials, legal structures, and expert consultants who make decisions for citizens. A bureaucracy and hierarchy of government agents are necessary to govern. Citizens at large are capable of determining their representatives from election to election but do not possess the time, interest, knowledge, and intelligence to deliberate and solve issues for themselves. Thus, the rule of majority vote through elections and referendums is the key to sustaining society and ensuring the rights and responsibilities of individuals.

Participatory democracy is the belief in active participation of citizens in the ongoing deliberations and decisions of representative, republican government. It is assumed that citizens are as intelligent as those they elect and those who are appointed as civil servants. The solicitation, initiative, and involvement of citizens in public forums, *ad hoc* committees, and task forces to help shape government decisions are critical to the success of society. Thus, the focus of participatory democracy is not simply elections where voters determine preselected choices, but instead, having citizens deliberate and shape the choices and consequences of decisions.

Community democracy is the belief that society is largely improved by how citizens live in everyday, personal interactions. The concern is not with particular forms of official government or legalistic structures, but instead how people listen, learn, and mobilize together to change their associative conditions for the better.

These three definitions are simplified and in practice often overlap, but one might now glimpse how the word democracy resonates differently with people according to their definition. Liberal democracy is embraced most often by those citizens who have benefited from the existing governmental and legal structures and who have greatest influence on the republican political system. Participatory democracy appeals most to those who have been outside the liberal system but have found optimism in strategies of protest and resistance, forcing deliberations and changes in governmental decisions. Community democracy resonates mostly with those who view government as uncontrollable, or at best, as a noneffectual entity, and find value in the personal ways that people help each other.

To complicate matters a bit further, there are other conceptions of democracy, not academic or theoretical, that simply come from the lived experiences of individuals. Thus, democracy may be viewed as patriarchal by those who feel denied of their rights and as freedom by those who have experienced economic success in free market economics. Dixon (1997), in his careful analysis of educational reformers, has argued cogently that prominent educational leaders wrap their particular advocacies for change in schools in the cloak of democracy but often do so without explaining what they mean.

What is Meant by Democracy and Congruent Education?

Let me begin with five points. First, democracy in the sense of equality, freedom, and liberty for all its citizens has never been fully achieved in the United States. Second, the U.S. political system of state and federal governments is in practice more a designed liberal system of elected persons influenced most by powerful individuals, interests, and businesses than a participatory democracy of equal citizens (Arendt, 1963). Third, the essence of a community and participatory democracy, (which is what the Declaration of Independence advocated—rather than what the Constitution legislated) is an educative belief about how citizens best learn. Fourth, when community and participatory democracy is used as a guide for educational leadership and school reform, there is significant personal, empirical, and cultural evidence of educating students extraordinarily well. Fifth, before public schools can improve the education for all students, leadership must *practice* the rhetoric of a community and participatory democracy in all aspects of school life, including whole school renewal, and curriculum with culturally responsive and participatory pedagogy and assessment (Wilder, 1995). Participatory governance alone won't improve schools. In sum, each school in its local community needs to continually answer this question: What should we be doing in our schools, our curriculum, our placement, our scheduling of students, our allocation of resources, and our teaching that gives each child his/her inalienable right to life, liberty, and the pursuit of happiness? Thus, democracy is a means of decision making (shared governance) to achieve the ends of an education for students that helps them to achieve life, liberty, and the pursuit of happiness.

In answering this question, faculty, administrators, staff, parents, students, and citizens bring a strong sense of mission, teaching, and learning practices, standards of performance, and ongoing means for reflective, school-wide progress (Glickman,

1993). Powerful schools take democratic clarity and purpose seriously in everything they do. They create a pedagogy of learning—where participation, choices, connections, demonstration, and cultural respect and responsiveness foster high expectations for all. I define democracy as the belief that citizens can educate themselves well when a society ensures freedom of expression, a free press, the marketplace of ideas, the general diffusion of knowledge, and the pursuit of truth (truth with a lower-case "t") so that each generation may uncover new and different truths. In effect, it is individual liberty and community freedom as a way of learning (Glickman, 1998b).

Democratic Pedagogy

How can an espoused democracy be revitalized to support and encourage individual liberty and community freedom as a pedagogy for learning? Cognitive research, personal learning experiences, and ideological faith provide evidence that democratic pedagogy is the most powerful form of student learning. Not only is the pedagogy consistent with the aims of democratic education, it is also how students become knowledgeable, wise, and competent citizens.

What are democratic pedagogies? Democratic pedagogies aim for freedom of expression, pursuit of truth in the marketplace of ideas, individual and group choices, student activity, participation, associative learning, applications, demonstration, and contribution of learning to immediate and larger communities. Such pedagogical efforts are undertaken in the context of equality for all, consideration of individual liberty and group freedom, and respect for the authority and responsibility of the teacher to set conditions for developmental learning.

Let me clear up potential distortions of democratic pedagogy with examples of what it is and what it isn't (Glickman, 1996, 1998a & b).

Democratic pedagogy is *not:*

1. Students deciding for themselves if, what, or how they will learn.
2. Absence of such skills as reading, writing, arithmetic.
3. Absence of content studies in areas such as humanities, science, and art.

Nor is it:

4. All students learning the same material at the same time.
5. Students sitting and listening, passively.
6. Students categorized, labeled, and placed in fixed ability groups and tracts.

Democratic pedagogy is:

1. Students actively working with problems, ideas, materials, and other people as they learn skills and content.

2. Students having escalating degrees of choices, both as individuals and as groups, within the parameters provided by the teacher.
3. Students being responsible to their peers, teachers, parents, and school community that educational time is being used purposefully and productively.
4. Students sharing their learning with each other, with teachers, and with parents and other community members.
5. Students deciding how to make their learning a contribution to their community.
6. Students assuming escalating responsibilities for securing resources (of people and materials outside of the school) and finding places where they can apply and further their learning.
7. Students demonstrating what they know and can do in public settings and receiving public feedback.
8. Students working and learning from each other, individually and in groups, at a pace that challenges all.

There are a number of research studies on learning practices that increase student achievements, learning satisfaction, and success in later life. These results have been consistent across socioeconomic, "race," ethnic, and gender compositions of students. There is a strong case that such learning is culturally responsive in that it takes into account diversity of student history and background. For example, students who graduated from 30 high schools using education and democracy as the central concept of curriculum and instructional practices outperformed students who graduated from traditional high schools. It was found that in 1,475 matched pairs of students, studied through four years of high school and followed four years afterwards, that graduates from democratic schools had higher grades, received more academic and nonacademic honors, had a higher degree of intellectual curiosity, and participated more in groups and international issues (Aiken, 1942). In a 1977 study of 26 urban and rural schools, the greater the democratic effort made in a school — in process and organization — the greater was the achievement of students (Joyce, McKibbing & Weil 1977). In 1995, a study of 820 high schools and 11,000 students, under the direction of Fred Newmann, found schools that reorganized their academic programs around active learning and where this type of instruction was widespread throughout the school had significantly higher student gains on all measured achievement domains of mathematics, reading, social studies, and science, as measured by the national Assessment of Educational Progress (Newmann et al. 1995). The same results held true for longitudinal studies of elementary and middle schools (Newmann & Wehlage, 1995).

There have been instructional studies around specific active and participatory methods such as cooperative learning, role playing, the jurisprudence model, inductive thinking, and concept attainment (see Joyce & Weil, 1996). For example,

Shlomo Sharan's work shows that democratic process teaching generates twice the student learning as passive lecture/recitation teaching (Joyce & Weil, 1996, p. 8).

The same type of effective pedagogy, when incorporating cultural differences of students, can be seen in the work of several recent scholars. For example, Norbert Hill (1993) wrote that successful Native American teachers provide "assistance and guidance, rather than domination and control" and that teachers "encourage students to engage their curiosity through cogenerating and participating in a variety of activities." Sonia Nieto and Carmen Rolin (1995, p. 22) summarized studies of Latino (or Hispanic) students and found that successful teachers increased "students' active participation and leadership responsibilities inside and outside the classroom." Gloria Ladson-Billings (1994, p. 140–41) described ideal learning in a school culturally responsive to African-American students, "The student learning is organized around problems and issues. . . . The students have studied cities in ancient African Kingdoms, Europe, and Asia. They are studying their own city. They have taken trips to City Hall. . . . Groups of students are working on solutions to problems specific to the city."

To summarize, those teachers and schools that define democracy as participatory and community-oriented appear to have much greater success with all their students. It is a pedagogy that respects the students' own desire to know, to discuss, to problem solve, and to explore individually and with others rather than learning that is dictated, determined, and answered by the teacher. It is the belief that all students can participate and excel. School leaders facilitate and develop such a school community through their love, care, and belief that each student is equal and educable and that each can learn to become a valuable citizen of society (King, 1994; Scheurich, 1995).

Conclusion

Education is not public because it is publicly funded; rather, it is public because of public purpose (Barber, 1992). That is why it is publicly funded. Therefore, all schools in the United States with the public purpose of preparing the next generation of citizens for a democratic society need to define carefully what democracy means and what are appropriate practices in and across classrooms, within a school, and within its larger community.

The Declaration of Independence stated that "all men are created equal, that they are endowed by their Creator with certain inalienable rights; that among those are life, liberty, and the pursuit of happiness." It stands to reason that educators need to ensure that students have an education that will allow each and every student the attainment of those inalienable rights. Therefore as schools study and determine their future changes and improvements, they need to first define democracy and then make direct applications in the ways that they group, schedule, assess, and teach students.

I do not wish to leave the reader with the impression that once educational leaders help to define what democracy means that solutions to practice are simple, obvious, and uncontested. But what I do believe is that with reworking, shared definition, U.S. educators, with parents, students, and other citizens, will be answering the essential and perennial question of why schools exist.

So as I conclude, I welcome others to this conversation. What do we mean by democracy? What are our obligations to our students? Are we willing to practice a form of democracy in our everyday actions in schools that make possible a societal form of democracy that we have not yet reached?

Section 2

Commentary: The Grave Dangers in the Discourse on Democracy

James Joseph Scheurich

Numerous scholars and educators have given pride of place to democracy both for society at large and for schools and school reform (Glickman, 1993, and Raywid, 1990, among others). In emphatic contrast, I would like to suggest that this is a *dangerous* choice. However, in making my brief points I do not want to speak "against" any particular individual who privileges democracy in this way. Instead, I want to speak against the ways democracy, as a linguistic vessel of meaning, discursively circulates both in educator and scholarly discourses. I want to try to show those who participate in these circulations that they are involved in a complex, discursive enactment that has deleterious effects. I would like for us to think together, to consider certain difficult problems in the discourse on democracy, to critically examine some serious dangers in this discourse. Specifically, I want to discuss how the promotion of democracy as the principal underlying value in society or in schools and school reform is not only particularly *harmful* to national minority groups, like African-Americans or Mexican-Americans, but also, in the long view, harmful to everyone. This discussion, though, should not be taken as a comprehensive critique, archaeology, or genealogy of the discourse on democracy (certainly something that is needed); what I provide here is but a bare beginning.

Before I can make my points, though, it is necessary to address and then move beyond the emancipatory claims for democracy. In this regard, democracy is appropriately taken to be a reallocation of power from a small elite to the citizenry at large; however, as everyone knows, in Athens, democracy, like the early U.S. democracy, was relegated only to certain citizens, like white, male property owners, so the application of democracy is not necessarily coterminous with the entire adult population. The most well known example of democratic emancipation in the United States is the revolution that overthrew British royal rule of the 13 colonies. Other subsequent U. S. examples are the expansion of democracy via voting rights to women and to people of color. In addition, internationally there are courageous movements whose principal goal is to establish democracy in their societies. One clear example would be the successful movement to end Apartheid in South Africa.

It is exceedingly important, therefore, that it be understood that, for the discussion that follows, I strongly support these efforts to develop and expand democracy in whatever context—from countries to corporations, from societies to schools. Democracy rightly holds a critical significance in any context in which relatively small elites subjugate or have subjugated majorities. I do not dispute that democracy, in this regard or context, is emancipatory; I strongly agree that it is. However, it is precisely when democracy has been obtained and implemented, precisely at this point, where the dangers arise and thus where we must begin our critical interrogation. More specifically, when a democracy has been established in a societal context that encompasses minority groups along with a dominant majority, we have a context that is literally dangerous for minority groups.

Said most directly, democracy is not equity, nor is it any guarantee of equity. This is the point that Glickman implies at the very beginning of the preceding discussion, but I think we need to consider this issue in more depth and centrality than he does. This point—that a society is democratic, no matter how democracy is defined, does not guarantee that it is equitable—seems, on a kind of superficially logical level, an obvious point. However, at the level of human practices and their effects, at the level of how democracy gets discursively enacted and thus "materialized" as practices, such as in personal conversation, speeches, writings, school reforms, classroom pedagogy, administrative actions, laws and policy, etc., this point is not widely discussed and thus is not socially obvious.

Indeed, the context that Glickman presents us with at the very beginning of his piece is instructive: Glickman gives a speech about keeping "education rooted in the spirit of American democracy." The audience responds warmly, but a Native American woman approaches the speaker after the speech to suggest that democracy for her and her people has literally been genocidal. Her suggestion to the speaker is to be extremely careful about how democracy is defined, a point Glickman addresses by discussing his definition of democracy. However, I would suggest that proposing a definition of democracy, however radical the definition, and then proceeding to build a view of educational reform (or societal reform) on that definition without taking serious and careful account of dominant social assumptions and practices is dangerously naive (and by "dangerously naive" I mean that the naivete itself is a social practice with dangerous effects).

I will illustrate what I mean. Affirmative action arose as a relatively limited policy to address the historical sedimentation of inequity that had become deeply embedded in a broad array of social practices, like hiring personnel or the letting of government contracts, and to redress the inequitable distribution of power, resources, awards, etc., like education, that resulted from that long-term sedimentation. Nonetheless, besides the fact that the policy chiefly benefited white majority women and besides the fact that the white public held exaggerated and distorted views of the policy and its limited effects, the majority has begun to move democratically against this policy. The clearest example of this is the passage by a democratic majority of Proposition 209, which makes affirmative action by the state government illegal in California.

Perhaps a more metaphorically compelling example is provided in a story, called "The Space Traders," by Derrick Bell (1992), an African-American legal scholar. In this story aliens come to the earth and offer to the United States

> ... gold, to bail out the almost bankrupt federal, state, and local governments; special chemicals capable of unpolluting the environment, which was becoming daily more toxic, and restoring it to the pristine state it had been before Western explorers set foot on it; and a totally safe nuclear engine and fuel, to relieve the nation's all-but-depleted supply of fossil fuel. (pp. 159–160)

And what do the space traders want in return for all of this: "to take back to their home star all the African-Americans who lived in the United States." This "bargain" is put to a vote, and the democratic majority chooses to make the exchange. The aliens are democratically given all of the African-Americans.

This story and the California move against affirmative action highlight the naivete I mentioned earlier. To invoke democracy in the current societal context is not an innocent practice in its effects in contrast to the intentions of the speaker. It does not matter that the speaker wishes to provide a more radical definition of democracy; the discourse that the speaker speaks into, the receiving of the discourse, must be considered along with the speaker's intentions. It is socially naive to believe that speech simply circulates as input from the individual speaker to reception by the individual listener. Speech (its meanings, categories, rhythms, etc.), as a social practice, circulates within social discourses that are structured by complex social assumptions (Bakhtin; 1986, Butler, 1993, Williams, 1991). What speakers say and what audiences hear is not only typically incongruent but also, and more importantly, socially structured or constructed.

In this specific case, the social structure in place is long-term inequities around the relationships between the majority and various minorities. In these historical relationships the majority has established what could be called a normativity, a standing ideology (or archaeology) of socially reinforced or iterated norms. For example, what this means in terms of race is that a white cultural normativity is and has historically been dominant, and this historical dominance is deeply embedded in virtually all aspects of social life, from the nature of an individual or of schooling to assumptions about what democracy is and means (see Banks 1995, or Scheurich & Young, 1997, for reference lists on this). Consequently, when a speaker speaks to an audience, it is a mistake not to understand that the speech is spoken into this racialized normativity.

My contention is thus that within this racialized normativity, democracy discursively performs or circulates, whether it is consciously intended or not, as a code word for white majoritarian racial domination or supremacy. On the one hand, it is as if to whites the word "democracy" has this positive, appealing surface as it is circulated within the dominant normativity. It is seen by whites as the heart of a heroic story, an indication of the special character of U.S. society. It is central to what, to whites, makes the United States great in human history. It has thus become, in its invocation by whites, central to white nationalistic patriotism. However, while it is not on the surface, not explicitly discussed in public, whites know that democracy is, majority-wise, white power. And it is this understanding that politicians and others stoke with the promotion of fears about increases in immigrants, increases in the percentage of racial minorities in the national population, and "unfair" increases in minority gains in the job market through affirmative action. It is thus this understanding that drives the white majoritarian democratic attack on affirmative action.

On the other hand, members of historically dominated minority groups, like the Native American woman cited by Glickman and like Derrick Bell, see "democracy" in a very different light. They see that democratic majorities historically supported the slavery of African-Americans, the genocidal destruction of Native Americans and their ways of life, the murder and suppression of Mexican-Americans, and the labor exploitation and oppression of Asians. People of color see and experience daily acts of racism, acts that are constantly being discounted by whites as "things are better," the exaggerations or paranoia of people of color, and other such dismissals. People of color see who has the largest proportions of their population in poverty and relegated to a kind of geographical apartheid in substandard housing. They see whose kids are well treated and helped in school and whose are not. They see whom bankers and real estate agents and supervisors treat well and whom they do not. They see whom the police favor and whom they do not. That is, they constantly see the white normativity and its deleterious effects, while whites repeatedly state that they themselves are increasingly fair, open, and democratic—beyond racism or, at least, getting better. This, then, is the dark heart that travels within the circulations or invocations of democracy, for people of color, whether the speaker intends or not.

What I am addressing here is the politics of reality itself. Whatever is thought to be or taken to be reality is a social construction. Different groups historically come to construct reality differently. In a complex democratic society in which the majority—in this case, whites—has historically dominated and continues to dominate minority groups, such as Native Americans, African-Americans, Hispanic Americans, and Asian-Americans. Over time, reality itself (the normativity I spoke of before) comes to be defined by the dominant group, the racial majority in this case. Furthermore, the dominant group takes its view of reality to be real reality, to be natural, the nature of things. In contrast, minority groups see, live, experience, survive within substantially different perspectives, normativities, realities. Thus, what democracy means to the majority and what it means to a minority are often vastly different. This, then, is political because minority "realities" are dominated, suppressed, ignored by the majority "reality," hence a politics of reality.

Given this, it is crucial that we critically understand the reality politics of the dominant group in terms of democracy. In terms of analyzing and understanding these reality politics, it is naive to invoke a key social concept, like democracy, without considering how it discursively functions and circulates within the reality politics (the dominant normativity) of contemporary U.S. society. Invocations of democracy, in the terms of the contemporary and historical experiences of racial minorities, easily sound like invocations of white supremacy. And, indeed, I would argue that these invocations, to a significant extent, act or perform in this way; invocations of democracy among whites ignite a complex discursive circuitry of supremacy, a circuitry that is woven into the individual subjectivities of whites and that links them as the dominant racial group.

In other words, when a white audience responds positively or warmly to invocations of democracy, the complexity of that response includes an invocation of the emancipatory gains of the past *and* white majoritarian power *and* the often deadly racial oppressions of the past and the present. Invocations of democracy do appeal to and stimulate whites, but what is being appealed to and what is being stimulated is not simple, is not just positive and emancipatory, but also is destructive and oppressive. Being unreflective about such invocations, then, is highly dangerous to racial minorities because the very utterance of the invocation turns on a racial dominance circuitry among whites, a circuitry that is not necessarily conscious, but a circuitry that is often highly dangerous to people of color in the United States.

I have said, then, my brief piece. I have tried to provoke some thinking together about a complex and central issue in U.S. society and in schools and school reform. I have tried, though my effort is in response to the piece by Glickman, to keep my comments away from individuals and directed at discursive enactments of democracy in the contemporary United States. For example, I know Carl and his work. I appreciate his voice, and I appreciate the work he does in schools. I believe that he is committed to schools that work well for both white children and children of color. That does not mean, however, that I do not think he is in some deep, dangerous waters with his invocations of democracy in his writing and in his work in schools. I hope then that I have been provocative and useful in that regard.

I know, though, from numerous past experiences, that it is at this point that I am expected to provide an answer, to provide suggestions about how we can address or, even better, change the situation as I have described it. What is my solution to the problem I have raised? I refuse to answer; I cannot answer. We whites and people of color are in a room together called the United States. We have a horrible history of the most destructive racial oppression. While in the present (which contains in complex ways our past together) the forms of that oppression have evolved in some cases and not in others, racial oppression continues throughout society and especially in schools, where children of color are overwhelmingly the least served and ill served by our schools, often to the point of the destruction of their very belief in themselves.

Indeed, we whites are in denial about our conscious and unconscious addiction to white majoritarian power and about the destructive effects of that addiction. If you "read" our democracy from the viewpoint of people of color—insane percentages involved in the "justice" system or prison, insane percentages failed by schools, insane percentages relegated to poverty, insane percentages exploited for cheap labor, insane percentages forced to live within Apartheid-like geographical areas of substandard housing—which is how we whites must "read" for it is by the least among us that we know ourselves, we are living a racial nightmare. That the media and much educational scholarship only provides and thus reiterates the dominant normativity as real reality and not the nightmare is but more of the same. In fact, to many whites my invocation of "the racial nightmare" may seem outlandish or extreme, but ask scholars of color, ask Cornell West, ask Gloria Anzaldùa, ask bell hooks, ask Richard Valencia, ask Frances V. Rains, ask Laurence Parker, ask Henry Trueba, ask Michelle Foster if I am being outlandish or extreme. That we whites do not "see" the nightmare is but racial reality politics at work inside our minds, business as usual.

Consequently, while I have no business offering an answer to people of color, I also have no answer for whites. For me to offer whites an answer would be to think that I could do the work we all need to do together. It would be to merely intellectualize. Intellectuality, such as that I have practiced here, is good for analysis; it is good for gaining an understanding or for critiquing the *status quo*. But, it is not the doing of change, the journey of transformation. This journey cannot be prescribed, cannot be told or figured out ahead of time; it has to be lived. It has to be carried through by the people involved. It has to be done by you and me. Ending this racial nightmare is our journey; it is still the same one, the one that Sitting Bull and Sojourner and Martin Luther and Cesar and Rosa and thousands of others have repeatedly urged us to take.

Section 3

Commentary: A Response to the Discourse on Democracy: A Dangerous Retreat

Carl D. Glickman

In the inaugural issue of the *International Journal of Leadership in Education,* I (Glickman, 1998a) wrote an article entitled, "Educational leadership for democratic purpose: What do we mean?" In the same issue, Jim Scheurich (1998) followed with a critique entitled, "The grave dangers in the discourse on democracy." His response was that the word democracy used as a premise for educational change circulates to audiences . . . consciously intended or not, as a code word for "white majoritarian racial domination or supremacy" (Scheurich, 1998, p. 58).

He then writes that . . . "it is naive to invoke a key social concept, like democracy, without considering how it discursively functions and circulates within the reality politics (the dominant normativity) of contemporary U. S. society" (Scheurich, 1998, p. 59). And finally, he concludes with his concern that the promotion of the word democracy obscures the terrible issue of racial exploitation. "In fact, to many whites my avocation of 'the racial nightmare' may seem outlandish or extreme, but ask scholars of color, ask Cornell West, ask Gloria Anzaldùa, ask bell hooks . . . " (Scheurich, 1998, p. 60). He wanted me to know that my invocations of democracy for educational leadership and school renewal get me into "deep and dangerous water" (Scheurich, 1998, p. 59). Before I respond to his concerns, I want readers to know that I have great respect for Jim Scheurich—his thinking, his manner, and his work. He wished not to offend me personally, and I took no offense.

So without repeating my entire article, let me review a few of the major points. First, democracy has various definitions to different people, and as a guide to school change I believe that educators, students, and community members need to deal with the central question, "What should we be doing in our schools, our curriculum, our placement, our scheduling of students, our allocations of resources and in our teaching that gives each child his/her inalienable right to life, liberty and the pursuit of happiness?" (Glickman, 1998a, p. 49). Thus, I point out that democracy needs to be viewed both as a governing means for achieving certain ends and that these ends are best achieved through classroom and school learning, which is active, participatory, and contributory. I cited that such democratic-based pedagogy results in greater success for all students "across socio-economic 'race,' ethnic and gender composition of schools" (Glickman 1993, p. 51). I conclude my essay by reinforcing my point that American democracy must be viewed as more than representative, majoritarian government, but as a way of day-to-day life in schools that again achieve the democratic goals of ". . . life, liberty and the pursuit of happiness" for all students (Glickman 1998a, p. 52).

Now let me respond to Jim's analysis. I understand Jim's argument. I agree that the word democracy, when not carefully explained, can be a comfort to those in privileged positions and keep the dominant status quo intact through majoritarian vote. There is a need for me, and others, to explain the progress, struggles, and failures of American democracy. There are two realities out there—one of great progress, the other as Jim defines of "insane" inequities. I concur with the statement of African-American scholar Louis Gates, Jr. that "we need something we don't yet have, a way of speaking about race and poverty that doesn't falsify the reality of racial advancement, and a way of speaking about racial advancement that doesn't distort the enduring realities of poverty" (Gates & West, 1996, p. 33). The great tragedy of America today is that so many people have gained material wealth, and yet at the same time there are so many poor persons left in despicable conditions. I believe that any discussion about democracy needs to delineate the practice of American society—both the good, the bad, and the ugly—with the espousal of democratic ideals.

Jim says that all education reformers—white and/or of color—are being naively dangerous in using the word democracy as central to educational improvement, "the promotion of democracy . . . in schools and school reform is not only *particularly* harmful to national minority groups, like African-Americans or Mexican-Americans, but also in the long view, harmful to everyone" (Scheurich, 1998, p. 55). So in one stroke, Jim dismisses the work of democratic educators across the spectrum of human color as doing more harm than good to minority groups. Again, I understand Jim's perspective about institutional racism and unintended collusion with internalized power structures, but I could not disagree with him more. I simply have seen and studied the positive results of such democratic inspired reform efforts on previously disenfranchised youth to believe that such work, in the present and long-term, is harmful. Rather, I would argue that a retreat from democratic education is what is most dangerous in the long-term for minority groups and everyone.[1] Lastly, Jim undercuts his own position by saying that the examinations of "insane" inequities can be found by listening to scholars of color, beginning with Cornell West. I suggest that Jim carefully read Cornell West. My work about democracy has been greatly influenced by West (see Glickman, 1998b). Cornell West puts American democratic ideals at the center of his hope for addressing the inequities of his own and other oppressed people. West wrote, "the greatest experiment in humankind began in 1776." He goes on, "it didn't apply to white men who had no property. It didn't apply to women. It didn't

apply to slaves. . . . But that is not solely the point. It is in part the point. But it is
not fully the point. The courageous attempt to build a democracy experiment in
which the uniqueness . . . [and] sanctity of each and every one of us who has been
made equal in the eyes of God becomes at least possible" (1993b, p. 8).

In another book, *Race Matters,* Cornell West (1993c, p. 158) wrote, "Since
democracy is, as the great Reinhold Niebuhr noted, a proximate solution to insol-
uble problems, I envision neither a social utopia nor a political paradise." But he
continued, "we simply cannot enter the twenty-first century at each other's
throats, even as we acknowledge the weighty forces of racism, patriarchy, economic inequality, homophobia and ecological abuse on our necks" (Cornell West
1993c, p. 159). So if we look to a scholar such as Cornell West, we don't retreat
from the greatest experiment in humankind; we embrace it as our very best hope
for a better society.

Finally, I disagree with Jim's postmodern, critical theorist perspective on
language usage. He attacks the concept of democracy as carrying imperialist, colonial baggage ("white cultural normativity" and "historical dominance") by citing
an experience that I wrote about, the Native American woman who confronted me
about a convocation address that I gave in which I discussed American democracy,
Thomas Jefferson, and the Federalists" paper. She reminded me that what happened under that word, and time, was the systematic eradication of her people.
She—as well as Jim and others—are correct to challenge all of us who use the word
democracy to examine the hypocrisy of ideals of liberation versus practices of subjugation. *But,* she didn't ask me to stop using the word, instead to explain it carefully and publicly. Jim wants me and others involved in educational leadership and
school change not to use the word at all. Again, we are totally apart on this issue.

The ideals of a democracy—equality, liberty, fraternity; justice and freedom; life, liberty, and the pursuit of happiness—are, in my opinion, constantly
worth struggling for. Perhaps Jim wants to replace the word democracy as a guide
for educational leadership and school renewal with different terms; i.e., equity,
emancipation, transformation, liberation? But where do those replacement words
come from? Is he trying to find words that come from a tradition and culture free
of exploitation and hypocrisy? If so, they won't be easy to find. Instead, I wish to
keep the word (and concept) of democracy, recognized by virtually all Americans,
and examine it in all its beauty and ugliness. It is only by doing so that we can re-
vive the goals of democracy to accomplish more, for all its people, than ever before.

Democracy does not belong to white people alone, and to suggest that it
does is an insult to all those people—of color and of white—who have struggled
to redefine it as being far more than voting rights or majoritarian government, but
instead, ideals that give a common hope to so many different people (Maier, 1997,
p. 208). For example, the Reverend Joseph Lowry of Atlanta, a lifetime civil rights
leader and president of the Southern Christian Leadership Conference, recently
received "The Spirit of Democracy Award" (Freda, 1997). He should be proud,

not ashamed, to be recognized as an espouser and promoter of a better democracy. As feminist scholar Seyla Benhabib writes, "postmodernism can teach us the theoretical and political traps of why utopias and foundational thinking can go wrong, but it should not lead to a retreat from utopia altogether" (1992, p. 230).

To conclude, I want to thank Jim for his critique. He has captured the paradoxes, dissensions, as well as conscious and unconscious harm of democracy (Massaro, 1991, p. 230). At the end, this argument is a very dear one as it gets to the essence of what hopes and aspirations we have for education, individuals, and society. It is too important an issue to be bandied about by two white European male professors at American research universities who write papers to each other. Jim and I agree this discussion is not between us. It's really an issue about the future and the best ways of realizing it for all our children. It's an issue that needs to be confronted, defined, and practiced in every school and community in America.

Note for Chapter 4, Section 3

1. Educational reform and renewal which uses participatory, community based ideals of democracy as central can be found in the works of such contemporary persons as James Comer, Deborah Meier, Linda Darling-Hammond, Ernesto Cortes Jr., Hank Levin, Ted Sizer, Roger Soder, George Wood, and John Goodlad.

Chapter 5

Preface

Chapter 5 came out of a similar situation to Chapter 3. Recently, a *Handbook of Research in Educational Administration* (1999) has been published. Again, the Editors of the journal *Educational Administration Quarterly* asked various scholars to respond to different chapters in this new handbook. Jay Scribner, one of my colleagues, was asked to respond to the first three chapters of the *Handbook*. He talked to me about working with him on this. We decided to have a "conversation" among ourselves and some of our doctoral students, Gerardo Lopéz, Jim Koschoreck, and Kanya Mahitivanichcha. This chapter, then, is that published conversation. Thus, this is another example of me as a white scholar trying to address white racism, but in this chapter my comments are part of a conversation involving a colleague and our doctoral students, and two of those students are themselves students of color.

Chapter 5

The Building Blocks of Educational Administration: A Dialogic Review of the First Three Chapters of the New *Handbook of Research in Educational Administration*

Jay D. Scribner, Gerardo R. Lopéz, James W. Koschoreck, Kanya Mahitivanichcha, and James Joseph Scheurich

The first author (Jay Scribner) was asked to write a review of the first three chapters of the *Handbook of Research in Educational Administration*. Rather than approach this task in the conventional way, he decided to involve several others in his department. He asked three of his doctoral students, Gerardo R. Lopéz, James W. Koschoreck, and Kanya Mahitivanichcha and one of his colleagues, James J. Scheurich, to work with him. The five then began to discuss how this might be done.

What we decided to do is a kind of structured dialogue. In this dialogue, there are three "blocks." For "Block 1: Introductory Comments," each of us independently read and responded to the first three chapters of the *Handbook*. This means that none of us knew what the others were writing for Block 1. For "Block 2: Response," each of us continued our response to the first three chapters but also responded to what everyone else had said in Block 1. For "Block 3: Final Comments," each of us, once again, continued to respond to the *Handbook*'s first three chapters as well as respond to what others had said in Blocks 1 and 2. Included in this last response are our respective conclusions. In this regard, the resulting blocks reflect both our structured dialogic interaction as well as our understanding of the diverse epistemological foundations (building blocks) of the field as discussed in the first three chapters of the *Handbook*.

We understand that our format is somewhat unusual. However, once we finished, we all thought that this approach made for a provocative review and reaction to the *Handbook*'s first three chapters and to each other's thoughts about those chapters. We hope that our dialogue provokes further thoughts, feelings, critiques, and reactions.

Block I: Introductory Comments

Jay D. Scribner

Flashback. When I entered the doctoral program at Stanford University in 1963, my idea about a knowledge-base in educational administration consisted of such courses as finance, personnel, school plants, and curriculum. My prior experience was to search the textbooks for those foolproof lists of how-to-do-it prescriptions one needs to survive on the job or to take copious class notes of the exhortations of my infallible, expert professors. Culture shock awaited me when I arrived at Stanford. Arthur Coladarci, co-author of *The Use of Theory in Educational Administration* (Coladarci & Getzels, 1955), offered a course on "hypotheses making"; H. Thomas James, a national leader in school finance research, offered an Economics of Education course; Dean James Quillan taught the Sociology of Education; Nathan Gage taught Theories of Learning; and James McDonald taught a Social Psychology/Group Theory course. I also was literally sent away from the intellectually familiar surroundings in the School of Education to Spindler in Anthropology, Dornbush in Sociology, and LaPorte and Prewitt in Political Science.

However, I learned very quickly that it is not enough to arrive on the job with a valise full of formulas, forms, charts, and other sundry recipes for dealing with real-world problems. I learned that the university is neither a widget factory nor a packaging plant producing how-to-do-it survival kits for eager administrators. I learned that to go about the task of knowing, I needed to become armed, like the other members of that new breed of 1960s "young Turks," with a repertoire of theories, conceptual tools, and new methodologies for mapping the social territory of schools and their communities. And I had changed my career goal from school administrator to university professor, from the reality-based practitioner to the ivory tower expert.

Flash-forward. Now, almost four decades later, I find myself asking, "What did it all mean?" What did it mean to set out to inquire deeply and persistently into a given subject matter? What did it mean to refuse to be satisfied with trivial or shoddy standards of reliability and to make use of trustworthy knowledge? What did it mean to pursue a career in which everything seemed to be related to a single central vision of science and where there was only "one gate to the kingdom of knowledge" (Halpin, 1966)?

Answers to sweeping questions such as these can never be conclusive, and after reading the first three chapters of the new *Handbook of Research on Educational Administration*, neither are they likely to be even moderately satisfying. For me, the Willower and Forsyth chapter tends to validate my earlier years, reinforcing my expectations for great returns from one way of knowing. Donmoyer's chapter, on the other hand, allows for a much broader, more pluralistic outlook, hovering comfortably under one large tent. And finally, Leithwood and Duke demonstrate how difficult it is to define the concept of leadership when possessed with a universal organizing principle for all human experience. After reading and reflecting on these chapters, my initial reaction is to admit disgrudgingly that the time is ripe to liberate educational administration from the mind-set of an outmoded or exaggerated paradigm and reduce our dependence on the quick fix of using timeworn methods to answer all questions of administrative/leadership behavior.

Ironically, I had found the answer back in graduate school in John Gardner's (1964) little classic, *Self-Renewal,* and failed to recognize it. Writing about how we settle into rigid and unchanging social and political views by the time we are 30, he says, "Unlike the jailbird, we don't know that we've been imprisoned until after we've broken out" (p. 9).

Gerardo R. Lopéz

Donmoyer suggests that the field of educational administration has, for the past 22 years, been involved in "big tent politics": divergent knowledge is allowed to coexist alongside traditional perspectives, maintaining the status quo of traditional administrative and organizational pursuits while simultaneously giving the appearance of inclusion and acceptance of difference. Donmoyer believes that this political strategy has resulted in a lack of discussion among our peers, fragmenting the field of educational administration in favor of a hierarchically organized smorgasbord of acceptable knowledge that serves traditional modalities and ways of knowing as the main course while relegating alternate epistemologies to mere side dishes. In other words, this chapter in the second edition of the *Handbook* suggests that the knowledge-base in educational administration is a buffet of paradigmatic thought, in which the side orders periodically change but the main dish has remained the "specialty of the house" for more than 100 years.

In contrast, Willower and Forsyth's introductory chapter suggests that the side dishes of alternative epistemologies have functioned to both enhance and dilute the main dish/knowledge-base. In other words, they argue that side dishes have always been on the menu, but certain side dishes are tastier than others. The focus, they argue, should not be on the variety of dishes (or knowledge) available to choose from — as Donmoyer has in his discussion — but on the side dishes that best complement the main course. It is inevitable, the authors suggest, that individuals will serve themselves different proportions of both main and side items — after all, humans have unique palates and appetites. However, Willower and Forsyth also suggest that we are all in the buffet line for similar reasons — because we are hungry (for understanding/meaning, for reform, etc.) or because we believe the food that we receive will help us to be better researchers and/or practitioners of administration.

On the other hand, Leithwood and Duke take a different approach to the buffet of knowledge in the field, arguing that different epistemological side dishes have played unique and important roles in the development of a knowledge-base on leadership. They agree with Donmoyer that the "smorgasbord effect" has resulted in a fragmented understanding of leadership, yet they also agree with Willower and Forsyth that such diversity does not preclude a conceptual understanding of the field. In other words, they suggest that epistemological side dishes do not make (or break) a meal, but an eclectic assortment of side dishes makes the meal heartier.

Like Donmoyer, I believe there is promise to the marginal perspective, forcing those of us in the tent to think outside of our proverbial boxes. However, I am still unsure whether Donmoyer is suggesting an expansion of the tent (to include more marginalized voices) or whether he wants to do away with tents as such. If it is the former, he is, in essence, advocating for a type of "big tent politics," which would be contradictory to his argument. If it is the latter, marginalized voices will no longer be marginal to the big tent of knowledge, and his whole argument surrounding the promising nature of such knowledge loses its effectiveness. If the field is as open and participative as Willower and Forsyth claim, then diversity of all types ought to be well received by its membership. If it is not, then either these authors have painted an overly pretty picture of the democratic nature of educational administration or their systematic critique of diverse perspectives (i.e., critical theory, postmodernism, poststructuralism, standpoint theories, etc.) is an inherent contradiction in their argument.

Like Leithwood and Duke, I subscribe to a different understanding of diversity, in which "difference is not opposed to sameness, nor synonymous with separatism" (Minh-ha, 1990, p. 372). In other words, I believe differences are not what separate the field as much as our understanding of those differences and our receptivity toward them. As Leithwood and Duke suggest, we should not be so much concerned with stringently defining the corpus of knowledge surrounding educational administration but with what those processes mean for research and practice.

James W. Koschoreck

One of the key thematic threads underlying all three of the pieces under consideration, as I see it, is the notion of a community of scholars joining together in a quest to create a common body of knowledge in the field of educational administration. Yet, even as this community is bound by the pursuit of democratic, participatory ideals with a goal to improve public education, differences of opinion abound as to how to achieve that goal. Although all of the authors generally agree that these differences produce a fragmentation in the field, how they interpret this fragmentation varies from author to author.

Willower and Forsyth, for example, hold that the elements that unify the field "deserve greater attention than they have received." Briefly, these elements include a commitment to democratic principles and open administration, a reliance on logic and evidence in research, and an association of professionals that recognizes achievement and excellence. Fragmentation, in their view, arises as the result of an alliance with alternative epistemological viewpoints. Still, despite their occasional expression of disdain for some of these alternative paradigms, they are hopeful that the fragmentation will not lead to a state of incommensurability. They base their hope (a) in the belief that scholars are open to new ideas and (b) in the reality that dissident voices have already created forums in which to discuss their concerns.

Donmoyer contends that the existing forums will not lead to a diminution of incommensurability. He claims that the field has taken an additive rather than an integrative approach to competing perspectives, resulting actually in very little sharing of ideas across different ways of thought. As one who moves easily back and forth across perspectives that rely on logical evidence and those that seek to create knowledge from alternative bases, I am puzzled at times by the communication that fails to occur among scholars whose theoretical proclivities place them at opposing ends of an epistemological spectrum. Tierney (1997) recently called for a community in which "we honor the unique talents individuals bring, and we work to use and develop such attributes instead of seeking to smother and assimilate them" (p. 5). I believe that these unique talents are not merely expressions of personality and ability; rather, they include the richness of ontological and epistemological diversity.

In reflecting on this notion of multiple acceptable approaches to research and administration, I have remembered something that my aunt told me years ago. I was raised in a working-class family and had been away at college for several years. I was the first in my extended family to attend college, and there was admittedly a certain mystique around my pursuing a career in higher education. Yet, she told me one day that what most impressed her about me was my ability to move comfortably between worlds. Which world was more real? Which world led to a better understanding of life and human relationships? I believe that each of these experiences in different realms has created a type of knowledge to which I would otherwise not have had access. I suggest that the field of educational administration will be the richer by opening up to the possibility of a similar sense of multiplicity.

Kanya Mahitivanichcha

It may be important to ask ourselves the following fundamental questions prior to this discussion: Who are the participants in the field? Whose voices have we most often heard from? Who controls the content in such dialogues? It is clear that much of the discussion in these three chapters, particularly the first chapter, assumes a large amount of background knowledge and a significant depth of familiarity with the internal political structure of the field. Although such a dialogue may challenge those already in the loop to acquire a higher level of understanding, its immensely exclusive nature may distance more people (especially practitioners) from the discourse via the intellectual gap it subconsciously creates.

Moreover, it is interesting that much of the discussion presented in the first two chapters of the *Handbook* appears to emerge from one particular tension that is persistent in the intellectual arena—that between the objective and subjective construction of meaning and the models that result from it. Willower and Forsyth seem to suggest that such tensions (or fragmented perspectives) should be valued in the light of diversity rather than independently rejected as irreconcilable differences. In addition, the authors suggest that we should give more attention to the elemental objectives that bind these differences and the common vision on which the pillars of American education rest. Whichever way we choose to view these tensions, few would disagree that the existence of diverse theories and approaches signifies a field that is dynamic and one that is continually growing and redeveloping. This is good news in and of itself. Nonetheless, we need to take a step further and ask ourselves these questions: Where are we going with the richness of understanding and the broader knowledge-base that now exist in the field of educational administration? Should our responses and actions stop at this very stage of intellectual exploration? This leads to other questions that need to be addressed: How can we capitalize on such diverse theories and better use them to meet the needs of an equally diverse community in the schools? In our dialogues, are we generating viewpoints, frameworks, and theories that merely act to sustain themselves? As professionals and intellectuals in academia, are we merely firing ideas that generate higher volumes of publication? Are we engaged in the aimless effort of theorizing what never gets across to others in the field who might in fact be the agents of educational change? Are such efforts thus self-defeating?

It is also interesting that the dichotomy of thoughts along the line of objective and subjective truths parallels the concept of concrete and abstract realities that has been acknowledged for centuries by the Greeks. (In a previous conversation, Jay brought up the abstract and concrete components in the Greek word *teoria*, which is the root word for theory. I believe he will discuss this later.) The Greeks also have a concept of time that is both concrete and abstract in nature. In fact, time is expressed via two terms: *kairos* and *chronos*. Kairos denotes the qualitative nature of time, the quality of the occasion — an idea of time that is more abstract and subjective. Chronos is the root word for chronology, which speaks of time in its quantitative dimension — a historical measure that is more concrete and objective. Interestingly, the Greeks used two words to express the concept of time, which our modern world only attempts to capture in one. To the Greeks, it appears that the idea of something holding both abstract and concrete shares of realities could coexist as complementary and reconcilable ideologies. Could the tension between our two seemingly opposing theoretical frameworks (the objective versus the subjective) be reconciled in a similar manner? How can this be applied to our current knowledge-base and understanding as we continue to approach the diverse theories and practice models in educational administration?

James Joseph Scheurich

Each of the authors of the first three chapters, if queried formally or if overheard talking casually to a friend, would, I have little doubt, give strong support to equity throughout education, from kindergarten to research institutions, although each would probably define equity somewhat differently. To give this a more specific focus, I believe all of them would publicly and privately say that they strongly support racial equity throughout education, and I believe this support is sincere on the part of each. Furthermore, I think it is likely that if any one of them were accused of racism, they would be emotionally and intellectually upset that someone thought this about them. Finally, I think that all of them would agree that racial equity is a critical issue to educational administration and to schooling. Indeed, I think I could extend these same conclusions to all of the authors in the *Handbook*.

I am not, then, interested in, nor do I find it useful to question, the intentions (good, I assume) or politics (liberal, I assume) of these authors. What I am deeply interested in, however, is thinking about how scholars might problematize whether individual conscious intentions, beliefs, and thoughts (and the scholarly products of these, like the chapters) are an adequate way to evaluate whether we scholars are reproductive of racial biases. For example, as far as I can determine, more than 90% of the authors in the *Handbook* are white, and most of the scholars of color are involved in only one chapter (chapter 9). Although pointing this out may be upsetting to the authors or readers of this book, I think it is a provocative point in terms of how we perceive ourselves, our beliefs, and our actions in regard to racism. Surely, in 1999, in educational administration in the elite research institutions in a *Handbook* put together by our most prestigious scholars, we would expect a more conscious, and more successful, effort to ensure a broader racial diversity than this. Of course, the authors of the first three chapters cannot be expected to control who the authors of all the chapters are, although I doubt anyone would question that the authors of the first three chapters are highly influential scholars who could, if they chose to, influence the racial representation among the *Handbook*'s authorship. It may simply not have occurred to them to raise this issue (which, if true, raises again the racial issue). More important though, I would like to argue that beyond the authors' intentions and beliefs, all three chapters are, in effect, white, racialized histories; white, racialized stories; and white, racialized representations—again, beyond the authors' intentions and beliefs.

Block II: Response

Jay D. Scribner

Where one stands on issues of relevance is determined not so much by the specifics of any particular issue (say, unity/diversity, inclusiveness/exclusiveness, objective/ subjective constructions of meaning) as by a more general world view. This world view includes one's assumptions about the meaning of change and the nature of knowledge and discovery. Lopéz makes it abundantly clear that "differences are not what separate the field but our understanding of those differences and our re-ceptivity toward them." Koschoreck finds comfort in knowing that educational administration is opening up the possibility of having access to "multiple accept-able approaches" and "alternative epistemological viewpoints" similar to his own life experiences, which included many different worlds from which he acquired knowledge that he otherwise would never have had access to. Scheurich penetrates beyond the obvious, making us see something much deeper in the development of the *Handbook*, something we either fail to see or, if so, something we fail to act on: the issue of racial equity in our field. In Mahitivanichcha's response to the first three chapters of the *Handbook*, she asks, "Are we engaged in the aimless effort of theorizing what never gets across to others in the field who might in fact be the agents of educational change?"

Implicit in these discussions of the *Handbook*'s first three chapters is the issue of personal capacities to change—not our local work group, not our profes-sional reference group, not them but us, our individual capacity to change. Appre-ciating differences, gaining access to those differences, penetrating beyond the obvious, and bridging the theory/practice gap are new experiences for most of us, experiences that tempt us to retreat to personal and familiar constructions of real-ity. As I see it, my colleagues find some solace in the major divides emerging from the chapters authored by Willower and Forsyth, Donmoyer, and Leithwood and Duke. For instance, Lopéz found inconsistencies (the side dishes) within consis-tencies (the main dish); Koschoreck asks us to consider dissatisfaction (producing fragmentation) within satisfaction (embracing fragmentation); Scheurich shows us how intolerability (latent, white, racialized representations) too often exists within tolerability (manifest sincerity on the criticalness of racial equity); and Ma-hitivanichcha urges us to consider the coexistence of subjectivity (the abstract) within objectivity (the concrete). One must not underestimate the power of our world views and tendencies to evoke initial conservative impulses toward what at the outset is unclear, uncertain, and new. Inconsistencies, dissatisfaction, intolera-bility, and ambivalence, as set forth above, can be powerful conditions for initiat-ing changes in one's most valued assumptions, assumptions about the meaning of change and the nature of what we know and the way we know. Authentic change ain't for sissies!

Finally, I would like to say something about Mahitivanichcha's reference to the Greek word *teoria*. Many years ago, Karl W. Deutsch's (1971) presidential ad-dress, titled "On Political Theory and Political Action," was delivered at the an-nual meeting of the American Political Science Association. In it, he told a story about how spectators upon the aftermath of enjoying a Greek tragedy would en-gage in teoria, or as he translated it, "passionate contemplation," about what the event meant to their innermost emotions, needs, and desires and to how they viewed the world around them. Thus, the classic tragedy left them "heightened in awareness and shaken and purified in their emotions" (p. 1). Thus, I believe, as my colleagues have indicated in their initial reactions to the three *Handbook* chapters they reviewed independently, that the major dividing issues that they acknowledge have a double context and like the inextricable intersect between objectivity and subjectivity found in the origins of the concept of theory, the perceptions of the *Handbook* authors include both inner and outer contexts that are reconcilable and capable of being shared.

Gerardo R. Lopéz

It appears to me that a common thread in our initial responses is the debate between unity and difference, that is, what brings us together as a field and what tends to push us in seemingly opposite directions. Our discussion overwhelmingly suggests a strong belief that difference can only enrich the field of educational administration. This position—best exemplified in the responses by Koschoreck, Scribner, Mahitivanichcha, and me—not only suggests that diversity in epistemological positions is important but is also critical if the field is to capitalize and build on subjugated or alternative knowledge-bases. In his response, Scheurich has a different take on the unity/difference debate, highlighting the taken-for-granted assumptions undergirding our research and representational practices. By suggesting that diversity in racial representation is largely relegated to one chapter in the *Handbook*, he makes a Donmoyer-like argument that "big tent politics" (however well intentioned) serve the interest of a traditional, white power structure. I would argue that his take on difference is not far removed from the perspectives of the other respondents. I believe that in questioning the obvious omission of racial representation in the *Handbook*, Scheurich seems to position himself in favor of difference because he suggests that different "racialized histories" could possibly tell a different story of the knowledge-base problematic.

Nevertheless, not all of the respondents have a similar understanding of the unity/difference debate. Mahitivanichcha, for example, attempts to reconcile unity and difference by asking critical questions about a field that is "continually growing and redeveloping." Rather than seeing unity and difference as contradictory elements, Mahitivanichcha opts for a more conciliatory position grounded in the Greek concept of time that allows for both concrete and abstract understandings of time to mutually coexist. It is a similar argument that I make in my own response—where difference is not necessarily the opposite/antithesis of "sameness," the "Apartheid type of difference" (Minh-ha, 1990, p. 372) rooted in friction, antagonism, and incompatibility. Rather, we suggest that "Difference . . . does not necessarily give rise to separatism. There are differences as well as similarities within the concept of difference" (Minh-ha, 1990, p. 372). In this regard, both Mahitivanichcha and I believe that difference is neither uniform nor pure.

This different understanding of "difference" is unlike the understanding posed by Scheurich, Koschoreck, and Scribner. From their perspective, "different" knowledges are "on different sides of the spectrum" (Koschoreck), something other than "timeworn methods" (Scribner), and something other than "white, racialized representations" (Scheurich). This position fails to acknowledge that there can be differences on the same side of the spectrum, that timeworn methods were never absolute, and that white, racialized representations are not homogeneous.

What does it mean, then, to include/exclude different perspectives and epistemologies into the knowledge-base discussion? If we assume a unitary and/or stagnant definition of difference, then we tend to think of alternate knowledge as homogeneous, all-encompassing entities—"critical theory," "postmodernism," "race-based," "feminism," and so forth—and fail to interrogate differentiated pockets of heterogeneity within respective world views. If, however, we assume a more dynamic interpretation of difference, we will see that there are an indefinite number of possible perspectives and positions within the same world view (e.g., postmodernisms, feminisms, etc.). This suggests that unity does not necessarily equal homogeneity, because it is possible to have differences within the concept of unity. Audrey Lorde (1990) once stated, "We have many different faces, and we do not have to become each other in order to work together" (p. 321). Let us take her advice as we interrogate the concept of unity and difference in our quest for a knowledge-base.

James W. Koschoreck

I am struck that in their variety of observations and reflections, my co-authors have coincided in their insistence on how issues of (ir)relevance and reconciliation operate as significant modalities of critique of the first three chapters in the *Handbook*. Scribner questions, for example, the relevance of outmoded paradigms; Scheurich takes issue with the relevance of an overwhelmingly racialized representation in the *Handbook*. Lopéz suggests that the task of defining the authoritative body of knowledge in light of an active pluralism of dissident scholars might be addressed and replaced by a deeper reflection on the implications of the nature of the processes of such a colossal undertaking. In his discussion of difference, he seems to be posing an argument for reconciliation without approaching the Hegelian sort of synthesis that Mahitivanichcha appears to endorse.

Despite various differences in focus, however, it seems that there is a loud call to end the resistance in the profession to debate the issues that divide educational scholars into discrete camps. This is not a demand for yet another argument in which an either/or mentality prevails, in which perceived adversaries "dig in their heels" to declare dominance. Such a simplistic adherence to paradigmatic principles is stultifying at best. Rather, what is proposed is a provocative, clamorous discussion in which the plurality of voices transcends their ideological allegiances to explore the points of contact. The ability to create a relevant corpus of knowledge lies not in the power of any one philosophical approach to define the discourse for the entire field. The power to create a meaningful, diversified body of knowledge resides in the ability of each individual scholar to assume the responsibility of redefining the professional structure in such a way that the oppositions at the margins and the center refuse to be reinforced.

I would venture to agree with Scheurich, for instance, that no scholar in this profession would refute the notion that equity is a desirable social outcome of all of our efforts in public education. I would further postulate that this universal commitment to equity is not even simply the professional manifestation of a political correctness gone awry. I believe, rather, that the term has taken on such a level of abstraction as to render unintelligible any communication among those who would seek to employ it. It is time to move from the abstract to the concrete. If social justice and equity are agreed-on goals, then it is time to contextualize those goals and to talk specifically about how racism, sexism, ageism, classism, heterosexism, and other systems of inequitable domination continue to be reinscribed on all students in the public schools. It is time to dismantle the panoptical surveillance that precludes a visceral discussion of the particular injustices that have particular material effects. To the extent that any epistemological and/or methodological perspective can draw us closer to the goal of social justice, then to that extent I applaud the understanding that emerges from such an effort.

Kanya Mahitivanichcha

I agree with Koschoreck that the authors, despite their differences in opinions, share a common fundamental pursuit—that of improving and advancing what is currently contained in the field. What binds, or rather what should bind, all these differences and inconsistencies ought to be the common democratic principles, such as racial equity, as mentioned by Scheurich. In this light, it appears that the discrepancies within the collective knowledge-base and theoretical framework are merely different means toward achieving the same end. Nonetheless, given our differences in definitions of what it means to improve or advance education, are we really pursuing the same goal? And what exactly is this goal? In this nation, there appears to be a distinct lack of consensus on the goal or purpose of education. Of interest, the American society appears to value independent development and individualism more than many other societies, yet it is also one in which the ideology of public welfare, collective good, and human rights is highly espoused. Given the broad societal interests and demands, it is not surprising that the purpose and multifaceted roles of education would be difficult to define in this country. It is thus of no coincidence that we would encounter such diverse and often conflicting views on what it means to govern or manage this educational system.

Nonetheless, such a wide array of opinions characterizes most well-established multidisciplinary fields, particularly education, which encapsulate our immediate societal demands. The question is, How do we reconcile and integrate all the differences in opinions and discrepancies in the theoretical frameworks? Like

Donmoyer, Koschoreck, and Lopéz mentioned, the current "big tent" approach has resulted merely in "addition" rather than the actual "integration" of diverse opinions. Yet, how far can we really go in mediating such differences and administrating education when the education of the community is in fact very intertwined with the education (and thus the growth) of the individuals who call themselves educators? How do we manage a system and lead others in their education—a system in which we ourselves are submerged? This is to say that schooling is a common experience in which we as educators have all been a part of at some point in our lives and still continue to be a part of. Hence, capable as one may be, one can only attempt to fix the pipes from the inside. As Scribner mentioned, we do not know what lies outside unless we manage to break free from the cell that confines us.

Nonetheless, what exactly have we been trying to break free from? Amid this era in which change and reform have much intellectual appeal, it is easy to pursue reform simply for the sake of reform or change for the sake of change. Seldom do we ask ourselves: To what purpose? Clearly, it is important to ask ourselves where we are heading with all the novel ideas and theories that we have chalked up in our knowledge-base. It is clear from the first two chapters of the *Handbook* and our discussion here that we are wrestling with our own education and understanding and at the same time trying to define what this should all look like for the larger school community for whom we assume responsibility. We are historical beings with backgrounds that undoubtedly bias our opinions and affect the way we perceive education, what it means, and how it should be run. Nonetheless, does this mean that we are incapable of understanding what lies outside the sphere of meaning constructed by our own personal biases? I agree with Lopéz that the tensions among the differences observed in our knowledge-base may not be inherently embedded in the separate realms of thought. Rather, these tensions signify the limitations of our own personal understanding of ideas and schemes that lie outside of our scope. Much of the tension, as suggested by Lopéz, rests not in the differences in world views themselves, but rather in our reactions and responses toward them.

Clearly, there is a need for us to take some time to reflect on and not simply react to the inconsistencies that we see in our system and knowledge base. Having said that, how do we then confront, reflect, and respond to the differences in opinions and theories without compromising the richness of each? In the presence of such diverse opinions, how do we ensure that we do not fall into a "crisis of knowledge" (Cassirer, 1944, p. 22)? How do we ensure that we do not end up in a "complete anarchy of thought," a "mass of disconnected and disintegrated" ideas that are void of all frames of reference and one that "[lacks] all conceptual unity?" (Cassirer, 1944, p. 22).

James Joseph Scheurich

All three of these chapters are representations of, mostly, the last 50 years of educational administration. Willower and Forsyth tell one story of this history, the more traditional one, and Donmoyer tells a different story, the alternative one. Leithwood and Duke try to synthesize all the stories, focusing on leadership research. In one sense, then, we have the "traditional," the "alternative," and the "synthesis" stories (Hegel, once again). But all of these stories are inside the domain of educational administration's conversation with itself, and I want to reference what is outside that domain, although it is explicitly interdependent with it.

Let us imagine that there is a small, shining city set on a hill (the university), which is surrounded by many cities. These cities have schools for their children, but those who lead these schools come to the shining city, in which they spend four to eight years learning their craft. Those who teach these future school leaders, professors of educational administration (who are overwhelmingly white), occasionally study the schools, which are led by those the professors have trained. Based on these studies (and other commentary on studying itself), these professors have a conversation (the inside domain). But, once in a while, these professors develop a guide to what this conversation looks like to date (the *Handbook*). There are, however, multiple connections between the professors' conversation high up within the shining city and the schools themselves, both in terms of the professors' studies of the schools and the school leadership they train.

Within the schools themselves, children of color comprise from about 15% 50 years ago to about 25% today of the total student population (although much higher in the larger states and cities). Because of centuries of societal racism, a disproportionate percentage of these students are from low-income families. In parallel with the racism and economic status, these children disproportionately do less well academically than the white majority, particularly the white middle-class (which is where most of the professors and school leadership come from). Throughout these 50 years, both the school leaders trained by the professors and the professors themselves in their conversation are thoroughly immersed in negative or deficit-based theories, studies, assumptions, and stereotypes about these children; at the very same time, these professors and leaders profess to be committed to democracy and equity. As would be expected, this deficit-oriented perspective has led to the creation of schools that, on average, yield success for middle-class, white students and little success for children of color.

What emerges from my story is a strange, peculiar, and provocative contrast between, on the one hand, the professors' representations (such as those in the *Handbook*), the work of the leadership they trained, and the espoused views of the professors and school leaders about democracy and equity and, on the other hand, the ways that children of color are treated in schools, including disproportionate relegation to lower academic tracks, a cultural/race-biased curriculum and pedagogy, disproportionate assignment to discipline, and so forth. This results in little academic success, high percentages of students who drop out (or escape), and virtual destruction of these children's fundamental belief in their own academic abilities, all of which results in assignment to low-paying employment for the rest of their lives.

However, this strange, peculiar, and provocative contrast only rarely appears in the professors' conversation and does not seem to disrupt their reflexive understanding of their commitments to democracy and equity, as if they have had nothing to do with creating and sustaining the contrast. What gets largely left out is their historical role and responsibility for the treatment of children of color in the schools, a reflexive recognition of the deficit-oriented nature of their past and present representations of these children, and the cries of pain of these children and their families.

How, though, does my point relate to that of the previous comments by my colleagues? To an extent, I agree with Mahitivanichcha's questions about who speaks and who gets heard, but she soon turns to limiting herself to the professors' inside conversation. Lopéz does the same thing; he takes the conversation itself as his limit, as does Koschoreck. Scribner, though, raises the issue of whether we professors need to free ourselves from our conversational prison. I would then challenge my colleagues to take Mahitivanichcha's questions, Lopéz's call to get outside of our "proverbial boxes," Koschoreck's ability to move across different worlds, and Scribner's call for us to escape our prison for the purpose of including both what happens inside the schools themselves and what the role and responsibility, past and present, of professors is for that which has occurred in the schools.

Block III: Final Comments

Gerardo R. Lopéz

It appears to me that Scribner, Koschoreck, Mahitivanichcha, and I are all trying to reconcile what we believe are major tensions in the field as implied in the first three chapters of the *Handbook*. Not only do our collective responses suggest that such a task is necessary, but they also posit that such conciliation is critical if we are to overcome our paradigmatic and epistemological baggage and work together toward socially productive ends. Throughout this discussion, however, Scheurich has consistently rejected such conciliatory strategies, arguing that such a discussion is not only misplaced but also limited by its own discursiveness. According to his arguments, the shining "city on a hill" (and by extension its departments of administration and leadership) is simply engaged in a racial/gendered/heteronormative conversation with itself. Therefore, any and all knowledge claims produced or proffered within the great city are simply a reification of the same conversation.

In this regard, Scheurich suggests that this conversation is not only circulated among ourselves but also fails to translate into specific actions and/or remedies for a large number of students who do not have access to the great city or its academic departments. Scheurich makes the argument that if we want to break away from such nihilism, we ought to be having a different type of conversation — a conversation that focuses not on the "state of the field" but on how our own discursive practices fail to address the contradiction between what we espouse and the lived reality of students. Although such a gesture is indeed quite stimulating/ thought-provoking, forcing those of us inside the shining city to rethink our own implication in the reproduction and reification of our own discursive strategies, I nevertheless find Scheurich's argument rather ironic because he, too, is a community member of the city and speaks/writes/proffers discourse mainly to other scholars in the field.

Therefore, Scheurich's own response is part and parcel of a reified conversation. Are we, then, to disregard his own contribution because it, too, emerges from a particular discursive space? I would hope not. I agree with Scheurich that most (if not all) of us in the academic hill are, to some extent, discursively distanced from the lived reality of students, but I still believe that this fact should not stop us from building across our differences in an attempt to have a positive conversation about the multiple ways that we can all contribute to substantially affect the lives of all children.

James W. Koschoreck

Several weeks have passed since we first began this project, and in this short time, I have watched myself waver between a cautious advocacy for reconciliation and an angry plea for the silent (muffled) voices of the dispossessed to claim their legitimacy in this space that we call educational research. The task at hand being "to pull it all together," as it were, it is time to try to make sense not only of the chapters in the *Handbook* but also of why we have bothered to undertake this project at all.

(The voice of The Academician fades as the light that had focused on him moves around the stage to illuminate various events. Upstage, Stage Right, a tremendous explosion is heard as we witness the wreckage of a high school in Colorado. As the light moves forward Downstage, we find a gathering of people saddened, angered, and bewildered as they come together as a Nation to try to make sense of the tragic incidents. They are unified by the inability to comprehend the complexity of the circumstances, despite the occasional voice that would claim to have discovered The Cause. The light moves quickly to Stage Left where a national conference of educational researchers is taking place in Montreal. The Voice of Reason bellows loudly through the corridors while the muffled echoes of dissenting convictions struggle to testify to the plurality of visions that must be brought to bear if they are to approach the complexity of the educational problems that they all must face. As the light comes once again to focus on The Academician, we see that he is weeping. He fears that the Structured Arguments and the Well-Turned Phrases that characterize his profession have lost their connection to an educational system that continues to be riddled with social inequities.)

And so, it seems to me that the great task before us is to consider how, as educational researchers (and as conscientious citizens), we will decide to face up to the persistent inequities and social problems that plague our schools. To quote from Tony Kushner (1994), "The Great Question before us is: Are we doomed? The

Great Question before us is: Will the Past release us? The Great Question before us is: Can we Change? In Time? And we all desire that Change will come" (p. 13).

And just as long as these "Great Questions" are before us, then for that time, are we obliged to continue to enter the dialogue, to bring forth our convictions, and to seek change in educational research and policy that would promote social justice?

Kanya Mahitivanichcha

That our discussion would indirectly and symbolically converge on the subject of values is of no surprise. Scheurich and Koschoreck have consistently redirected us back to the universal commitment and values that theorists and scholars hold — values that promote racial equity and social justice. López and Scribner point us to the contexts in which our differences and inconsistencies are rooted and their capability of being shared via rightful appreciation and understanding of each. This takes us back to the warning issued by Willower and Forsyth and the challenges put forth by Donmoyer. In the first chapter, Willower and Forsyth posit the warning that unity needs to be awarded its proper value and seen in the light it deserves. Currently, when and where unity is acknowledged, it tends to be "portrayed as undesirable or even malevolent, as of bland conformity or of oppressive dominance, arranged to serve the interests of privileged elites" (p. 20). Simultaneously, Donmoyer challenges scholars to look beyond the current system that is in place (a system that merely works) and reconsider the values that may be "implicit in the criteria we use to access utility" (p. 38) in the field of administrative research and practice. Diverse as they may be, these comments direct our attention to the values that knowingly and unknowingly guide our opinions and beliefs, values that form the engine on which our theories and administrative approaches emerge and diverge.

We are here not only to acknowledge our unity and differences, but also to consider the ways that these elements are being portrayed (as put forth by Willower and Forsyth). We are here not simply to construct and maintain something that works. Rather, we ought to go beyond that step and ask ourselves the question posited by Donmoyer: "For whom does it work?" (p. 38) Thus, our commitment does not rest in getting something done or getting a system in place but rather, getting it done right or at least going about it the right way. Needless to say, this requires that we consider the values that permeate the field of educational administration as well as those that underlie the intentions behind research and practice agendas. Nonetheless, values in educational administration are packed with ambiguity, as are the goals and purposes of education. In a pluralistic society, it seems almost impossible to talk about values without any explicit or implicit reference to a specific group or subgroup or without claiming by default a reference point of judgment. In talking about public values, societal values, or democratic American values, much is assumed without being defined. When we talk about public values and public education, we often leave undefined the notion of the public. Who is the public? And to whom do these values belong? Yet, who decides or who should decide on the values on which administrative practices are constructed?

Clearly, many of the questions raised in this discussion are ones to which there is no single or simple answer. Similarly, we might not be able to put forth an easy means of containing all our differences in opinions, beliefs, and values on which our theories are founded. Nonetheless, we cannot afford to ignore a question that is of equal, if not more, importance: How can we mobilize the wealth of intellectual resources entrapped in the different theoretical frameworks? Scribner reminds us of the power embedded in the different and diverse world views that should not be left dormant. López calls us to examine the wealth and richness that exist in the broad spectrum of perspectives that characterize our collective knowledge-base. Scheurich directs us back to the schools and alerts us to the needs that have remained unmet: the problem of racial and social equity that has remained stubborn. Koschoreck suggests that we "contextualize" these "agreed on goals" (of racial equity and social justice) and channel the efforts and wealth of resources in research and academia toward these functions. As suggested in these comments from my colleagues, the diverse theories, opinions, and values, although difficult to reconcile or integrate, can clearly serve as a rich template from which educational and administrative change can germinate and take root. As Scribner reminds us, the power entrenched in the diversity of our collective intellectual resources cannot be ignored.

James Joseph Scheurich

The authors of the first three chapters in the *Handbook* were all trying to survey a particular territory of actual research and epistemological discussions of research. My colleagues in this discussion are trying to survey the territory of both the three chapters and our discussion here. In a salient sense, both the chapter authors and my colleagues are involved in a conversation at some considerable distance from the lived reality of children in schools. I think this distanced, decontextualized territory, as Koschoreck suggests, is a dangerous one for the children and a dangerous one for us. I think it allows we scholars, including myself, to feel comfortable while many children are in serious pain.

I am aware that many children's school experiences are positive or acceptable. I am also aware that the opposite case is true for many. What does our conversation do for a young child of color being taught by a teacher who thinks that this child will never do well in school and teaches the child to think the same, while the teacher is certain that she or he is a good person and certainly not a racist? What does our conversation do for a feminine-acting boy being harassed on a daily basis by peers and even some teachers? What does our conversation do for the self-hatred he is being taught? What does our conversation do for a girl who is being taught that she does not have what it takes to succeed in science and math, that she cannot learn those subjects, that she is dumb in those areas? What does our conversation do for a girl about whom the boys, and even some of the male teachers, are constantly making remarks regarding her attractiveness, or lack of attractiveness? What does our conversation do for a child who experiences in school that there is something wrong with his home language, that his home language is somehow of less value than English? What does our conversation do for the poor, white girl who is taught that she is dumb and that she does not know how to dress or talk right?

Why do our schools disproportionately assign children of color to special education, discipline, and lower tracks? Why do our schools disproportionately assign boys to upper-level math and science classes? Why do our schools allow children to harass other children who do not fit by appearance, by behavior, by language, by culture, by sexual orientation? Why is school success so substantially related to being white, male, middle- class, heterosexual, and reasonably attractive?

Why are these issues not at the center of these chapters and our conversation here? Why do these issues not appear in every chapter and everyone's comments? Why do these issues not run out of the *Handbook* and out of our computers onto our hands and into our minds, leaving us unable to avoid them, unable to make ourselves feel comfortable and safe and so proud of our intelligence and our arguments for our point of view? How can we talk abstractly, pushing one epistemological position over another or attempting to synthesize various positions when there are so many real children in real pain, a pain that is caused, at worst, by the system itself, its prejudices, its ignorance, its lack of care and, at best, by us—administrators, teachers not paying attention, having excuses, espousing distant theories, and carrying on paradigm wars in some far-off, shining city on a hill?

Jay D. Scribner

After reviewing "A Brief History of Scholarship on Educational Administration," "The Continuing Quest for a Knowledge Base: 1976–1998," and "A Century's Quest to Understand School Leadership" and synthesizing what my colleagues and I have had to say about the contents of the first three *Handbook* chapters, I have set forth the following sets of questions that seemed to emerge from our discussion.

Scribner asks: What does it all mean? How do we free ourselves from the legacies of our past and disengage from looking at the world through a straw? The first questions call for a re-examination of the theoretical assumptions, which sustain our field, and for bringing our most contentious assumptions under critical scrutiny. To do this, we need to broaden our perspective (beyond the narrowness of the "straw") and examine the conceptual presuppositions and methodological commitments that have constricted our understanding of our field. We might find, as others have done, that the empiricist foundation that has shaped our scholarship may be fundamentally flawed. How will we know this unless we are willing to adopt new frames of reference, new outlooks?

Lopéz asks: How do we get outside our "proverbial boxes?" How do we look beyond differences and begin to understand and become more receptive to them?

The questions derived from Lopéz's contributions to this dialogue draw our attention to the notion that differences can enrich and diversity can empower. He makes it abundantly clear to me that "difference does not necessarily give rise to separatism" and that diversity is inevitable within different world views. It seems to me that if we assume, as Lopéz does, that unity does not equate to homogeneity, then we can begin to understand and be more receptive to multiple perspectives.

Koschoreck asks: How do we foster openness in communication and a commitment to democratic principles? How do we foster movement between diverse and often oppositional worlds? Koschoreck's questions ask us to make a conscious effort to transcend our "ideological allegiances," to engage others in the search for common ground, and above all, to search for ways to celebrate diversity and movement among and between what often are perceived to be oppositional worlds. He argues that we must "face up to the persistent inequities and social problems that plague our schools." At issue appears to be two views that can be described here as social conservatism and social liberalism. The former includes beliefs about separatism, individualism, and differences among people, including class, race, gender, sexual preference, and so forth; any deviation from these existing differences and established norms must be justified. The latter includes beliefs about distributive justice, freedom, and equality; any deviations from these established norms must be justified in terms of what is good for all.

Mahitivanichcha asks: Are we engaged in an aimless effort of espousing theories that are neither understood nor put to use by our counterparts in the field-of-practice? How do espoused theories become theories-in-use? After reviewing the *Handbook* chapters, Mahitivanichcha's chief concern seems to be that we appear not only to be on the inside but that we are also constrained by looking inward. She suggests that what we need to be doing is learning about what lies outside our own personal biases. More important, she contends that we need to do a better job at communicating between two worlds: the technical knowledge we derive from our scholarship and the craft knowledge we derive from our practice. In an applied field, who can argue that we must never lose sight of the need to translate our espoused theories into theories-in-use and to provide a bridge between the personal knowledge, experience, and wisdom of the practitioner and those who espouse theoretical knowledge.

Scheurich asks: Are we guilty of reproducing racial biases? Why are there hardly any racial minorities represented in the development and interpretation of scholarships in the field of educational administration, as presented in the *Handbook*? Finally, this set of questions gets directly to the heart of the matter! Scheurich constantly reminds us of that which we do not wish to hear. We are racists. Why? We were born into a society that has lived with institutional racism for generations. Scheurich appeals to our sense of justice and equity to do something about it. Personally, I find it difficult to ignore his appeals, and I hope others will listen before the next *Handbook* is published so that we might construct a new, more accurate historical account of our scholarship in educational administration.

Chapter 6

Preface

Chapter 6 is based on a request from Henry Trueba to respond to the methodological work of Harry Wolcott. As is well known, Harry Wolcott believes that research methodology is fairly apolitical. In contrast, as can be seen in "Coloring Epistemology" in Chapter 2 of this book or in a prior book of mine, *Research Method in the Postmodern* (1997), I do not believe that it is possible for any researcher or any methodology in the social sciences to be apolitical. In my critique here, I argue that Wolcott's neutrality toward white racism in society is itself an example of that racism. This, then, is a third example of my anti-racist critique of the scholarship of other white scholars.

Chapter 6

The Destructive Desire for a Depoliticized Ethnographic Methodology: Response to Harry Wolcott

James Joseph Scheurich

In many ways, critiquing Harry Wolcott is not easy. He comes across in his books as this friendly, helpful person. I sometimes use his books in the courses that I teach, and I am using one of them now, *Transforming Qualitative Data*, so I am re-reading it. Once again, I have an experience of this warm, open person who simply wants to share his knowledge and expertise in a helpful way. I have also heard him speak one other time, besides today, and I got the same impression from that experience. Here is a person who is not as egotistical as many well-known academics become.

Another part of this friendly persona is that while he certainly indicates an awareness of paradigm and political debates throughout his written work, he always seems to *not* take them very seriously. He will make minor comments, almost like asides, about such debates, and then will proceed to do his ethnography or discussions of ethnography.

I am afraid, however, that this is part of what makes an approach, like that of Harry Wolcott's, dangerous. Having read several of his books and articles, but certainly less than half of them, I have come to realize that his comments, or asides, on various debates, especially political debates, are highly problematic. It is not, as I used to assume, that Harry Wolcott is not political; he is in fact *very* political. His brand of politics, like many Americans, particularly white Americans, is that all of those words and actions about inequity and oppression by other, more politicized researchers have only a little to do with "reality," and certainly nothing to do with research methodologies, like ethnography. Otherwise, how could he go on this meandering travel, writing about, musing about the nature of ethnography without ever addressing the politics of epistemology and methodology, of research and the university.

You cannot just discuss what ethnography is when our society sends an extraordinarily disproportionate percentage of men of color, particularly Hispanic

---

Presented at the Critical Ethnography Conference, The University of Houston, Houston, Texas

and African-American men, to prison. That over the past ten or more years we have embarked on this incredible expansion of our prison system, easily the largest among the so-called advanced nations, and stocked these prisons with men of color is hideous. In fact, 25–50% of young men of color in many urban areas are somehow involved with the law enforcement and the penal systems. What does this say about our society, about us? How is this one situation so ignored? Surely, this has nothing to do with ethnography in general, nothing to do with methodology and epistemology, nothing to do with the social functions of social science research and the university.

You cannot just discuss what ethnography is when in our schools, kindergarten to graduate, students of color are mistreated so badly that their self-esteem is often destroyed as is their belief that they too can be smart and knowledgeable. Children of color in our schools get disproportionately the most discipline, the most assignment to special education, the most tracking in the lowest educational tracks, the least positive and the most negative attention of the teachers, the least assignment to programs for the gifted, the least attention in the curriculum, and the least understanding of their culture. Surely, though, this has nothing to do with ethnography in general, nothing to do with methodology and epistemology, nothing to do with the social functions of social science research and the university.

Adults of color disproportionately hold the lowest paying jobs. The hierarchy of most corporations in Houston is a color chart. As you start at the bottom with those earning the least, the color is brown and black. As you work your way up the hierarchy, the color slowly turns lighter, until by the time you get to the top, it is almost all white. People of color are largely segregated inside the worst housing in any city. As a person of color you will have much more difficulty getting loans, buying houses, obtaining rentals, and being treated decently by clerks at retail counters. A good example of this comes from a recent report that indicates that for every one dollar of family wealth the median white family had in 1999, the median African-American family held barely nine cents. While most of the white faculty in this room, including myself, are likely to be above the median for whites, just think, at a maximum, for every $100 dollars you have, an African-American family has $9 dollars, and I doubt that the wealth of Hispanic families is much different than the latter.

Our society is, in fact, this massive hierarchy of inequality by race that at a minimum substantially limits the potential of people of color to succeed in school, to earn a decent salary, to live in decent housing, to be treated as an equal human being, and to enjoy a decent life. At a maximum, this hierarchy literally destroys people of color, particularly children of color, in a thousand different ways, and then usually blames them as the cause of their own destruction. We simply do not live in a free and clear world; we do not live in an apolitical world. Our society is massively political, outrageously inequitable. Surely, though, this has nothing to do with ethnography in general, nothing to do with methodology and epistemology, nothing to do with the social functions of social science research and the university.

/Our world, our society, is a social construction. I don't mean that the streets or trees are social constructions. I mean the meaning we make of the world is a large social construction. And the dominant social construction in our society, whether it is in the popular media or in the university, is a white racist one. Ethnography did not just pop out of a historical hat like a rabbit, though if it is a rabbit, it is certainly a white one. Social science research in general has a social function, a conservative social function with an apolitical white face, to help create and legitimate a certain kind of inequitable social construction of what we then come to think of as "reality."

Consequently, inequity and white racism are ontological. That is, our socially constructed world, which is historically and daily constructed through semiotic categories of all kinds (including but not limited to language), in its most fundamental being is a white racist construction. It is not that white racism is just an action at the surface of human thoughts and actions, so that as long as you are not an explicitly racist individual, you are free and clear to think and write about just ethnography. The very nature of reality as we know and live it in our society is a white racist one. Thus, the inequity cannot be critiqued and fought as if reality, or ethnography, just exists apolitically. Social reality, at the level of its deepest assumptions, is a white racist reality. Research epistemology and methodology, at the level of their deepest assumptions, are racist.

The ontological and epistemological struggle to critique and remove this racism obviously has many implications for ethnography and for critical ethnography, many more than I can address in my time frame. What I want to do, then, is to turn to one issue this struggle raises, an issue I think Anglo critical ethnographers have in general not sufficiently addressed. And in these remarks to follow I only address other Anglo critical researchers like myself. In my view of white racism, it is none of my activist or philosophical business to be critiquing the subjectivities of researchers of color. I want to repeat this point: the remarks that follow are for me part of my efforts as a white scholar to address other white scholars on the issue of white racism.

Our selves, our subjectivities, do not stand outside of ontology, outside of the social construction of reality. This view that the self walks through history rather than is deeply constructed by history is one aspect of white racism. The idea that an individual self is separate from history, that an individual self can autonomously choose her or his life, this is the self of the elite Anglo man. Only those in this category possess the power and resources to come anywhere near to accomplishing this positionality. This so-called individual self, which we all live under the sign of, is the creation of modernism, the individual that Lacan called the transcendental signifier of history. In other words, the individual, autonomous self we are taught to have as our "birthright" as a person is an elitist, masculinist, heterosexist, white racist trope.

And this trope haunts all of us as we daily try to live it. It is inside all of us, including me. In other words, emancipation, revolution, struggle, transformation is not just an issue of the critique of the socially constructed, inequitable world; it is an issue that comes home to our own subjectivities. In general, I find that we white critical theorists want the critique and political struggle to be out there in the world. In general, I find that we are very good at criticizing the inequitable world. But this overload, this imbalance in one direction toward the critique of the world out there is itself a failure of critical theory, an instance of reproduction within ourselves of the white racist ontology. In other words, by not attending to the nature of our own subjectivity, and the roles it plays in the reproduction of an inequitable *status quo*, we too are guilty of participating in the creation of that status quo. We can criticize the world out there day after day, but if we don't also criticize our own subjectivity, we leave one of the main tropes of white racist modernism not only untouched but also active in reproduction.

In fact, we white critical researchers can live a good life, gets lots of attention, live in nice houses and drive nice cars, travel around to conferences staying in nice hotels. We can become well paid and well known criticizing the world. Consequently, in my view, Anglo critical theorists, including myself, have a serious problem. Because we have not been sufficiently ontological in our critique, we often leave the socially constructed, white racist nature of reality itself off our table. Then, when we do address this, we still leave our own subjectivities off the table. And I don't mean just subjectivity as another general category. I mean we leave who each of us criticalists are in our selves off the table. How is the self that I live, not the self of someone else, but the self that I live, how am I reproductive of the inequitable status quo? Am I living the egotism of the white racist, transcendental signifier? Yes, I am. It is in and of me. The way that I talk to myself, the way that I talk to others, the way that I see myself, the effects of my white skin privilege are inside me, deeply a part of me.

Thus, we cannot just operate freely in the world as critical researchers. We cannot just critique the world out there. We have to place our selves, our subjectivities, our personal selves inside the circle of critique and struggle. Our critique of the world out there is very fine; it is complex, it is deep, it is thorough. Our critique of ourselves as selves, our struggle with our selves in collaboration with each other is virtually non-existent. We offer the world a fine critique of inequity, but we leave out subjectivity, we leave out the personal space in which we live. When we do this, we end up as just another elite white group.

The question for me then is how can we participate in the world in a way that acts to create a world of sister and brotherhood both that is open, supportive, and loving and critically struggles with each other about our own subjectivities? How do we participate in the world as researchers in a way that brings our subjectivities inside the circle of our critique and struggle? Transforming the world is not just about critiquing it, while living safe and easy lives in our elite white subjectivities. Transforming the world requires, through a loving struggle with others, our very selves becoming part of the ongoing social struggle for transforming society.

Returning to where I started this brief, almost completed, journey, I want to say that I do respect Harry Wolcott for placing his subjectivity inside the circle of his work. With his Brad trilogy, which I am sure most of you are familiar with, and generally throughout his writings, Wolcott has, to some extent, placed himself inside, and he advocates others doing this, also. I think his Brad trilogy does provide us with a useful example. However, what is dangerously missing from this example, as with Wolcott's work in general, is a critical perspective, about himself, about his work, and about the white racism that is deeply "indigenous" to reality itself, to research epistemology and methodology, and to social science research and the university. However, what I hope can receive some attention as this conference proceeds and what I am most concerned about among those of us Anglos who consider ourselves to be critical theorists, is our strong tendency to only critique the world out there while leaving our selves, our lives, and our lifestyles, outside of the struggle. In my view, university-based critical research will continue to have little effect on the society at large until through our own loving struggles with others from both inside and outside the university we have learned to critique and change our own subjectivities in parallel with our critiques of the appallingly inequitable world.

Part III
ANTI-RACIST REPRESENTATIONS
OF THE RACIAL "OTHER"

Part III is composed of four chapters. All four examples relate directly to my belief that for the present historical moment there ought to be an embargo on white scholars working alone or just with other whites to study adults or children of color. The good intentions or even radical political intentions of white scholars are simply not sufficient protection given the dismal history of such well intended, white scholar-driven research in the past. Because of this white racism embargo, I have proposed that when studying the racial other, white scholars, for the present moment, need to work with scholars of color as equal colleagues in the research. Chapter 7 is an early example of my failure to do this in my own work. Chapters 8, 9, and 10 are all examples of my more recent commitment to *not* do research on people of color without being involved with people of color as equal co-researchers.

Chapter 7

Preface

As mentioned earlier, chapter 7 is an example of my failure to observe the white racism embargo. Thus, I now consider it as an example of my own participation in white racism. I wanted to show that I too have had the same problems that I criticize others for, that I too am a white racist. While many, both scholars of color and white scholars, often consider this chapter a valuable piece of research, I have since decided that white scholars doing this kind of scholarship alone or just with other white scholars is too dangerous to countenance.

Chapter 7

Highly Successful and Loving Public Elementary Schools Populated Mainly by Low SES Children of Color: Core Beliefs and Cultural Characteristics

James Joseph Scheurich

> Rather than asking "what are the correlates of marginally greater success within the parameters of traditional schools?" we are asking, "what entirely different parameters for schooling appear to enable far greater numbers of students of all kinds to succeed in ways that are not found within traditional schools?" (Darling-Hammond, 1996, p. 13)

The fact that elementary public schools, urban and rural, that are highly successful for low-socioeconomic-status (SES) students of color do exist is unquestionable (see, e.g., Burka, 1996; Daniel, 1996). In fact, such schools are more common than most educators or the general public realize, although certainly not common enough. The schools are ample enough in number to provide the basic outline of the type of school that is needed to provide both a loving environment[1] and strong academic success for low-SES students of color, a level of academic success that is definitively higher than that often reported for "successful" schools populated principally by low-SES children of color.[2] These elementary schools are also sufficient enough in number and consistent enough in terms of their characteristics to undermine the widespread assumption that the source of academic failure for low-SES students of color is themselves, their parents, their genetics (i.e., Herrnstein & Murray, 1994), their neighborhood, their SES, their race, or some combination thereof (see e.g., Berliner & Biddle, 1995; Hacker, 1992; or Shulman, 1990, for discussions of some of these latter assumptions). In other words, if there is a schooling model that consistently works academically, especially at the highest levels, then the problem for educators is not anything about the students, the problem is that we are providing the wrong type of schooling for them.

What is needed, then, is a research-based description of these highly successful and caring pre-K to fifth-grade schools.[3] But, before I provide this description, I first need to emphasize that the schools on which this model is based are not simply ones in which students of color do acceptably well on state-based high-stakes tests. They are ones in which these students do exceptionally well, placing them in direct academic competition with what are considered the better Anglo-dominant schools in the state. Second, I need to emphasize that the educational environments provided for the children in these schools are genuinely caring and strongly child-centered. Third, I need to emphasize that the model described here was developed not at the university level, like Comer's, Levin's, Sizer's, or Slavin's, but was developed at the grassroots level of education by school-level educators, principally educators of color who were working essentially on their own. My purpose here, then, is to describe the model that these schools have operationalized, although it should be understood both that there may well be other models that are equally successful[4] and that this generalized model is definitely not a formula that can be applied in the same way in every school. I will not, though, provide a thick description of each of the core beliefs and cultural characteristics of this model.[5] Instead, my purpose is to name these and to provide a brief discussion of each one, resulting in a remarkably coherent model, a model that I and many of those who have led such schools[6] have begun to call HiPass (High Performance All Student Success Schools).[7]

However, before I describe the HiPass model, I briefly discuss the source of the model, and then I describe the sources of data from which this model was drawn. I begin my description of the model by discussing the core beliefs that virtually all of the administrators and teachers in a school must hold to create a highly successful and loving school for low-SES students of color. Next, I depict the characteristics of the organizational culture[8] of these schools. Last, I discuss some implications of this model for education, for other organizations, and for society in general.[9]

What Is the Source of the HiPass Model?

The HiPass model did not come from the reform literature or from the leadership or organizational literatures, although those who created the model individually drew some pieces from these. Indeed, those who developed the model were not self-consciously developing a model; in their view, they were just developing schools that were successful for low-SES children of color ("their" children). That the schools they developed had sufficient similarities to be called a model is a product of the research that is discussed here.

The answer to the question about what is the source of the HiPass model, I would suggest, is that it arose principally from the loving and passionate commitment to the schools' children on the parts of the principals, who in every case has been a person of color, although it also arose from the commitments of the school staffs, who represent all races. These grassroots educators, particularly the principals, were simply unwilling to accept the widespread negative assumptions about the children in their schools, and they were unwilling to accept any other course of action than one that would lead to the highest levels of academic success. They knew that their children were just as capable as any other children—they just had to create a school that would prove this.

It must be especially clear, then, that neither I nor any university researcher developed this model; the principals and staffs of these schools developed it. It was their deep love for their children and their passionate commitment to making a difference for those children that created the model. Each one of them, like Toni Morrison (1992), could have said, "I intend to outline an attractive, fruitful, and provocative critical project, unencumbered by dreams of subversion or rallying gestures at fortress walls" (p. 3). Accordingly, they went beyond subversive critique or gestures of resistance to "an attractive, fruitful, and provocative critical project." However, more fundamentally, the answer to what is the source of this model goes beyond these educators to communities of color.

Communities of color have had to endure over many generations daunting economic odds and debilitating racism.[10] Within this harrowing context, they have had to survive, cope with the dominant Anglo culture, and still collectively raise their young and sustain themselves with a life-nourishing dream that a promised land did exist. What that dream is, how to get there, and what the promised land ought to look like had to be drawn dynamically, both from internal cultural resources (i.e., Mexican, African, Native American, Asian, etc.) and from historically evolved, hybrid, or borderland interfaces with the dominant Anglo culture, interfaces in which there is often a selective, creative appropriation of aspects of the dominant Anglo culture.

It should be understood, though, that these particular schools are not self-consciously or explicitly culturocentric,[11] as has been described by Lee, Lomotey, and Shujaa (1990) or Faltz and Leake (1996). For example, no one in the schools described here ever said that they were an Afrocentric or a Latinocentric school, and they did not talk in terms of culturocentric discourses. Indeed, most of them, although dominated by African-American or Latin-American students, also had students from other races, and some of the schools had no majority race. However, advocates of culturocentric schools will, I think, find much to value in these schools because the schools incorporate such culturocentric features as highly valuing the racial culture and the first language of the child; treating children of color with love, appreciation, care, and respect; believing and proving that all children of color can achieve at the highest academic levels; and focusing on community more than competitive individualism (what Shujaa & Afrik, 1996, have called "communalism," p. 256), none of which typify Anglo-dominant schools, whether or not they include students of color in their populations.

Nor are these schools what might be called "critical" schools, that is, schools in which "critical pedagogy" is applied on a systemic or school-wide basis.[12] I would surmise, however, that criticalists would find much to value in these schools because these schools include various features that the criticalists promote.[13] They are highly collaborative and democratic, with all participants, including parents, empowered; they do not treat the student as a passive consumer of knowledge; and they deeply value the racial culture and language of the child.[14] In a sense, then, the schools described here represent a different alternative — not traditional (Anglo-dominant), culturocentric, or critical but a different, hybridic possibility, a possibility of nonracist treatment of children of color, their racial culture, and their language within loving, highly successful educational environments. It could be said, then, that these schools are both within and against traditional mainstream schooling.

However, although these schools do not descriptively fit within culturocentric discourses or criticalist discourses, they may fit within postcolonial discourses as hybrids. Within this latter discourse, cultures of color within the United States can be seen as internal colonies, the members of which have historically, because of their race, not had equal power, resources, or access when compared to members of the dominant Anglo culture. Instead, these cultures have been, and still are, used as cheap, disposable labor, depending on the condition of the economy. This inequitable or colonized status has been particularly true in relation to public institutions such as public schools, which have historically been controlled by members of the dominant Anglo culture, by dominant Anglo culture perspectives, or both. Because of the rejection of key elements of these dominant perspectives, particularly elements that have had destructive effects on children of color; because of the assumption of leadership by educators of color dedicated, in the name of communities of color, to the academic success of children of color; and, thus, because of the exercise of what Appiah (1992) has called "a space clearing gesture" (p. 149), it could be argued that the schools described here are postcolonial.

As is apparent, though, within numerous examples of postcolonial discourses, being postcolonial does not always mean that all aspects of the dominant Anglo culture have been erased, creating, thus, a return to a precolonial, culturocentric past. Instead, postcoloniality has often been said to be hybrid, meaning, in this case, that it is a complex intersection of cultures of color and of the dominant Anglo culture, an intersection that problematizes the simplistic binary of same-other or dominance-resistance (e.g., Minh-ha, 1989). What Sangari (1995) says about "the hybrid writer" is true about these schools; they are "already open to two [or more] worlds" (p. 144). I would suggest, then, that these schools are hybrids[15] for the following reasons: (a) They build and sustain a powerful, positive sense of people of color and their racial cultures; (b) they create wonderful, loving environments for children of color; (c) they provide a "lived" critique of traditional schooling, without being "always directly oppositional" (Ashcroft, Griffiths, & Tiffin, 1995, p. 3); and (d) they incorporate a selective, creative appropriation of some aspects of the dominant Anglo culture (such as using high-stakes tests to drive instruction) that they see as useful to them and their visions.

Because of this hybrid nature, these schools represent a "strategic intervention" (McCarthy & Crichlow, 1993, p. xvi) for this particular historical moment, an institutional possibility (not just a theory but a lived practice, not just critique but critical action) that sufficiently fits within current conceptions about school reform, organizational change, and the leadership needed for such transformations, enabling these schools to survive and sometimes even thrive within public school districts and public educational discourses. Thus, they are able to create exceptional educational environments for children of color while not being undermined or attacked for being too different or too exclusively racial or too radical, again, a highly significant, strategic accomplishment (see Lytle, 1992, for one, on the difficulty of this challenge).[16] They, as Ernst and Statzner (1994) said, are

> . . . active agents in complex social sites wherein powerful societal forces shape the limits of what is possible . . . [and they] have the laudable dedication and exemplary ability . . . to manipulate the educational system and transform the social world they inhabit. (p. 203)

In parallel with and respect for their hybridity, then, the description of these schools that follows interweaves discourses of color; criticalist discourses; and mainstream reform, leadership, and organizational discourses to show, as these schools do, that it is possible for leaders, schools, and communities of color to construct positive institutional spaces in which children of color can endure and flourish and that these spaces can be seen as credible from several different perspectives or discourses, including being seen as credible by the dominant Anglo culture. However, I want to end this section by returning to my earlier point that the true sources of these highly successful schools, beyond abstract discussions of postcolonial hybridity, are communities of color and their lived, historical struggles to first survive and then to create powerful, loving, communal spaces for themselves and their children.

The Research on Which the HiPass Model Is Based

The analysis on which the HiPass model is based is actually a kind of meta-analysis of four sources of data (meta in the sense that it is a step of abstraction above a single study or data source). First, my colleagues, our doctoral students, and I have recently been involved in a study of successful schooling practices for low-SES Mexican-American students.[17] We spent more than two years in various phases of the research project, first collaborating with educators in the border region of Texas on the choice of the schools we would study, then interviewing and observing teachers and administrators in the chosen schools, and finally, writing our reports. We visited the schools in two teams of five to nine faculty and doctoral students, with one to three researchers assigned to study particular aspects of the school, such as classroom instruction, leadership, parental involvement, special programs, and so forth. We took notes on observations and we interviewed parents, teachers, administrators, district staff, and other school staff (all of the interviews were recorded and have been archived).[18] We then wrote reports detailing our results (P. Reyes & Scribner, 1996), which we have discussed at several conferences (e.g., Paredes Scribner, 1996; P. Reyes, 1996; P. Reyes et al., 1996; Scheurich, 1996; Scribner, 1996; Wagstaff, 1996).

My second source of data is my own interviews with urban and rural principals who have transformed low-performing schools with predominantly low-SES students of color into high-performing schools.[19] At the University of Texas at Austin, we have a Cooperative Superintendency Program that draws some of the best principals around the state who want to become superintendents. A high percentage of these principals have previously been assigned to schools that were low performing, but these principals were able, typically within a 3- to 5-year period, to transform these schools, while keeping 80% to 90% of the teachers, into schools that were competitive with the better schools in the state. For example, one high school principal was able to take a predominantly low-SES African-American high school with less than 20% of the African-American students passing the state math test and, within five years, have more than 60% of these same students passing the math test.

Third, several of the above-mentioned doctoral students, who have themselves, as principals, led low-SES schools populated mainly by children of color to high performance, and I meet on a weekly basis. Some of these students are working, with me as their chair, on dissertations that are case studies of these highly successful schools. For example, one student is studying acts of leadership that began with the arrival of a new principal and extended through the achievement of high levels of academic success three years later at a low-SES African-American urban school. A second student is studying math curriculum and instruction for African-American high school students at a highly successful school populated principally by African-American students. A third student is studying how superintendents aid in the creation and maintenance of these successful schools. Consequently, my third source of data comes from my ongoing interactions with these students and my guidance of their in-process dissertations.[20]

My fourth source of data is drawn from the fact that a group of these same doctoral students and I have formed a team to work together to assist low-performing schools whose students are mainly low-SES children of color. Not surprisingly, this work with those who have led these highly successful schools also pervasively informs my knowledge of the features of these schools. For example, recently, two of these students and I spent from 7:30 A.M. to 5:30 P.M. in a low-scoring, low-SES school as part of our ongoing effort to help them become highly successful. During the drive back and forth and during the time there, we spent more than four hours discussing what was needed to transform the school from low to high performing. Such discussions and our experience in working with low-performing schools deeply inform the description of the HiPass model that follows.

Finally, as to the trustworthiness (Lincoln & Guba, 1985) of the description that follows of the core beliefs and cultural characteristics of these highly successful schools, I asked, as a member check, several of those who led these schools to read this description and to give me feedback on whether it was a good description. Their response, without exception, was that I had been able to communicate a real sense of their work and their accomplishments. For example, one said, "Dr. Scheurich's description . . . is excellent . . . I am very pleased with the way that Dr. Scheurich synthesized our experiences into a model." Another said, "The research within this paper is very much in line with my experiences. . . . It reflects and validates our efforts to reform curriculum and instruction to better serve the needs of underachieving children." Additional trustworthiness measures included other member checks, prolonged engagement, triangulation, and persistent observation (Lincoln & Guba, 1985).

Results

Core Beliefs

According to those who are working or have worked in these schools, especially the principals, the absolutely necessary foundation for achieving high academic success with low-SES students of color is a set of five interrelated core beliefs. Without these, the educators in these schools emphatically and repeatedly say, high performance is not possible, that is, no core, no high performance. In addition, it is the actual operationalization of these core beliefs that is, in my view, chiefly responsible for making these schools superior to academically high-performing Anglo schools. In the latter schools, as in most traditional schools, the bell curve rules; there is an emphasis on selecting and sorting students into tracks (Oakes, 1985; see also Meyer & Rowan, 1983), and teachers and administrators are often detached from the success and well-being of every child (see e.g., Carlson, 1992; Smith, 1993). In contrast, in the highly successful schools described here, high performance for each and every child, delivered in a passionately committed and loving way, is the only way.

Core Belief 1: All Children Can Succeed at High Academic Levels—No Exceptions Allowed
Although many proponents of excellent schools, from Ron Edmonds' Effective Schools to Sizer's Essential Schools (Wohlstetter & Smyer, 1994; see also Deal & Peterson, 1990), have emphasized high expectations, the way that those in HiPass

schools define this core belief exceeds the common definition of high expectations. In that common definition, the belief is that high expectations remedy the supposed deficits that the children bring to school with them and the negative effects of low teacher expectations for some children. There is, also, often a kind of harshness that sometimes accompanies this that children should not be coddled or spoiled but should be pushed to achieve or taught the discipline of achievement. In contrast, in these highly successful schools, the focus on high expectations is based on the revolutionary belief that the natural condition of all children is high performance (see Hopfenberg et al., 1993, or Henderson, Greenberg, Schneider, Uribe, & Verdugo, 1996, for similar views) and that this high performance is not based on pushing children but on providing loving, facilitating conditions that deliver learning in a way that fits, supports, engages, and energizes the child (see also Core Belief 3).

Although many educators and schools commonly espouse this belief, especially in their mission or vision statement, few, in my experience, are truly committed to enacting it. In fact, to say of the educators in these highly successful schools that they are truly committed to success for all is an understatement. They are fiercely committed, not just to holding out high expectations for all children but for achieving high levels of success with all children. The question is not whether it can be done; the only question is how is it to be done for all—not just for a few, some, or many, but for all—of the children in the school. Consequently, these educators are running counter to the long-term, fundamental belief of U.S. educators that only a small percentage are academically superior (Oakes, 1985). They have, thus, disposed of the bell or normal curve as a guiding principal for academic success and replaced it with what in statistics is called an extremely negatively skewed distribution, meaning many scores are near the high end. They have accomplished this, however, not by lowering standards, which is how such a skew is typically attained, but by reconceptualizing what is possible for all children and by refusing any other result. As Ladson-Billings (1994) said, successful educators of children of color "believe that students are capable of excellence, and they assume responsibility for ensuring that their students achieve that excellence" (p. 18).

Core Belief 2: Child- or Learner-Centered Schools
Directly related to the first core belief is the belief that high-performance schools require that the entire school community be focused on the academic success and the holistic well-being of the students. Although many educators would say that their schools are focused this way, the educators at these highly successful schools mean something different. They mean that the pedagogy, the curriculum, the organization of the school itself, the conduct of students and staff, parental involvement, and staff development—all aspects of schooling—are driven by whatever it takes to achieve high levels of academic success and a positive, healthy environment for

all students. "If the child is not learning, the teacher should find another way to work until she or he finds the solution" (Lima & Gazzetta, 1994, p. 245).

There is, thus, an open, even aggressive, willingness to alter any aspect of schooling for the purpose of achieving these goals. As Sergiovanni (1996) advocates, the staff of these schools "place 'doing what's best for students' at the center of decision making" (p. 121). Or, as Darling-Hammond (1996) suggests, "It is clear that ordinary schools can succeed in extraordinary ways when they refocus their work on the need of students rather than on the demands of the bureaucracy" (p. 14; see also Henderson et al., 1996). For example, if the pedagogy that teachers have learned in college does not work with children, either in terms of academics or well-being, these schools find one that does. If the organizational structure is getting in the way of these goals, they change the structure. If the way they conceive of or accomplish parental involvement is not supporting student academic success and well-being, they change it. Literally all aspects of schooling are shaped and reshaped to achieve high levels of success and well-being for every child. The center of schooling, then, is the child, not the teachers or administrators, not the parents or the community, not the bureaucracy or rules, and not the pedagogy or the curriculum; it is the child.

Core Belief 3: All Children Must Be Treated with Love, Appreciation, Care, and Respect — No Exceptions Allowed

This third core belief is my favorite, and one that I think may be the most powerful factor in the success of these schools.[21] One principal said that one of her chief "nonnegotiables" is that no teacher or administrator can ever treat any child with disrespect. This same principal has said frequently that we must truly love all of our children, that all of our students need to know that they are loved by us, and that we need to constantly communicate this to our children. Many would say that this approach is useful for helping children to develop positive self-esteem, but for the educators in HiPass schools, it goes beyond self-esteem. These schools are educational communities, learning communities, totally devoted to the well-being of the whole child and to successful learning for that child (for somewhat similar perspectives, see Comer, 1986, 1993; Darling-Hammond, 1996; Haberman, 1995; Sergiovanni, 1996). The educators of these schools, as called for by Henry (1992), act as "caring parents," creating a "family ethos" (p. 399) in the school. These are environments that children truly want to go to every day; they are environments within which they feel treasured, valued, and loved.

Creating such loving environments, though, requires caring for or, better, loving the children, an approach or orientation that has begun to gain some legitimacy in academic circles, principally with the work of Noddings (1984, 1992, 1994) but also with that of Raywid (1993) and Beck (1994). However, I would suggest that the loving orientation that I am describing here is somewhat different than that described by Noddings, Raywid, or Beck. First, the "love ethic"

(West, 1988, p. 10) of HiPass schools is rooted in a historical communal practice of communities of color, as they have survived within extremely deleterious circumstances. This is well exemplified by the Black Christian church. As West (1988) said,

> The black [Christian] church was a communal response to an existential and political situation in which no penultimate reasons suffice to make any kind of sense or give any type of meaning to the personal circumstances and collective condition of AfroAmericans. (pp. 4–5)

Second, Foster (1994), in her description of exemplary African-American teachers, uses words such as *connectedness, solidarity,* and *common affiliation* to indicate how she saw these teachers' "loving" relationship with their students (pp. 226–230). Combining West's (1988) historical focus with this latter one of Foster's (1994), it is as if in particular the principals (again, who all were persons of color) have a sense of historical solidarity or union with the children of color, so that the plight of the children is their plight, the needs of the children are their needs, and the successes of the children are their successes. In fact, some of them have said to me that they constantly see themselves in the children. Thus, the kind of lovingness I am trying to describe is not some particular action or interaction. It is more like a way one has become or successfully earned through a specific historical crucible of experiences. For the principals of these schools, based on my experiences with them, this lovingness is always there. It is pervasive; it inhabits everything they do or say. It also seems, to me, to be a source of endless energy to always do more for the children, no matter how committed these principals already are. It is as if on some deep level they are saying, "These are all my children, and my mission or meaning in life is to ensure that they all get a positive, successful schooling experience." What is most impressive is that against immense odds, they have succeeded in facilitating this mission.

Core Belief 4: The Racial Culture, Including the First Language, of the Child is Always Highly Valued—No Exceptions Allowed

From our studies of these successful schools and from my conversations with those who led them, it quickly becomes apparent that these schools value highly the racial culture and first language of the student. They use what Ladson-Billings (1994) calls "culturally relevant teaching . . . a pedagogy that empowers students intellectually, socially, emotionally, and politically by using cultural referents to impart knowledge, skills, and attitudes" (pp. 17–18). As Trueba (1994) contends, "The very possibility of developing a positive self-concept and ethnic identity depends on the recognition and celebration of one's own social, linguistic, and cultural heritage" (p. 380; see also Lipka & McCarthy, 1994; Merino, 1991).

One of my colleagues tells a story from his childhood, a story of being marked with white chalk dust from an eraser and being made to leave this stigmatizing mark on throughout an entire school day to punish him because he spoke Spanish at school. In sharp and total contrast, in HiPass schools, no matter what the language and racial culture of the students is, that language, or culture, or both, is positively integrated (in a substantive way, not in a trivial way like focusing on just food and holidays) into teaching and learning within the classroom and into the overall organizational culture of the school. As Smith (1993) contends, "Instead of ignoring or denigrating local culture, as has often been the case in schools serving nonmainstream students, teachers must strive to make that culture pivotal to students' learning activities" (p. 12), an approach Hollins and Spencer (1990) call "respond[ing] in positive ways to the home culture" (p. 92).

　　Like the teachers and principals in these successful schools, scholars have increasingly begun to emphasize the critical importance of what has been called "culturally congruent" (Au & Kawakami, 1994), "culturally centered" (King, 1994), or "culturally relevant" (Ladson-Billings, 1994) pedagogy. Au and Kawakami (1994) have recently reviewed the research on this issue, dividing it into five areas: (a) nonmainstream English dialect speakers, (b) classroom participation structures, (c) English as a second language (ESL) students, (d) classroom narrative and questioning styles, and (e) peer group interactions. Summarizing this research, they suggest that typical practices that appear ineffective for students of diverse backgrounds are those that devalue the home language or dialect, rely too heavily on classroom recitation, fail to recognize community variations in styles of narration and questioning, and ignore peer group dynamics (p. 23). As Trueba (1991) has said, "The school cultural environment and the organization of classroom work should reflect sensitivity to the ethnic cultures of minority students and [in] this way maximize their participation in learning activities" (p. 159). (For an excellent collection of work on this issue, see Hollins, King, & Hayman, 1994; see also Garcia, 1986, 1994; Lomotey, 1989; and Merino, 1991, among many others.)

Core Belief 5: The School Exists for and Serves the Community—
There is Little Separation
In these schools, the traditional separation between the school and its community has been erased, often moving beyond "Parents as Partners" (Boyer, 1994, p. 31) or "Reforming the Relationship Between Schools and Clients" (Elmore, 1990, p.18) to what Tyack and Hansot (1982) have called "a community of commitment" (pp. 249-262). These schools have created many different but creative ways to interweave the school and the community, to create what Estes (1994) has called "the high performance learning community" (p. 28). But "this does not mean [that these schools are] resocializing [for instance] African American parents to white middleclass ways" (Hollins & Spencer, 1990, p. 93); instead, these schools experience themselves as being in union with the community—the community's needs and dreams are their needs and dreams, and vice versa.

One school has parents working with teachers in nearly each class. Another school takes its meeting with the parents to sites that are comfortable to the parents. At still another school, at the beginning of the school year, the teachers ride the buses; at each stop, the teachers get off the bus and meet the parents to show their respect and appreciation to the parents. Several teachers have turned their schools into aesthetically pleasing environments because as they say, the school building is the best, most expensive building in the community. Some teachers have turned their schools into community centers, incorporating nonschool-related activities that serve the community. But the orientation of these schools goes beyond what they specifically do: These schools work "to truly bring parents and the community into the learning circle" (Henry, 1996, p. 193; see also Comer, 1984; Edwards, 1996; Hopfenberg et al., 1993) and to truly bring the school into the community circle. Therefore, what Siddle Walker (1993) has said about a successful, predesegregation African-American school could be said of the schools discussed here:

> The community–school relationship is a two-way process . . . [the] involvement should not be defined simply as how to bring the parents into the school, but also how the school can be "in" the community. (p. 179)

In fact, one principal said that the school's commitment to the well-being of its community was its first and primary commitment, taking precedence, if necessary, even over its academic commitments to the children. Another school, when asked by the district office to provide parenting training to its parents, asked the parents what they wanted from the school. The parents said that they wanted training on computers, so the school provided this training rather than parenting classes, responding primarily to the parents rather than to the district office. These schools see parents and themselves as collaborators in the education of the children, and so the schools do everything they can to positively promote this collaboration. Most importantly, though, no matter what the education or income level of the parents, the school staff treat all of the parents with respect, appreciation, warmth, sensitivity, and care.[22] Consequently, these schools have developed the "six qualities" that Raywid (1993) contends are key features of building community: "respect, caring, inclusiveness, trust, empowerment, and commitment" (p. 40).

Organizational Culture Characteristics

Sergiovanni (1996), following Deal and Kennedy (1982), summarizes the concept of organizational culture as a metaphor that refers to the values and rituals that provide people with continuity, tradition, identity, meaning, and significance, as well as to the norm systems that provide direction and that structure their lives (p. 20). Although a concept that is so comprehensive in definition tends to lose its analytic value, the concept or metaphor of organizational culture continues to have heuristic value. In this latter sense, then, describing cultural characteristics is one way of providing a sense, even a metaphorical sense, of the nature of the successful schools described here. It should be recognized, though, that there are other ways or heuristics that could be used to describe these schools. It should also be recognized that, as with the core beliefs, the cultural characteristics are interwoven, mutually reinforcing, and cannot, thus, actually be separated into the seven separate characteristics; they are what Smircich (1983) has called "shared meanings" (p. 55).

Organizational Culture Characteristic 1: A Strong, Shared Version
In the 1990s, saying that successful schools or successful organizations have a strong vision is like repeating what everyone already knows (see, e.g., Boyer, 1994; Burns, 1978; Roueche & Baker, 1986). But these successful schools, and their leadership, do not just have a strong vision, they have a particular vision. The core of their vision, and the core of the HiPass model is, thus, driven by their passionate commitment to their belief that there are ways to do schooling so that literally all children do well. Many of them, particularly the leadership, are deeply disturbed by the widespread school failure of children of color, and they know this is unnecessary. Some of them have seen the difference they could make as teachers in their own classrooms, and they wanted to make that same difference for a whole school. At the beginning, they typically did not know how to do this in its entirety, although they had ideas. Nonetheless, they were powerfully committed to their vision that it could be done and that they were going to figure out how to do it, no matter what it took. Driven by their vision, they, in short, became transformational.

However, for them, being transformational does not mean forcing a vision on the entire staff and on the school's community. The approach of the leadership is closer to what Sergiovanni (1996) calls an "invitational mode" (p. 83). As he says,

> . . . the emphasis in community leadership is building a shared followership and the emphasis in building a shared followership is not on *who* to follow, but on *what* to follow. Community members are not asked to comply in response to clever leadership processes or in response to aspects of the leader's personality. They are asked to respond to substance . . . to develop a broad-based commitment to shared values and conceptions that become a compelling source of authority for what people must do. . . . In establishing . . . [this] leadership, principals have a special responsibility to share their visions of what schools can become, but they must do this in an *invitational mode* [italics added]. (p. 83)

But even this description by Sergiovanni, although substantially better than most conceptions of communicating vision, is insufficient for HiPass schools. The leadership and many of the teachers have this heightened, energized belief that "together we can be highly successful with children" and that together there is nothing else more important in the world; they communicate this in a way that literally melts the typical separation between people. They facilitate a kind of loving community focused on a higher purpose, a higher ground. But it is not charisma, it is love, love for children; love for what, given the right conditions, children can achieve; and love for school staff, in cooperation with the parents and the community, accomplishing this together. In other words, "it calls . . . to higher levels of commitment. It calls . . . to higher levels of goodness. [And] it calls . . . to higher levels of effort" (Sergiovanni, 1996, p. 95).

Organizational Culture Characteristic 2: Loving, Caring Environments for Children and Adults

One of the schools that my colleagues and I studied in the border area of Texas served almost exclusively low-SES Mexican-American children who entered school speaking Spanish. The staff at this school have created one of the finest schools I have ever seen, and one of its most outstanding characteristics is that they have created an educational environment that is loving and caring for both children and adults. Although several scholars, such as Ladson-Billings (1994), have found that successful teaching for children of color depends on treating children with love, care, respect, and appreciation, the HiPass schools have discovered that if the goal is to create a whole school, a whole system, that is successful for children of color, the adults working in the school must be treated in the same loving, caring manner. In short, these schools are wonderful places to work for adults, too, and not just because of the pride of success.

Indeed, a key to transforming a school from low- to high-performing, according to those who have guided these transformations, is transforming the way that staff are treated and the quality of the work environment that is created. When the principals of these highly successful schools enter low-performing schools, they typically find dispirited, disconnected, alienated, conflicted staff whose teaching is often less than the best and often ill-fitted to the children that they serve. To convert or transform these negative environments and those who work within them requires that the principal communicate trust, openness, connection, and caring to the staff.

If the staff does not feel this from the principal, they are simply not going to change either their attitudes or their teaching. As even Peters (co-author of *In Search of Excellence* with Waterman, 1982), the guru to bottom-line, profit-oriented corporate managers, said, "*Caring—a must!* . . . If you don't get this one right, you will scuttle the rest" (Peters, 1992, p. 749).

This point cannot be underestimated. To go from low performance to high performance is a total conversion of an entire organization encompassing numerous, complex individuals who are engaged in numerous, complex tasks with numerous, complex students. To accomplish this requires a formidable paradigm shift on the part of all of the staff. To get the staff to achieve this requires that the principal act out of love—no other word really suffices. When the staff feel this kind of powerful commitment from the principal to them and to the children, they will, as the Christian scriptures say, move mountains, and no less than moving mountains is what must occur, given the distance an alienated, low-performing school must move to become high performing and loving. Consequently, from the beginning of their transformations, these successful schools develop an environment of love, care, respect, and appreciation for both children and adults (see Beck, 1994, for an advocacy of this approach for all schools).

Organizational Culture Characteristic 3: Strongly Collaborative— We Are a Family
One of the most common statements I have heard from teachers and administrators in HiPass schools is that "we are a family here" (see also Beck & Murphy, 1996, pp. 87–96, for a similar conclusion). Virtually all of the staff have bonded together in a deep way so that they feel they are doing the work of schooling together, as a family. These educators have created what Sergiovanni (1996) calls "communities," which he defines as "social structures that bond people together in a oneness, and that bind them to a set of shared values and ideas" (p. 47; see also Darling-Hammond, 1996). And in these communities, "all decisions are ultimately the responsibility of the whole staff" (Meter, 1992, p. 607; see also Beck, 1994; Comer, 1993; Henderson et al., 1996; Thompson, 1992). In other words, these educators could say, like the participants in the Brazilian *Projeto Inaja* that "We lived moments of transformation together. . . . This made us all part of the learning" (Lima & Gazzetta, 1994, p. 243).

One principal said that when she interviewed a potential new teacher, the most important characteristic she looked for was whether this new person would be able to bond with the school staff because this principal saw that bonding was the key, the foundation to their success. In addition, this principal said that no matter how talented the person was as a teacher and no matter how excellent the person's credentials and training were, without that ability or willingness to be part of the family, the person would not be able to contribute to the success of the school. Thus, although Haberman (1995) has concluded that successful teachers of low-SES children must create an extended family in the classroom, these highly successful schools have been able to extend their family to include the entire school and, typically, the community.[23]

Organizational Culture Characteristic 4: Innovative, Experimental, Openness to New Ideas
Mohrman and Mohrman (1993) defined innovation as

> . . . a process that generates something new—products, applications, processes, practices, or systems. It is a creative process of seeing new applications for existing knowledge, combining different bits of knowledge to create a new capability, or "inventing" new solutions. (p. 93)

In addition, they indicated that it is typically not individuals but "teams of people" (p. 93) that develop innovations. Both of these are accurate descriptions of innovation in HiPass schools. For example, in one school there are always new experiments being conducted. Even though this school is ranked more highly than most middle-class suburban Anglo schools, they are always trying to find new ways to become even better. They have, thus, done what Fullan (1991) has called for, that is, a "redesign [of] the workplace so that innovation . . . [is] built into the daily activities" of the school (p. 353).

Teachers, other staff, and administrators in this particular school are "always questioning existing practices" (Glickman, 1993, p. 16) and always looking for new ideas; they are practicing what Gideonse (1990) has called "practitioner-orientated inquiry" (p. 102). When they find what they see as a good idea, they investigate it, read about it, go study it in action, discuss it, and, if they decide it sounds worthwhile, they try it out in a small way. If the pilot works, that is, if it improves their work in a significant way, they implement it on a wider scale (Levin's "accelerated schools" use a similar approach, which is called the "inquiry process" [Hopfenberg et al., 1993, pp. 95–137]; see also Glickman, 1993). As one principal said, the only criterion is whether it will improve education for their children; thus, the principals have decided that any new possibility must be studied and justified before the experiment is piloted. If the experiment does not work, no one is blamed. It is simply dropped, and they move on to another new possibility. They, in fact, expect that finding successful new teaching methods, curriculum, and so forth, requires an openness to the failure of the experiment.

Organizational Culture Characteristic 5: Hardworking But Not Burning Out
As several teachers in one school said, teachers just do not apply to this school unless they want to work hard because that is the reputation we have. All of the educators at these schools, not just some, as with many schools, work hard. At one school, when they decided to offer a Saturday morning math academy, they needed staff to volunteer to take turns operating the academy, but they did not have sufficient funds to pay anyone. However, they had no trouble gaining ready volunteers from among the staff. In addition, many of these schools offer individual, teacher-conducted tutoring before school and after school. Furthermore, many work hard in the sense that they have put in a major effort to learn to teach in entirely new ways rather than rely on old ways that were not successful for their students. They have also learned to create classrooms in which children are almost always on task, that are child-centered rather than teacher-centered, and that engage all the children rather than a few or some, all of which takes much more focused attention than a traditional, teacher-centered classroom.

Some scholars and educators have worried, however, that this hard-working orientation expects too much from teachers and will burn them out (see, e.g., Sarason, 1982). What I have found, however, is that contrary to the burnout theory, these teachers are energized because they are integral members of a team working collaboratively and experiencing success together. Burnout, I would suggest, tends to happen more often to those who must work hard in a school in which many teachers are failing to do well and in which there is little of a loving, collaborative spirit. These successful schools, some of whom have been doing well for many years, are not peopled by tired, burnt-out teachers who are using their last grain of energy to be the best. They are peopled by teachers who evidence pride in their success, who continue to be committed to hard work with their students, and who maintain an energized environment for themselves and their students. They are, in a sense, successfully fulfilling a higher calling or commitment, a process or an accomplishment that increases rather than depletes their willingness to work hard.

Organizational Culture Characteristic 6: Appropriate Conduct is Built into the Organizational Culture
One sure sign that someone is not in one of the successful schools that I have been describing is a room full of students waiting in line to be disciplined or an administrator working with discipline cases all day long. For these schools, discipline cases are rare. In fact, one principal told me that she disliked the word *discipline*, and thought that those who use this word do not understand how to develop a successful school for all children. For HiPass schools, appropriate conduct, for children and adults, is built into the organizational culture (the importance of this to multiracial schools, as some of these schools are, is discussed in Schofield, 1996). There are, as has been reported about the focus schools of the 1990 RAND study titled *High Schools With Character,* "strong social contracts that communicate the reciprocal responsibilities of administration, students, and teachers" (Hill, Foster, & Gendler, 1990, p. vii). And, this contract is expressed repeatedly and reinforced constantly, but "not in the tough, inspectoral sense suggested by factory images of inspection and control" (Sergiovanni, 1996, p.91).

When someone, adult or child, violates the standards of conduct, consequences are immediate but always fair; they are respectfully but equitably delivered. These schools "aggressively mold student attitudes and values" (Sergiovanni, 1996, p. viii; see also Shipley, 1992, for similarities with Comer's schools). At first, I personally was uncomfortable with the strength of the focus on conduct; it did not fit my idea, at the time, of a good school. As Delpit (quoted in "Scores Count," 1996) has recently said, progressive Anglo educators and progressive educators of color hold significantly different views in this area. However, as I have seen more of these schools and talked to their principals, I have seen that virtually all of them consider the establishment of strong and powerfully reinforced expectations of appropriate conduct as a key feature of a successful school.

Of course, a safe and orderly environment has always been one of the components of Edmonds' Effective Schools. In addition, Edmonds has said that everyone in an effective school agrees on the rules of conduct and that everyone enforces them (O'Neill & Shoemaker, 1989). A similar focus on conduct is also a feature of Comer's school, according to Shipley (1992), a principal in one of those schools. Kuykendall (1992), in *From Rage to Hope: Strategies for Reclaiming Black & Hispanic Students* (a book that many administrators and teachers in successful schools and classrooms of color respect), says that everyone in the school—from teachers and administrators to cafeteria workers and bus drivers—must constantly communicate responsibility and appropriate behavior. However, it needs to be clear that for HiPass schools, discipline or order, as traditionally construed, is not the focus. The focus is on embedding an understanding of appropriate conduct (conduct that applies fairly and equally, even lovingly, to both adults and children) into the organizational culture of the school itself.[24]

Organizational Culture Characteristic 7: School Staff as a Whole Hold Themselves Accountable for the Success of All Children
In HiPass schools, the educators hold themselves as a whole accountable for all children in the school, in a way similar to that advocated by Clark and Meloy (1989; see also Darling-Hammond, 1996; Henderson et al., 1996). In addition, the administrator holds herself or himself accountable for the success of the whole school. Of course, many schools do this in this era of state-based, high-stakes tests results that are communicated in the public media. What is different, though, about HiPass schools is that all of the school staff truly believe that they are all collaboratively accountable for all children, what Ouchi (1981) calls "a collective sense of responsibility" (p. 40; Levin's Accelerated Schools take a somewhat similar approach [Wohlstetter & Smyer, 1994]). This means that just succeeding with the children in one's classroom is not sufficient; each teacher must work together with administrators and other teachers to ensure success for all children. In some cases, this holistic approach to accountability has been expanded to include the parents and the community. In others, the children are taught and modeled to be responsible for each other's success; that is, they learn to aid one another in the teaching and learning process.

   In addition, these schools use high-stakes state test data as a whole-school accountability measure that drives instruction. Originally, this was also a problem for me. I have long been an outspoken opponent of these tests because I felt that the research was abundantly clear on the negative effects (see Darling-Hammond, 1991; Darling-Hammond & Wise, 1985; Jaeger, 1991; Madaus, 1991; Shepard, 1991; and Stake, 1991, for research-based arguments against these tests). However, the staff in these schools, in their view, have appropriated these tests to their own purposes, such as Michael Johnson did in his Science Skills Center in New York City ("Scores Count," 1996). For example, several educators in these schools said that although they were skeptical, based on their own reading of these tests, that state high-stakes tests were racially culture-free; they felt it was self-defeating to oppose such tests because such opposition would only further contribute to the racist attitudes that many have toward low-SES students of color and their schools.

Instead, these educators' decision was that, through their success, they would show that their children and their schools were the academic equal to other children and schools, even if they had to surmount unfair barriers, such as culturally-biased tests. According to them, having to be "several times better to be equal" was nothing new in a racially-biased society.[25]

Conclusion

I have briefly discussed the source of the model and the sources of the data, the core beliefs, and the organizational culture characteristics of highly successful, caring, public elementary schools populated mainly by low-SES children of color, all of which together form what some of those who have led such schools and I call the HiPass model. However, it must be understood that describing these schools using these various conceptual categories only creates a heuristic, analytical scheme with which to communicate and dialogue about them within researcher and educator discourses. Other ways of describing them, such as narrative or story-like ones, would be an equally useful alternative. In fact, all of the beliefs, characteristics, and qualities that I have described here could be more appropriately described as a holistic, interwoven tapestry, with all aspects influencing and reinforcing the other aspects. Even that metaphor, though, does not indicate that they are always in process, never done, and always changing. These highly successful schools are truly rich, vibrant, complex, collaborative creations, creations that have major, critical implications for education, for organizations, and, even, for society in general.

For education, there are two implications. The first is, as I have suggested in the introduction, that the very existence of multiple examples of such schools undermines the widespread assumption that low-SES children of color are to blame for their lack of school success. If the traditional model of schooling does not work for children of color, then we as educators ethically cannot use the traditional approach with these children. In addition, the differential school success of children of color is being used on a daily basis to justify racism, even by educators. In fact, when you talk to many educators about why their students of color are not doing as well as their Anglo students, the typical explanations, although they are often stated obliquely, are that it is the fault of the children's or parents' lack of commitment to education—the students are not disciplined, they are not prepared, they are not helped at home, and so forth. However, if these educators can begin to see and understand the successful schools discussed here, they will begin to see and understand that we educators have ways, a model, to provide high levels of academic success to literally all children, regardless of their race or class. They will see and understand that we do not need to lay blame on someone and that, instead, we do know, as Edmonds (1979) has said, "We can, whenever and wherever we choose, successfully teach all children whose schooling is of interest to us" (p. 24).

The second implication for education is that this model of schooling is simply a better way to do schooling, and it is not just some theory; it is a living reality from which all educators can learn. This model is clearly better for children of color. It is, in many regards, Ladson-Billings's (1994) successful teachers writ large to a whole system. Although successful teaching of children of color by individual teachers is critically important, we need, as Ladson-Billings suggests, to create whole systems of such classrooms, and this is a model that can create such a system. This model is also better, in my opinion, than high-performing, traditional, Anglo-dominant schools. Although high scoring, they are tracked and stratified; they do not serve all of their children equally well and they certainly do not believe that all children can succeed at the highest levels. They do not highly respect the racial culture and the first language of the child unless that culture is the Anglo culture and that language is the English language, and they are not deeply loving, caring places in which to work or school. Finally, the HiPass model is better because it does not, like most schooling, reproduce academic differences by race, class, or gender. In these successful schools, children of color do not perform more poorly on average than Anglo children, low-SES children do not perform more poorly on average than middle-class children, and girls do not perform more poorly on average than boys. Instead, these schools are passionately committed to high academic success for literally all children, and they fulfill that commitment. It is ironic, indeed, that a better way of schooling has emerged from low-SES schools and communities of color.

I want to end by suggesting that these HiPass schools, those who have created and worked within them, and the communities of color that midwived them, have given all of us a gift that is larger than just education, as vitally important as education is to our society. In terms of organizations and life in those organizations, these schools have given us living examples of a kind of organization that is wonderful to work within and that performs at the highest levels; in other words, they have given us organizations that are both loving and high performing. All of us who work within or lead any kind of organization—which is virtually all of us—should be looking with great interest at the model for these successful schools because they just may be providing us with a substantially better way to do organizations. In fact, the very idea that our work environments could be both loving and high performing is truly startling for most of us, given our typical experiences in organizations. Could, for instance, General Motors, Intel, or research universities be both loving and highly productive places to work? It would be ironic, indeed, if a better kind of organization has emerged from low-SES schools and communities of color.

In terms of society at large, these schools also speak to us about the communities and cities we live in and the current models we have for those communities. In the recent presidential campaigns and also in our daily lives, we see the social conflict, strife, pain, corruption, and alienation that divide along axes of race, class, gender, sexual orientation, age, and disability in our communities and in the nation. Perhaps the models we use, consciously or unconsciously, for our communities need to be reconsidered. Perhaps these successful schools offer us some new ideas about how we ought to be leading our communal life together.

For example, given the model of these schools, what if we, as members of our communities, were dedicated to the beliefs that a commitment to the whole well-being of all citizens was primary before anything else, including consumer goods and money; that everyone could be highly successful, and that together we would do whatever was necessary to accomplish this; that everyone was always to be treated with love, appreciation, care, and respect (no exceptions); and that all racial cultures and first languages were to be appreciated and respected? What if, for instance, as communities we were all committed to creating a loving, caring environment for everyone; to collaborating as if we were a family; to building community cultures in which appropriate conduct was built into that culture rather than forced or enforced; and to holding ourselves accountable for the well-being and success of all of the members of our community? What if, for instance, we were able to create communities of equality without alienating divisions of race, class, gender, sexual orientation, and disability—truly loving communities committed to the well-being and success of all citizens?

Although such conjecture may seem hopelessly idealistic, many would have thought, and still do, that the possibility of highly successful and loving, low-SES schools populated mainly by children of color is a hopelessly idealistic conjecture. Perhaps we should heed these successful schools. It would be ironic, indeed, if a better way to live together has emerged from low-SES schools and communities of color.

Notes for Chapter 7

1. I know that there is a growing use of the word *caring* in education discourses (e.g., Noddings, 1984). However, based on my experience in these schools, my conversations with their principals, and my collaboration with them, I did not feel that this word was strong enough, focused enough, or committed enough. I feel that the word *loving is* substantially better, even though its use may make some educators uncomfortable. The schools I am describing here are truly loving environments for both the children and adults, and those working in them, particularly the principals, truly have a loving attitude toward the children, their work, and those with whom they work.

2. To illustrate what I mean by high levels of academic success at the time this was published, what follows are some 1995-1996 descriptive data on one of the schools on which this article is based. The name of this school is E. B. Reyna Elementary School, and it is located in the border region of Texas. Its student body was 99.3% Mexican-American and 88.6% economically disadvantaged. It had a 22.6% mobility rate, 69.1% were limited

English proficient, 64.8% were considered bilingual, and 7.1% were in the special education program. In other words, their students were overwhelmingly low-SES Mexican-American students who enter school with Spanish as the first language. Nonetheless, this school had a high attendance rate (97.1%) and scored at the "Recognized" level on Texas' high-stakes test, which included reading, writing, and math tests. In 1995, at the third grade level, 95.4% correctly answered 70% or more of all questions on all three of the tests; at the fourth grade level, 96.7% did the same; at the fifth grade level, 83.8%. In 1996, at the third grade level, 89.6% answered correctly 70% or more of all questions on all three of the tests; at the fourth grade level, 89.8% did the same; at the fifth grade level, 75.0%. To score at this "Recognized" level, a school must have 70% of all racial groups answering correctly 70% of the questions on each of the three tests, a 3.5% or less dropout rate, and a 94% or better attendance rate. For the 1996 testing, 17.1% of all rated Texas schools (5,870 were rated) at all levels were rated as "Recognized." Consequently, E. B. Reyna was in the upper fifth of all rated schools in Texas at the time. (All of these data are available on the Texas Education Agency's web page at http://www.tea.state.tx.us.) In addition, the *Texas Monthly* ("Our Best Schools," September, 1996) did a rating of all elementary schools based on the results on the same test. In their system, a school received four stars, the highest rating, if at least 70% of the students passed the test and the school's passing rate was in the top 15% of schools with a similar percentage of low-SES students. E. B. Reyna received four stars (less than 15% of the 3,172 elementary schools taking the test received this highest rating).

3. The research on Texas border schools that my colleagues and I have conducted, and that of others (e.g., Louis & Miles, 1990), shows that educators have generally been more successful at creating successful schools for elementary-level children than for secondary-level students. That does not mean that such success is not possible at the secondary level, but we have fewer examples and less knowledge about such schools (Louis & Miles, 1990). Secondary-school contexts are considerably different from elementary ones in many regards, as most researchers know. However, there is an emerging body of knowledge about what is necessary to achieve high levels of success with secondary-level, low-SES students of color. Trueba (1991), for instance, has reported success in the South San Diego Writing Project with low-SES Chicano students learning to write English through the use of student teams who had "full control of their own writing activities" (p. 156). The result was that "these Chicano high school students not only significantly sharpened their communicative skills but [also] realized that these skills are a powerful instrument in voicing individual and collective concerns" (p. 157). Another example comes from my conversations with a principal of a high school who was able to facilitate a substantial increase in African-American high school students who passed the state's math test, from fewer than 20% passing to more than 70% passing, by detracking these students and developing a "culturally relevant" pedagogy and curriculum. My suggestion at this point for high schools is that the model that is presented here should be used as the foundation. From that foundation, other steps should be taken, including the elimination of low tracks; direct involvement of the students in real decision making about all aspects of their schooling (what might be called student empow-

erment); engagement of the students in a curriculum that is open to critique of the *status quo* (because these students are constantly confronted with the race, gender, and class biases of the *status quo* and because ignoring this disconnects education from these students' lives); and an accumulation of research on successful pedagogical and curriculum approaches, such as those arising out of research efforts to identify successful educational materials and practices for African-American children (e.g., Hollins, King, & Hayman, 1994; Ladson-Billings, 1994).

4. In a brief article in *The New York Times Magazine,* titled "Scores Count" (1996), there is a discussion of a school that is highly successful with low-SES students of color. This school has strong similarities with the schools discussed here, such as high expectations and a strong positive attitude toward the students, but it also has some strong dissimilarities, such as the principal is "unapologetically autocratic" (p. 44). This school may, thus, be one that has successfully operationalized a different model than the one presented here, or the differences may be a function of the differences between successful elementary and secondary schools.

5. A discussion of the nature of the leaders of these organizations and of their organizational attributes, including some provocative issues raised by these attributes, will appear in a separate article.

6. I want to express my deep appreciation to Louise Smith, Glenn Nolly, Encarnación Garza, Ron Peace, and Juanita Garcia Wagstaff, all of whom have served as principals of successful schools populated mainly by children of color. Without their loving and passionate commitment to children and without their skills and knowledge, the highly successful schools discussed here would not exist; without their friendship, I could not have written this article. Working and talking with them, I have learned that they truly know how to turn dreams into realities. Helping to carry forward their dreams and the reality of loving and highly successful schools for children of color—for all children—is what each of us can do to repay these individuals and their communities for giving so much when even surviving was often so hard.

7. What is meant by high performance is not what Sergiovanni (1996) means by "High Performance Theory" (pp. 9-19). Although my use of it encompasses Sergiovanni's focus on decentralization, what I mean by high performance is the strong academic results produced by the HiPass model. In point of fact, much that Sergiovanni advocates in his 1996 work, which he poses in opposition to what he calls High Performance Theory, occurs in HiPass schools.

8. The word *culture* generally means the norms, values, assumptions, rituals, symbols, and other patterns, formal and informal, common to some group of people. However, "common" does not mean every member of the group equally adopts or evidences every aspect of the culture; it only means that these aspects are typical or common across the group's members. But, although most uses in education research of the word *culture* are based on this definition, it is still applied in many different ways. For instance, sometimes culture is taken to mean the culture of a racial or ethnic group, such as the culture of African-Americans. Other times, it means the culture of the dominant group within a society, such as the dominant culture of the United States is the Anglo culture. However, it can also mean

the culture of an organization, such as a school or a corporation. In the latter case, it means the norms, values, assumptions, rituals, symbols, and other patterns that are common to the organization. For this article, I use the term *racial culture to* represent cultures that are race-based and that have arisen both from cultures of origin—such as the Mexican-American culture arising from its Mexican culture of origin—and from the survival of U.S. racial cultures under the dominance of Anglo racism. This is the same kind of definition, I assume, that Hollins and Spencer (1990) meant by "home culture" (p. 92) or that Trueba (1991) meant by "ethnic culture" (p. 159). I also, though, use the term *organizational culture.* In the latter case, I apply the meaning given above for the word *culture* to the school as an organization.

9. I want to thank Larry Parker for his insightful comments on earlier drafts. His commitment to children and communities of color are similar to those of the principals that led the schools described here. I also want to thank my colleagues Pedro Reyes, Lonnie Wagstaff, Jay Scribner, and Deborah Kazel-Thrasher, for the numerous conversations we have had about these highly successful schools. The influence of these conversations is undeniably evident throughout my efforts to describe these schools, and the influence of their strong commitment to develop schools that work for all children is also undeniably evident.

10. See, for example, Anyon, 1995; Anzaldùa, 1990; Banks, 1995; Bell, 1992; Cose, 1993; De Leon, 1983; Feagin & Vera, 1995; Hacker, 1992; hooks, 1990; King, 1992; Nieto, 1996; Reyes & Halcon, 1988; Scheurich, 1993a; Scheurich & Young, 1997; Takaki, 1993; Valencia, 1991; West, 1993, among many others.

11. See Warfield-Coppock (1995) for a discussion of an Afrocentric organization in comparison to a Eurocentric one; see also Schiele (1990). See discussions of the Afrocentric perspective and education in an entire edition of *The Journal of Negro Education* (Gordon, 1992) and in several chapters in Shujja (1994); for a broader discussion of the Afrocentic perspective, see the work of Asante (1987, 1990, 1991). See Faltz and Leake (1996) for a discussion of African-American immersion schools in Milwaukee. Finally, see Shujja and Afrik (1996) for a discussion of "the Council of Independent Black Institutions (CIBI) [that] was founded in 1972 as a national organization to unify a far-flung, rapidly developing movement of Pan-Africanist-oriented independent schools in the United States" (p. 254).

12. *Critical pedagogy is* a term that has in the last decade gained considerable ground among educators. It is most typically drawn from the work of Freire (see e.g., Freire, 1970; Freire & Macedo, 1987), although it now encompasses a significant range of work, including, for example, that of Keith (1996), McLaren (1989, 1995), Shor (1992), Simon (1992), and Sleeter and McLaren (1995), among many others. A particularly good source is a *Harvard Educational Review* reprint, edited by Leistyna, Woodrum, and Sherblom (1996), which includes such advocates of critical pedagogy as Maxine Greene, Donaldo Macedo, Henry Giroux, Joe Kincheloe, and Peter McLaren. bell hooks (1990) provides a particularly good, succinct definition: "Critical pedagogy (expressed in writing, teaching, and habits of being) is fundamentally linked to a concern with creating strategies that will enable colonized folks to decolonize their minds and actions, thereby promoting the insurrection of subjugated knowledges" (p. 8).

13. When I make this point that these successful schools incorporate features of critical pedagogy, I do not mean to imply that this incorporation is a conscious appropriation from critical pedagogy discourses. It is not. When I encountered these schools, I immediately assumed that the leadership had come from the radical movements of the 1960s and 1970s, such as *"El Movirniento,"* or from the civil rights movement of the 1950s and 1960s, but this was not true. The critical features that have been embedded in these schools are endemic to the cultures that have had to survive racism and classism in this country. For example, a critique of racism and economic inequity in the United States is a deep and powerful aspect of African-American culture, communicated from generation to generation through families, churches, and social movements. As Watkins (1996) said, "Reforming African-American education is hardly a new enterprise. For the last century (and more), the African-American educational community has been critical of colonial practices in both the form and content of schooling and education. The various trains of protest and critique are deeply rooted in the social, economic, political, racial, and religious experiences of an oppressed and long-suffering people" (p. 25).

14. See Leistyna and Woodrum's "Context and Culture: What Is Critical Pedagogy" (1996) for a discussion of these features of critical pedagogy.

15. Because my contention that these schools are postcolonial hybrids is a complex one, there is not space here to give this contention its adequate due. Nonetheless, I will briefly suggest the direction I would take. Bhabha (1985) is, in my view, one of the most perceptive scholars on the complexities of hybridity. In one of his clearest, concluding statements, he said, "If the effect of colonial power is seen to be the *production* of hybridization rather than the noisy command of colonialist authority or the silent repression of native traditions [or cultures] [a point he has previously been arguing], then an important change of perspective occurs. It reveals the ambivalence at the source of traditional discourses on authority and enables a form of subversion, founded on that uncertainty, that turns the discursive conditions of dominance into grounds of intervention" (p. 154). In my interpretation of this passage, he is arguing, via a deconstructive or Derridian analysis, that colonization is not only not exclusively hegemonic ("noisy command of colonialist authority or silent repression of native traditions") but is also itself (internal to its own "ambivalent" discourse) "productive" of "subversive grounds of intervention." In other words, according to Parry (1995), Bhabha argues that the dominant "discursive system . . . constitutes [creates a field for, makes possible] a . . . native who by (mis)appropriating the terms of the dominant ideology, is able to intercede against and resist this [dominant] mode of construction" (p. 41). In the case of the schools discussed here, Bhabha's argument facilitates a space, an opening, in which these schools could be insightfully discussed in all their complexity as a postcolonial institutional possibility within the current social-historical context, as an instance "of transgression performed by the native from within and against colonial discourse" (p. 41).

16. I do not mean to imply that these schools are necessarily the ideal or best possible schools for communities or for children of color (nor do I mean to imply that I would know what is best for children of color or for communities of color). For example, I do not think

that these schools would fully meet the criteria advocated by Hollins and Spencer (1990), but I do think that they would find that these schools meet several of their criteria. Again, my point is that we ought to carefully consider the fact that these highly successful, loving schools are hugely impressive improvements over the schooling that is the common experience of children of color in the United States, that these schools do incorporate many features called for by advocates of culturocentric and critical perspectives, and that these schools are able to survive and sometimes even thrive within districts and states dominated by mainstream educational and political perspectives.

17. The research was led by Pedro Reyes and Jay Scribner, who, along with most of the other researchers, including myself, and many of the doctoral students, are in the Department of Educational Administration at the University of Texas at Austin. However, some researchers on the project were from other universities in the Southern Texas region.

18. Typically, the research team I was on would interview and observe all morning, meet at lunch to share what we had observed and heard (audio tape this lunchtime conversation), observe and interview all afternoon, and then meet again after or over dinner to discuss again what we had seen and heard (and, again, audio tape this conversation). Because of this schedule, we were able to magnify what each single researcher was seeing and hearing because each of us was twice each day able to get input from everyone else. One result was that each of us quickly had a strongly triangulated sense, drawn from a broad array of data collected by different researchers, of what were the best areas of price or programs in any particular school and of whether the school as a whole was generally successful.

19. One of my informants asked that I say that while he, as the principal, laid the groundwork for the success that followed shortly after he left, he cannot claim that he was the principal when the success occurred.

20. One of these dissertations is now finished. It is Glenn Nolly's *Effective Instructional Practices for Teaching Mathematics to African American Students* (1997).

21. This core belief also relates to the emerging body of research that identifies factors that promote resiliency (able to effectively cope with negative circumstances, such as poverty, racism, poor schools, etc.) among low-SES children of color. Although I do not discuss this work here, it does have a significant relationship to the features of the schooling model I describe, especially in the sense that HiPass schools would be resiliency-producing schools. For those seeking more information on this, see Vol. 24, No. 1 of *Education and Urban Socket,* edited by Winfield (1991).

22. For example, in one school, a principal (who returned as an adult to be the principal of the school in which he was mistreated as a child because he was a Spanish-speaking, Mexican-American migrant child) could not get his low-SES Mexican American students' parents to come to the school for meetings. He wanted to engage them in working with the school to improve the learning of their children. Instead of blaming these parents or complaining that they did not care about their children's learning (an attitude that is rarely true of low-SES parents of color [see e.g., Delgado-Gaitán,1992], but one that is frequently stated by many educators [Deyhle, 1991]), he went to where they were rather than expecting them to come to where he was. Because many of his parents lived in trailers in *colonias*

(collections of house trailers, often without electricity or plumbing, on small parcels of land), he set up meetings amidst the trailers, a place where most of the parents felt much more comfortable than they did at school. By respecting who his parents were and their needs, by coming to them, and by showing his commitment to them, he was able to gain a high level of involvement by his parents and a strong commitment by them to the school; thus he was able to build a vibrant merging of school and community.

23. Another causal factor in the facilitation of this collaborative, family orientation is open communication. As Galbraith, Lawler, and Associates (1993) have repeatedly said, the more that information is made available to everyone, creating an "information-rich organization" (Galbraith & Lawler, 1993, pp. 296–297), the more it is possible to create what Lawler (1988) has called a "high involvement" organization. Mohrman (1994), a close associate of Lawler, has called this "decentralizing information" (p. 38). Contrary to the traditional school, in which information is highly controlled and often stops at the principal's desk, in these highly successful schools, information was freely shared among everyone so that everyone understood as much as possible about the entire operation. As Wohlstetter and Smyer (1994) have said, "the nature of these schools seems to dictate an informed environment" (p. 97). It is this "informed environment" or free-flowing information that is a necessary thread in the weaving of a collaborative environment that repeatedly declares itself to be a family.

24. Another reason why these highly successful schools do not have many discipline problems, as repeatedly emphasized by one principal, is that the classrooms engage the students through a pedagogy that fits their culture and through a curriculum in which they see themselves reflected positively. In other words, there is a belief in these schools that when students are not engaged, feel alienated, and repeatedly experience failure, these experiences produce discipline problems. As Trueba (1991) found in the South San Diego Writing Project, when Chicano students who in the past have had problems with learning to write in English were engaged in a respectful way by a pedagogy and curriculum that valued them and valued their perspectives, these students dramatically improved their writing skills. Similarly, a principal who has had substantial success in raising the math scores of low-SES African-American students has repeatedly said to me that if what occurs in the classroom truly engages the students in learning that makes sense to them, discipline is not even an issue. Haberman (1995) found the same in the classrooms of his "star" teachers.

25. In addition, this use of high-stakes tests was focused and systematic, thus setting "clear performance goals" (Deal & Peterson, 1990, p. 10). In many of these schools, prior to the state test, they conduct one or more practice test sessions, using similar tests in similar circumstances, to prepare students and to determine progress. The results of these practice tests are then analyzed by student, by test objective, and by teacher to drive instructional focus and remediation. They are practicing what Boyer (1994) calls "measuring for success" (p. 32) or what Mohrman and Mohrman (1993) call "ongoing assessment of the efficacy" of the organization (p. 100). As Darling-Hammond (1996) has said of excellent teachers, the schools "constancy assess students to identify their strengths and learning approaches as well as their needs and to examine the effects of different instructional efforts. They

understand assessment as a measure of their teaching as well as a measure of student learning" (p. 12; see also Lomotey, 1989, pp. 141–142). It must be noted, though, that the data from this testing are used "for problem identification and redesign, rather than for punishment" (Mohrman & Mohrman, 1993, p. 101); it is used to assist the teachers, administrators, and parents to focus on instructional goals. More broadly and more importantly, though, the successful results on the high-stakes tests are used to prove to others that these schools, and their students, were among the best in the state. To the educators in these schools, and to their communities of color, the powerful result supersedes the limitations and biases of these tests.

Chapter 8

Preface

This chapter, along with the next two, are examples of my *move away* from any assumption that I can rely on myself as a white researcher or rely on working only with other white researchers to represent fairly people of color *and* of my *move toward* collaboration with people of color in doing research on people of color. In this chapter, Gerardo Lopéz, Miguel Guajardo, and I developed "A postmodern re-presentation of children in migrancy" for a special issue of the *Educational Administration Quarterly*. In this piece, we tried to provide readers with a substantially different approach to presenting research. It is a pastiche from many different sources, including government documents and migrant children's poetry, bounded by an introduction and a conclusion. The reason we chose this form was that we wanted radically to shift away from typical responses of white readers to representations of migrant children. Thus, our shift in representational forms was directly connected to both our political commitments and our epistemological ones.

Chapter 8

Windows/Ventanas: A Postmodern Re-Presentation of Children in Migrancy

Gerardo R. Lopéz, Miguel A. Guajardo, and James Joseph Scheurich

Living among us—citizens like ourselves—are migrant families who are dedicated to hard work, a strong commitment to the family, deep spirituality, and the critical importance of education for their niños (children). Through hard work these families, in a real sense, sit at our dinner tables as those whose toil brought us the affordable food we eat. However, these fellow human beings are paid unbelievably low wages, especially given that even the children have to work for the family to barely get by. Families are housed in substandard structures, often treated as slightly above slaves (sometimes patrolled by supervisors carrying guns), callously exposed to poisonous farm chemicals, and commonly mistreated by the educational system. Because the authors do not believe it is possible to accurately represent the complexity of these people, they offer a multivocal montage, a Bakhtinian carnival, of words and images focused on migrants and migrancy.

Prelude

As I (Gerardo López) was sitting down to write the introduction to this text, I noticed my one-year-old daughter being quite attentive to life outside our window/ventana. Curious to see what she was observing, I walked over and sat next to her. Together, we observed a slice of Austin life on a typical Sunday afternoon. After several seconds of observing, I began to describe to her all of the objects within our viewing area: "Look mi'ja! Those are cars, carros. Esos son pajaritos, birds." I repeated every object named—in that slow, melodic tempo that adults often use when talking to children. My daughter readily focused her attention on everything that was being named. I then proceeded to describe these objects in more detail. "Ese carrito es rojo. Esa es una camioneta azul. La camioneta es mas grande que el carrito" [The little car is red. That there's a blue van. The van is much bigger than the little car].

After several minutes of "naming the world": I began to sense that my daughter's attention span was decreasing. Thinking of a way to continue our learning exercise, I carried her to an adjacent window in another room. As we looked out this window, I immediately realized that from this vantage point, new objects suddenly appeared or were made visible to us — objects that were not evident or obvious from our previous vantage point. Similarly, objects that were once readily visible were no longer apparent. The carrito, for example, was no longer there. For all intents and purposes, it had disappeared. For a moment, I wondered whether it ever existed from the vantage point of this looking glass that framed our new perspective.

On this day, both my daughter and I learned a powerful lesson, one in which the tangibility of the Kuhnian paradigm became apparent. Just like the scientists in Kuhn's (1970) *The Structure of Scientific Revolutions,* we were busy defining reality from a single perspective. It was not until we switched windows (or our paradigm) that we shifted our vantage point and, thus, our understanding of the world. Windows, in this example, were both lenses and blinders. Each window served both as a discursive space to see and/or experience a particular "truth" and as blinder to hide competing "truth regimes" (Foucault, 1970, 1972, 1980b).

How could I communicate to my daughter that what we were seeing from Window B was indeed a different truth than what was observed through Window A? How could I communicate to her that truth was perspectival and that all claims to truth were partial at best? How could I convey that any representation of truth was filtered through a particular lens or window that allowed one to see a limited truth form? The more questions I asked, the more suspicious I became of both truth and truth regimes. Rather than engage my one-year-old in a philosophical discussion surrounding the malleability of truth claims, I set her down and let her play with her toys. I then returned to my computer, armed with a renewed suspicion of truth and a useful illustration of its falsity.

Introduction

The above illustration is a good example of the partiality of truth claims. In this example, the father (as the representer or author of the truth/reality/story) was describing to his daughter an oversimplified representation of what his frame/window allowed him to see. In other words, the story he communicated to her about the world revealed more about the framework (or window) that enframed his reality than any objective or "real" truth per se. This does not suggest that reality is nonexistent, but it does hint at the notion that truth is multifaceted, multivocal, and multiperspectival; it is much more complex than one can ever imagine, grasp, or represent.

In this discussion, we will re-present a story of migrant students and the economic, social, and political reality they face in contemporary America. Similar to the above story — as with any other story — what we re-present will only be one re-presentation of (the migrant) reality and, perhaps, a nonrealist slice at that. In other words, what we present in this discussion will only be a manifestation of the frames that encompass our perspectives and understandings of the migrant student experience. Therefore, the images we present can — and will — reveal as much about the frameworks that shape our understandings of the migrant reality as about the migrant students themselves and/or the conditions under which they live. It is obvious that this problem has implications for issues of representation, validity, and methodology and for other sticky issues that emerge in qualitative research endeavors. We will be discussing some of these sticky issues throughout this text.

For example, in curriculum research and in social science research in general, the critical issue of how the other is represented or narrated has, for good reasons, become highly contentious. In response, critical race theorists (e.g., Bell, 1992; R. Delgado, 1990) have called for privileging the narratives or stories of those experiencing racial oppression, whereas scholars and writers of color (e.g., Lubiano, 1991; Minh-ha, 1990; Saldivar, 1990) have called for privileging nonrealist narrative structures. In response, we will take on the challenges posed by these scholars by providing a nonlinear, multimodal narrative of the migrant story in order to invoke its polyphonic nature and multidimensional aspects.

Our aim, then, is not to document a particular migrant Truth (with a capital, authoritative T) but, rather, to trouble conventional forms of representation of migrants in order to let several migrant truths (with a small, indeterminate t) flourish. In other words, what we aim to do in this discussion is to access as many windows as possible, knowing full well that what we produce will never fully capture the totality of the migrant subject/story. Armed with such a recognition, the story we represent will undoubtedly be multivocal; it will be positioned within a communicative discourse that is itself fluid, incoherent, and complex (see also, Oliva, 1997).

On Reality and Its Re-Presentation

Undermining Representation Through Carnival

> The carnivalesque . . . de-familiarizes the recent state of affairs, to historicize that which is generally taken to be immutable and eternal, and to revitalize abstract claims to truth through a gay parody of official reason (M. Gardiner, 1992).

Because the world is polyphonic and because language is "bound up with the same semiotic process that governs the ideological environment as a whole" (Gardiner, 1992, p. 20), we will use the Bakhtinian notion of carnival (Bakhtin, 1968) to undermine the omnipotent/authorial single voice in issues of representation. Bakhtin's notion of carnival—based on Goethe's 1788 description of an Italian New Year carnival—aims to describe a "bewildering constellation of rituals, games, symbols, and various carnal excesses" (Gardiner, 1992, p. 45) brought together in this festive event. Such cultural forms, generally not sanctioned in everyday life—in our case, we take this carnivalesque excess to refer to voices and groups not generally heard in professional and public discourses—come together in a public setting, ultimately transgressing normative frameworks that govern legitimate discourses. In other words, on this day of carnival, people are allowed to break the rules without social repercussions. In this sense, carnival disrupts the arbitrary nature between signifier and signified by disrupting and exposing the normative frameworks/windows that discursively govern human discourses (see also Foucault, 1972). The result is the understanding that legitimated or professional discourses are social constructions and not the truth (Oliva, 1997).

In short, the notion of carnival is Bakhtin's vehicle to rupture "official" dominant discourses. It not only privileges a text with multiple voices—where the unusual and the magical, the stories and pictures of invisible groups, transgress our taken-for-granted assumptions of a single master narrative—but also invites these typically silenced voices and perspectives to intersect, contest, engage, disrupt, critique, and negotiate over discursive space to name reality. "Just as no single voice can constitute polyphony, no one viewpoint can be adequate to the apprehension and understanding of the object" (Gardiner, 1992, p. 94).;

Eavesdropping on an E-mail Conversation Between the Authors

Gerardo: I'm trying to get a [migrant] "reality" that is multilayered, more complex, that can be presented [in this text]. What we represent will be exactly that: a re-presentation of a slice of realism. How we choose to present that (and who we choose to be representatives) will be the hardest part of this task because, however we choose to slice it, we can't essentialize the migrant reality, on the one hand, and neither can we prematurely name individuals as being "representatives" of a larger group.

Jim: The problem of representation to me is the problem of realism. Realism requires that there be an accurate representation or at least a trustworthy one. If realism is deposed, the representational crisis disappears. There is no longer any purpose of accurately or trustworthily representing anything. There are, though, two problems. The first is what do we put in the place of realism; the second is who gets to decide what is in the place of realism. I would replace realism with a social constructivism. I think who we three are is intersecting with written material related to migrant students (our data), and some of the material is realist research and some is pictures, poems, short stories, etc. What we come up with as our final product will be a construction we created about this intersection. On the second issue—as to who gets to make the construction—we are the ones selecting the material and reconstructing it; it is not migrant students, and this is power, institutional, mine, yours; it is not great power because all we are doing is making an article about migrant students that few will read or attend to, but power nonetheless.

Gerardo: I totally understand that we are reconstructing or retelling this migrant realism or story. . . . But by privileging constructivism, we run the risk of proposing that the realism itself is a construction, a falsity. What I mean to say is that we may create a migrant "story," but our story will only be that: a story. It's not real, not tangible, not valid outside of the storyteller's frame. How far into constructivism dare we go?

Jim: Perhaps we are defining realism and constructivism differently. By constructivism, I do not mean there are not "real" effects. I would contend there is no really real; there is only our ways—yours, mine, migrant students', etc.—of constructing the real. To many educators, migrant students are invisible; to some educators migrant students are *at risk* or some other negative label. Different migrant students construct their own realities differently. There are thousands of different "real's," but which "real" gets to circulate and which is denied, marginalized, invisible? In the recent past, I have written in opposition to realism as a kind of imperialism, that it is very arrogant of anyone or group or strata to think it can name or describe or interpret the "real." Lately, however, I have been reading critical race theorists. Derrick Bell, I think, suggests a racial realism. This really struck a bell with me. It seemed to me a much more insightful idea, a more subversive idea, a more exciting idea—to proliferate realisms, to disestablish, undermine the dominant Realism with many realisms. Let a thousand realisms bloom. Mexican-American realism, migrant realism, African-American realism, radical feminist realism, etc.

Gerardo: I'm having some trouble with what it is you're trying to communicate. . . . I think your plea for a pluralization of difference (including difference within difference) is wrought with some problematic issues. Sure, the concept of letting "a thousand realisms bloom" sounds appealing—but on a deeper level, it reifies a potentially oppressive possibility. Let me be clear about this issue: I'm not against questioning the essences of identity as such. What I am against is the implications this line of questioning carries. . . . I can understand the notion that we can all "construct" reality differently. . . . But there comes a point, I feel, where such problematizing becomes problematic: when it threatens to erase the "real" that is really happening! Perhaps I'm having trouble separating the theory from the politics of the theory. I'm not sure I'm comfortable with such an artificial separation.

Miguel: I really am enjoying your dialogue, but I must say that after a while it becomes a pissing contest (pardon the vernacular) and I fail to see the relevance. . . . The struggle I have with postmodernism is that as it runs in circles, it never takes a stand or position. . . . I would like for our final product to be not only something that academicians can benefit from but [also] something that school administrators can also learn from. . . . My reason for working on this article is the same reason I'm working with kids: Their lives will impact ours now and in the future. Call it righteous, call it selfish, call it sustainable, call it what you want. My reality is that in the final analysis, we still have the responsibility (whether we accept it or not is another issue) of connecting this whole theoretical discussion to practice. If not, all we do is provide information for somebody else to quote, but it has very little—if any—impact on anybody's life, regardless of their "reality." And speaking of reality, I want to let you know that as a kid who worked in the fields of Texas, Michigan, and California, my reality was hard work, hard times, and many challenges in school! (G. Lopéz, J. J. Scheurich, & M. Guajardo, personal communication, June 17-19, 1997)

Validity and Carnival

The effacement of the referent in postmodern culture has made "the real" contested territory (P. Lather, 1993).

The concern for validity in conventional social science research is a concern over the relentless pursuit of Truth. In other words, if one takes the proper steps in her or his research design to guard against threats to internal and external validity, then the final analysis is accepted (within a certain community of scholars) to be a credible or trustworthy account of some definitive truth out there. The appropriation of the scientific framework, that aims to find/represent/unlock a particular truth form (with a certain probability of error), attests to the framework's immersion in a discourse of science, objectivity, neutrality, and Truth.

Many poststructural and postmodern researchers (e.g., Britzman, 1991;

Lather, 1986, 1991; Scheurich, 1991, 1995) and theorists (e.g., Derrida, 1977; Foucault, 1970, 1980a & b, 1984; Spivak, 1995), however, have taken the impossibility of truth as their starting point—appropriating the concept of language as an endless deferral of meaning to trouble conventional understandings of validity and truth claims. These theorists assert that "the real" is a socially constructed, multitextured, contested (and contestable) terrain. "Meaning is never truly present but is only constructed through the potentially endless process of referring to other absent signifiers" (Moi, cited in Ferguson, 1993, p. 17). Because the poststructural subject is not only irretrievable (Spivak, 1995) but also unrepresentable (Lyotard, cited in Flax, 1990), we must shift our research emphasis from the real to the "discourses of the real" (Britzman, 1991). This not only highlights the windows/frames that shape our seeing, but it also implies that researchers are "unreliable narrators" (Britzman, 1997, p. 1) at best.

In short, we will be using the Bakhtinian concept of carnival to disrupt traditional conceptions of validity (see also Oliva, 1997). We will present various sources of written and visual material, not to evoke a sense of triangulation (and thus, a closer representation of Truth) but to reveal the multiaccentual and polyphonic nature of the migrant story. We will also use "transgressive" (St. Pierre, 1997) or nontraditional sources of data—for example, excerpts of poems, songs, prayers, pictures, and so forth—not only to disrupt conventionally sanctioned academic data norms but also to "produce different knowledge, and to produce knowledge differently" (St. Pierre, 1997, p. 175).

Bienvenidos Al Carnaval

You are about to experience a ride that will take you from the valle de Tejas to los files de Michigan. From the agricultural heart of sunny Califas, to the pinche frio of Indiana. From the grueling pesca of the fresa to la chinga of the betabel. From the sudor of the laborers to a well-deserved pachanga at the labor camp. But be careful, the narrative you are about to read is in no way linear. In fact, it may at times be confusing, appearing to lack any organization, or just downright incoherent! If you find yourself frustrated with this text, please remember that we are purposely trying to avoid modernist paradigmatic assumptions that call for organization, linearity, and an authorial voice over the text—in our attempt to trouble conventional forms of representation. Now, buckle your seat belts and set your lowrider on cruise control; we are about to "take a trip through the barrio streets of your mind" (Salines, 1970, p. 39).

Narrative of the Migrant Journey

Song: Brown-Eyed Children of the Sun
Up to California, from Mexico you've come. To the Sacramento Valley, to toil in the sun. With your wife and seven children, they're working everyone. And what

will you be giving, to your brown-eyed children of the sun? (Contreras, Galan, & Valdez, 1968, p. 44)

Narrative: A Migrant Child's Story

When school ends, I go with my family to Indiana. We go in the back of a big black truck that is covered with a green tarpaulin. It takes us three days and two nights to get to Indiana.

In Indiana, we live in a little green house on the farm. At seven o'clock in the morning, we get up and go to work in the tomato fields. We are nine in our family, and we all work picking tomatoes. In the mornings, we take a big bag of lunch to the fields. We eat tacos of beans, potatoes, and steak pieces on tortillas and bread.

We work on the tomato fields until four o'clock. We pick a thousand hampers of tomatoes a day. We get paid twenty-five cents per hamper. Then we get home and take a bath and eat supper. We watch the movies on the little TV we bring from Dilley, Texas. (Gauna, 1982, p. 53)

Anecdote: A Voice from the Field

As we packed and boarded up the house in preparation for our journey, the process was never finished until the priest would bless the house and la camioneta [the truck] in preparation for the trip. (M. Guajardo, personal communication, March 3, 1998)

Migrant Adults' Narratives

Poem: Fiesta in the Labor Camp

The sun sets at seven. The music comes in with the moon. It fills the campo
    [camp].
Los chicos van por el parque [The little boys go through the park],
    cruising, checkando las girls.
Se oyen las novelas [You can hear the soap operas] in the houses—
María Mercedes, Corazón Salvaje [Wild Heart], Crystal—
I heard them all.
Los hombres [The men] gather by a compadre's [friend's] truck—
It broke down en el fil [in the field],
Juntos la componen—
Para eso son los compadres [Together they fix it—That's what friends are for].
Las mujeres hablan [The women talk] at the clothesline.
Tendiendo la clothes del trabajo.
"Oyó usted de la señora de 12-A" pregunta una.
"No, que pasó?" contesta mamá.
[Hanging out the work clothes. "Did you hear about the woman of 1 2-A?"
    one of them asks. "No, what happened?" answers mama.]
I learned early to be una esposa buena [A good wife].

Y las muchachas se pintan [And the girls put on makeup].
They go out to the parque
Where the boys have parked.
Oyen Los Bukis, y a veces
Los Invasores.
Allí se juntan y hablan de sus días en el fil. [They listen to The Bookies, and
    at times The Invaders. There they get together and talk about their
    days in the field.]
La fiesta en el campo se acaba a las ten [The celebration in the camp is over
    at ten].
At ten, you go inside.
Porque tomorrow—"a jalarle . . .
Tenemos que comer."
Pero a las siete again
Fiesta en el campo. [Because tomorrow—"you give it all you've got . . .
    We have to eat." But at 7:00 again celebration in the labor camp.]
    (Ledezma, 1996, pp. 98-99)

Research: An Ethnographic Study
The migrant families that I observed very seldom depended on outside agencies
for help. They took pride in the fact that they could work and immediately sought
work when arriving in a new location. Occasionally, especially when they first arrived and did not have money, some would go for food stamps. Two women who
were sick went to receive unemployment benefits. But, many expressed their desire
to work and not cause the government any problems. Some told me that there
were people who needed help more than they did. (Prewitt, Trotter, & Rivera,
1989, p. 74)

Migrant Children's Narratives

Narrative: Work To Do
I work in the fields. I clean the grass for seven dollars a day. I give the money to my
mother and father. My brothers and sisters help my mother and father clean the
grass in the field, too. I wear my jacket in the morning because it is cold. When it
gets sunnier and warmer in the day, I take my coat off.

When we finish one field, we work another field. Sometimes we do other
work, too. My family picks watermelons. I get the watermelons off the ground and
hand the watermelons to my father. My father throws the melons to two of my sisters. Then my sisters give them to my brothers to stack in the truck.

When dinner time comes, Mother makes dinner. We eat, and then I get to
play a little while. Soon it is time to put my hat on again and go back to the field
to work. We work until it is dark. We are tired. We go to bed to rest up for the
next day. (J. Delgado, 1982, p. 56)

Narrative: I Am Afraid of Not Making It
I am afraid of not making it. What I mean is, I hope I can get a good job and make enough money to support me or my family. I don't want to get welfare or something like that.

When I think of all that could happen, it makes you want to cry. You see everybody has a job, and they make it look so easy. But I can tell it's not.

I always thought we had enough money, but now I know we are not the richest people in the world. (Carroll, 1982, p. 108)

Narrative: A Successful Migrant Student
Francelia has migrated annually to Hillsboro, North Dakota, and Warden, Washington, since she was three years old. Despite her very late enrollments and early withdrawals, Francelia has maintained an 86 G.P.A. in college preparation classes. In addition to her busy academic schedule and her job, Francelia found the time to be a member of Business Professionals of America, President of the Migrant Club, and Vice-President of Youth Club of San Luis Gonzaga Church. When she resided in North Dakota, she worked as a volunteer reader for preschoolers. Francelia has applied for admission to The University of Texas—Pan American in Edinburg and at St. Edward's University in Austin. (University of Texas Migrant Student Program, 1997, p. 4)

Spiritual Narratives of or About Migrants

Portrayal: Chicano Theology
Chicanos have a spiritual affinity with the land. Most of them have worked the land; many still work the land for a living. Nature, the woods, the forests, the streams, the lakes, el campo (the countryside), have always had a special place in the hearts of all Chicanos. (Guerrero, 1987, p. 65)

Narrative: A Migrant's Relationship to the Land
When I work my land, the one I own, I work it the same way I work somebody else's land. It makes no difference; none, really. Land is land, and when all is said and done, or, as we say, when the music is over, one leaves the terrain—el terreno—for somebody else to occupy. But, one must leave the land clean, weeded, and ready for that somebody else who comes to it with that hope and that handful of seeds I spoke of. (Pogue, Hinojosa Smith, & Garcia, 1984, p. 6)

Portrayal: Chicano Theology
A large number of Chicanos are migrant workers who farm the land of agribusiness and multinationals. The growers get richer and the migrant workers get exploited and poorer. How does one reconcile the affinity of the land with the spirit of the people? (Guerrero, 1987, p. 65)

Migrant Contributions to the Economy

Research: The Agricultural Economy

Without the efforts of farm workers, it would not be possible to support the multi-billion-dollar fruit and vegetable industry in this nation. Agricultural production depends on the influx of seasonal labor at critical periods in crop development.

Migrant and seasonal farm workers provide this labor. Farm workers may be needed to hand-pick apples or peaches, harvest asparagus or chilies, stake up tomatoes, dig potatoes or beets, or work in a packing plant. Hand labor is especially vital to the production of the blemish-free fruits and vegetables which American consumers demand.

The fruit, vegetable, and horticultural industries in particular rely on the labor of migrant and seasonal farm workers. Over the last decade more than 85% of the fruits and vegetables produced in this country were hand harvested and/or cultivated. *(Fact Sheet: America's Farmworkers, 1995)*

Research: Migrant and Seasonal Workers in Michigan's Agriculture

It has been estimated that one farm worker produces an average of 107,000 pounds of food, equaling 53 tons of finished products each year. This same farm worker creates jobs for more than five nonfarm people who process, transport, and merchandise the crops as well as produce items farmers need (1988 Michigan Food and Fiber Facts). By this measure, nearly 25% of America's total labor force is involved directly in the food industry. (Rochin, Santiago, & Dickey, 1989)

Migrant Working Conditions

Research: Occupational Safety and Health of Migrant Farm Workers

According to U.S. Department of Agriculture's own data, agriculture is one of the most accident-prone industries in the United States. Although the occupational fatality rate for all private-sector industries is 4.3 per 100,000 full-time employees, the rate for the broad category of agriculture, forestry, and fishing was 23.9. Other data sources indicate even higher accident and fatality rates in agriculture.

Compliance with the regulations that are in effect is poor. In 1990 OSHA found field sanitation violations in 69% of its field inspections. The fact that OSHA can afford to inspect only a small portion of the establishments that are subject to the law raises questions as to the actual magnitude of noncompliance with the regulations. A recent North Carolina survey found that only 4% of farm workers surveyed had access to drinking water, hand washing facilities, and toilets. *(Fact Sheet: America's Farmworkers, 1995)*

Congressional Testimony: Ms. Filoxian—Farm worker for 36 Years

Last week I was in a grove supervised by a licensed contractor who had a small automatic belted to his hip. I would not file a complaint against him. The reason he

TABLE 1

Michigan Crops on Which Migrants Work—1987

Commodity	National Rank	Michigan Production	Unit	Value (in $)
Beans, dry edible	1	554,400,000	lbs	74,290,000
Budding plants	1	8,000,000	flats	38,000,000
Blueberries	1	54,000,000	lbs	36,000,000
Cherries	1	265,000,000	lbs	12,300,000
Cucumbers	1	308,200,000	lbs	20,800,000
Apples	2	1,050,000,000	lbs	90,000,000
Plums	2	32,000,000	lbs	2,000,000
Asparagus	3	24,000,000	lbs	14,000,000
Celery	3	114,700,000	lbs	13,100,000
Mushrooms	3	20,200,000	lbs	16,800,000
Carrots	4	192,500,000	lbs	14,000,000
Cherries, sweet	4	64,000,000	lbs	18,436,000
Nursery plants	4	27,055,000	pots	43,400,000
Tomatoes, processing	4	237,000,000	lbs	8,200,000
Cauliflower	5	7,200,000	lbs	2,100,000
Grapes	5	120,000,000	lbs	15,609,000
Sugar beets	5	2,911,000	tons	68,600,000
Cantaloupe	6	18,400,000	lbs	3,000,000
Peaches	6	60,000,000	lbs	9,500,000
Pears	6	16,600,000	lbs	1,844,000
Strawberries	6	13,200,000	lbs	6,266,000
Sod	7	—		15,000,000
Peppers, bell	7	13,500,000	lbs	3,300,000
Onions	8	190,000,000	lbs	16,368,000
Lettuce	10	21,500,000	lbs	4,300,000
Bulbs, flower	10	—	each	200,000
Cabbage	11	46,400,000	lbs	3,000,000
Soybeans	12	38,150,000	bu	202,195,000
Tomatoes, fresh	13	25,200,000	lbs	5,116,000
Total				757,724,000

SOURCE: Table reproduced from *Catalyst,* 1987, p. 8.

could wear the gun on his hip as he supervised his crew of fruit pickers is because our compliance officer couldn't get into the grove. They have no access. We have to work all day under the threat of this guy losing his temper and somebody being seriously injured. *(Implementation of the Helsinki Accords,* 1993, p. 90)

Anecdote: A Voice from the Field

One of the scariest moments I can remember was when we—my brothers and I— were working in the fields in Michigan. All of a sudden, these men in suits walk out of their cars and onto the fields! I was 11 years old then, and had never seen something like this before. I was pretty scared, because I thought they were going to take my mom and dad away. When we found out it was the "feds" enforcing the child labor laws, this scared me even more because I feared something bad would surely happen to my parents. (M. Guajardo, personal communication, March 3, 1998)

Cuento: Y No Se lo Trago la Sierra
"All right, since we're gonna catch the hottest part of the day hoeing up and down on the chop by those knolls there, don't forget to drink the water. You drink as much as you can, got that? Every now and then, okay? Don't go too long without it. And listen, it doesn't matter what the grower says if he comes over. If you're thirsty, you stop work and get yourself a drink. And do it! Never mind the grower; you get yourself some water.

"I don't want you coming down sick, now. You start feeling bad, you stop right there and do it! You just let me know . . . and as soon as you do, we go straight home. Okay? You remember what happened to Papa? Huh? You saw him, right? He overdid it, see? That sun'll eat you right up. . . . It will." (Rivera, 1987, pp. 80–81)

News: "Death of a Farm Worker Could Have Been Avoided"
Sergio Raúl Rodriguez, 19, was run over and killed by a trailer being pulled by a tractor on July 15 in a field near Mettler after his farm labor contractor ordered the driver to work boxing cantaloupes on the ground while the tractor was still running in third gear. The driver was assigned to help fill in for a shorthand field crew caused when some workers quit in protest over inadequate pay and bad working conditions. ("Death of a Farmworker," 1995, p. 13)

Play/Acto: Las Dos Caras del Patroncito
Patroncito: What do you want a union for, boy?
Farm Worker: I don't want no union, patron.
Patroncito: What do you more money for, boy?
Farm Worker: I don't want—I want more money!
Patroncito: Shut up! You want my problems, is that? After all I explained to you? Listen to me son, if I had the power, if I had the power. wait a minute, I got the power! (TURNS TOWARD FARM WORKER, FRIGHTENING HIM) Boy!
Farm Worker: I didn't do it, patron. (Valdez, 1971, p. 14)

Migrants' Exposure to Pesticides

News: "How Do Pesticides Hurt Me?"

Q: As farm workers we are often told that pesticides are dangerous, but how exactly do pesticides hurt me?

A: You can be poisoned if pesticides get on your skin, into your mouth, or if you breathe in through your nose or your mouth. Most farm workers get sick by getting pesticides on their skin.

Q: How do pesticides make us sick?

A: The poison travels from your skin or lungs into your bloodstream and then begins to affect you as it affects the insects it was supposed to kill. The poisons hurt the different organs and systems in your body in different ways. For example, many insecticides, which kill insects, stop your body from producing cholinesterase. This natural chemical helps your body control your nerves and your muscles. When you are poisoned, your body cannot produce enough of the natural chemical to control the nerves and muscles. ("How Do Pesticides Hurt Me?" 1982, p. 8)

Migrant Children in the Field

Congressional Testimony: Ms. Mull— Executive Director of the Association of Farmworker Opportunity Programs
A migrant farm worker child can be employed in agriculture even if they're younger than the age of ten. OK? A "fluke" in the law allows for a child younger than ten to work in agriculture. No other child can do that. Even without parental consent, ten- and 11-year-old migrant farm worker children can be used as hand-harvesters if the employer gets a waiver from the Department of Labor. No other child can do that.

A migrant farm worker child under the age of 12 can be employed on a farm that does not pay minimum wage if the child has written consent from his parent or person standing in the place of the parent. No other child can.

A migrant farm worker child can work in agriculture more than 40 hours a week, even during the school term. No other child can.

A migrant farm worker child can earn more than a 40-hour week, but is not eligible for overtime pay. No other child can.

A migrant farm worker child can work an unlimited number of hours performing agricultural services before school. No other child can.

And a migrant farm worker child 14 or younger can use knives, machetes, operate some machinery, and be exposed to dangerous pesticides, but no other child can.

Children who work in agriculture work long hours before, during, and after school. They're exposed to pesticides because they harvest the commodity. They may not be handling pesticides. Handling is classified as a separate activity from harvesting. If you're harvesting an agricultural commodity, you are exposed to pesticides, and these children are. *(Implementation of the Helsinki Accords, 1993, p. 98)*

Research: Fields of Toil
Dr. Don Gargas, a pediatrician at the Yakima Valley Farm Workers Clinic in Toppen-

ish, notes that agricultural work is the nation's most dangerous occupation and that 300 children die in accidents each year on farms across the nation. (Valle, 1994, p. 39)

Research: Challenges and Solutions for Educating Migrants
Migrant workers are a group of people who contribute billions of dollars to the U.S. economy and don't necessarily get the best of treatments for their families. Every year this nation has about 840,000 migrant farm workers who have 409,000 children traveling with them from one crop to another trying to make a living. Schooling for them is preliterate. Children of migrant workers are exposed to chemicals, social neglect, disrupted schooling, racism, and deplorable living conditions that would make our poor people look like aristocrats. (Leon, 1997)

Migrant Health Conditions

Research: Health and Social Services
Migrant farm workers have a Third World health status, although they live and work in one of the richest nations on earth. Unsanitary working and housing conditions make farm workers vulnerable to health conditions no longer considered to be threats to the general public. Poverty, frequent mobility, low literacy, language, cultural and logistic barriers impede farm workers' access to social services and cost-effective primary health care. Economic pressure makes farm workers reluctant to miss work when it is available. In addition, they are not protected by sick leave, and risk losing their jobs if they miss a day of work. These circumstances cause farm workers to postpone seeking health care unless their condition becomes so severe that they cannot work. *(Fact Sheet: America's Farmworkers,* 1995)

Research: Migrant Health Conditions
In many cases the frequency or intensity of a health problem is greater within the migrant population than in the population at large.

Some health concerns are clearly attributable to the occupational hazards of farm work. Dermatitis and respiratory problems caused by natural fungi, dusts, and pesticides are common. Lack of safe drinking water contributes to dehydration and heat stroke. The absence of toilet facilities leads to urinary retention, which is in turn linked to urinary tract infection. Farm workers suffer such infections more often than the general population.

Conditions such as tuberculosis, diabetes, cancer, and HIV, which require careful monitoring and frequent treatment, pose a special problem for farm workers who must move frequently. As a predominantly Hispanic population, farm workers are particularly vulnerable to diabetes.

The incidence of hypertension is significantly associated with occupational class and transition. Epidemiological studies support the view that psychosocial stress contributes to differences in blood pressure. Employment security and other work conditions play a pivotal role. The absence of decision-making latitude on the job, as experienced by farm workers, has been shown to be directly associated with the risk of cardiovascular disease and elevated blood pressure.

Depression is common among farm worker adults, where it is often related to isolation, economic hardship, and weather conditions. In addition, poverty, stress, mobility, and lack of recreational opportunities make farm workers especially vulnerable to substance abuse.

Migrant workers don't generally earn enough to pay for health care, and they almost never have health insurance. They may also lack transportation to the clinic or, since they don't receive sick leave, be afraid of losing wages or even losing their jobs if they take time off to seek health care. The U.S. Public Health Service funds some migrant health centers to help provide care to farm workers, but not nearly enough to meet the need.

Follow-up care and continuity of care for chronic conditions are serious problems. Mobile units are an effective means of reaching isolated clients, but too few health centers have the resources to establish mobile programs. Health care planners and providers, as well as migrant farm workers themselves, have to be very creative to ensure good health options. *(Fact Sheet: America's Farmworkers, 1995)*

Migrant Living Conditions

Research: From Chicken Coops to Trailers

"Chicken coops. We used to live in houses that looked like chicken coops," Marta Elena says with a serious look on her face. She recalls three years before when she, her husband, and their five youngest children lived in a one-room house while they worked the fields in Michigan. "I remember when we first got there I looked around and I said, 'Look at all the chicken coops!'" she recalls, laughing. "It was dirty. There were a few portable toilets for quite a lot of people, and they were always filled to the top. I knew I was going to get sick."

Marta Elena also recalls that showers were taken outdoors. There was a wooden fence that surrounded the camp; a curtain made out of sheets was then hung in one corner of the fence and that is where they stood to take their showers. "We had to carry the water in buckets from inside the house," she says.

The only furniture in the one-room house was a tiny stove and table. The family slept on bunk beds, although at times some of them left the crowded quarters to sleep in the car. (Valle, 1994, p. 21)

Research: Migrant Housing Conditions

The number of farm workers in need of housing exceeds the number of available housing units. The only national data on hired farm worker housing show that in 1980, available units could only house about 30% of the migrant farm workers in need of housing. Hired farm workers, particularly migrants, also face barriers to obtaining housing in the local private housing markets. Small rural communities may not have enough rental units available, or they may be unavailable to migrant farm workers because they cannot provide deposits, qualify in credit checks, or make long-term rental commitments. In the absence of housing, farm workers may be forced to sleep in tents, cars, ditches, or open fields. *(Fact Sheet: America's Farmworkers,* 1995)

Economic Exploitation of Migrants

Congressional Testimony: Ms. Mull—Executive Director of the Association of Farm- worker Opportunity Programs
Why do the parents allow the children to work? Well, the answer is very simple. It's a basic necessity of survival. If you can't make a decent wage and you want to provide for your children and have food on the table, they need a place to live, everybody in the family has got to work to contribute so that the family can sur- vive. We in America have allowed a situation where farm workers are forced to bring their kids to the field so that the basic family can survive? Why is that? *(Im- plementation of the Helsinki Accords, 1993,* p. 100)

Research: Migrant Economic Exploitation
Most farm workers earn annual incomes below the federal poverty level, and half earn wages below $7,500.00 per year. Farm workers rarely have access to Workers Compensation coverage, occupational rehabilitation, or disability compensation benefits. Although many farm workers fit eligibility profiles for programs such as Medicaid and the Food Stamp Program, very few are able to secure these benefits. Migrant health centers estimate that less than 12% of their revenues are derived from Medicaid, and it is believed that fewer than 25% of eligible farm workers re- ceive food stamps. After a lifetime of work, many farm workers are unable to prove their claim for Social Security benefits. *(Fact Sheet: America's Farmworkers,* 1995)

Negative Statements About Migrant Farm Workers

Research: An Ethnographic Study of Migrant Labor Camps
- Migrant farm workers are nonintellectual. They can't learn much, but can do things well with their hands, like an art. The kids are slow learners and so are placed in "special classes." The adults can only do field work. They have little ability to learn other skilled work. They really don't like indoor factory work.

- Migrants are satisfied with their life. They are simple, childlike, happy, passive, easily controlled, complacent, docile, nongoal-oriented, nonsuccess- oriented. So they have low aspirations. They are fatalistic. (God wants us to suffer.) Migrants don't try hard enough to help themselves. After all, we were poor, and we made it. They could, too, if they just tried harder.

Those who are second and third generation ought to be better off. We
made it up the scale.

- Migrants get a lot of welfare and government program aids. They depend
  too much on welfare. They are getting more aid than the people who live
  here all the time. The migrants just want charity and handouts. They
  cheat on food stamps.

- Migrants are not poor. They make $100 a day, and we've heard $10,000
  a year. Yet they get all kinds of aid. Are migrants overpaid? That's what
  I've been told by farmers. If migrants are so poor, why do they have a TV,
  a big car, or truck?

- Migrants are used to being poor. The Bible says, "The poor you have with
  you always."

- If being a migrant is so bad, why don't they get different work? If they really tried, they could get work. Mexicans are dirty, lazy, and so on. The
  camp housing is plenty good for them because it is better than what they
  have in Texas. There is no point in fixing up the camp housing because in
  a week or two the screens are broken and things are torn up. They did not
  take care of the flush toilets when we had them in our camp.

- They lie most of the time. The uneducated ones are this way. They are
  unreliable. They ask for a job and then don't show up. Or they quit before
  the job is done.

- They are just poor and have big families, and why worry about them?
  They are too dumb to understand family planning. They want big families anyway. Why don't they go back to Mexico where they belong? Why
  don't they stay in Texas? Why doesn't Texas take care of the migrant
  people? It's Texas's responsibility, not Ohio's.

- Why do Spanish people settle here in the North? How did they get into
  the cities? Why is it Spanish people are not interested in learning the English language? If they are second and third generation, why aren't they
  speaking English? (Hintz, 1981, pp. 7–9)

Migration's Effect on Education

Research: Challenges and Solutions for Educating Migrants
Migrant students are three years behind on average academically. Some can't
speak, read, or write English as well as their mainstream counterparts.

The system is rigged against migrant students. Many administrators don't know Spanish and don't have the means for testing language efficiency or correctness of any of the tutors and/or teachers.

Nine (9) out of ten (10) of Michigan migrant students are in grade levels K-8 and experience a myriad of other problems. Elementary schooling brings up other interesting factors. First, these students need extra help with social, health, and basic support services. Second, these students are trying to adapt to a different environment that is conflicting with their culture. Third, proper nutrition and care is essential for setting the correct stage for learning. These patterns are a representative sample of the national migrant conditions.

Over the years as a migrant education consultant, I have been able to identify six (6) major challenges. The following treats the challenges of migrant student education: (a) Interrupted Schooling, (b) Limited English Language Proficiency, (c) Lack of Health and Nutrition, (d) Social Isolation, (e) Economic Marginality, and (f) Lack of Self Esteem. (Leon, 1997)

Research: Migrant and Seasonal Workers in Michigan's Agriculture
Migrant children have the highest dropout rate of any minority group. Furthermore, about *half* of the parents have not graduated from high school. (Rochin et al., 1989)

Research: An Ethnographic Study
Sometimes there is direct interference with educational progress because of the economic necessity of child labor for family survival. Sometimes children as young as ten work daily in the fields to supplement the family income. Often older children miss school to care for younger children and thus free both parents to work in the fields. In either case, the ethnography shows clearly that these conditions directly interfere with children's education. New programs are necessary to ameliorate these barriers to the education and advancement of migrant children. (Prewitt et al., 1989, p. 65)

Research: An Ethnographic Study
"One of our teachers gave a lot of attention to the other students but none to us, the migrants. It was in a class of English. We felt bad and so sometimes we didn't go to classes. They never gave us sufficient attention. It is better not to go. The teachers made distinctions between the different students. They need to be strict with everyone, not just with us." (Prewitt et al., 1989, p. 89)

(In) Conclusion

Last Saturday morning, my wife and my daughter were watching television as I (Gerardo Lopéz) struggled to get out of bed. Half asleep, with morning breath, todo lagañoso, I stumbled into the living room and lay down on the sofa. Ignoring my early morning appearance, my daughter wobbled over to me and gave me my first hug of the day. She then sat on the floor and refocused her attention on the television set. Together, the three of us watched the last 15 minutes of *Sesame Street*.

In this episode, Elmo accidentally eavesdrops on Maria's telephone conversation with her husband. Maria, whose exact words were "Moving to Cleveland. Five o'clock," sends a disturbed Elmo rushing back to Sesame Street to spread the disquieting news. Under the impression that the whole Sesame Street family could dissuade Maria and her family from moving away to Cleveland, Elmo stages a protest outside Maria's family store. A provocation between Elmo and Maria then ensues—culminating with Elmo heroically throwing himself against the door to physically prevent Maria and her family from leaving. Maria—who does not have the slightest clue as to what is going on—angrily asserts, "Elmo, you're going to make us late for the movie." Elmo is at a lost for words. "A movie? But I thought you were moving to Cleveland!" Maria's husband laughingly interjects, "Moving to Cleveland? We weren't moving to Cleveland, Elmo. *Moving to Cleveland is* the name of the movie that we're going to go see" (Loman, 1997).

I immediately recognized Elmo's mistake: Not only was he constructing "truth" from a partial statement, but he was also interpreting the signifier *(Moving Cleveland)* literally, without recognizing that the phrase could also signify something else (in this case, the title of a movie). Elmo was an unreliable narrator (Britzman, 1998, p. 1)—confused by a system of signification that is not always straightforward.

For a minute, I pondered the pedagogic intentions of *Sesame Street's* producers—the Children's Television Workshop. Were they trying to demonstrate that eavesdropping could get one in trouble? Were they trying to demonstrate that Elmo should have asked for the complete story from Maria before he invented a faulty one? Or were they demonstrating the fluid relationship between words (signifiers) and what they mean (the signified)?

I then realized that their intention was somewhat irrelevant. In other words, what I took from the story was what my mind/eye was attuned to seeing. Since I am currently interested in the fluidity of language, I interpreted the *Sesame Street* text according to this linguistic lens. I doubt that my impression of Elmo would have been the same had I seen this episode three years ago—when I was interested in attributional processes. (Had this been the case, I probably would have interpreted Elmo's actions as an attributional error, with possible effects on his self-esteem, affect, and future expectations [Weiner, 1986]). I also doubt that I will have the exact same impression of Elmo's actions three years from now—when my own engagement with alternate discourses opens up different possibilities for viewing and understanding the world.

We hope the disparate array of images we have intentionally presented to you of and about migrant students will also take on different meanings as your own interactions with different discourses highlight different portions of this text and as further readings bring to the fore different issues surrounding children in migrancy. In this regard, the text is not static or rigid—a monocular representation of a migrant Truth that requires explanation, structure, and coherency—but a living, malleable, constructed entity. It is not a single linear story to be told but an indefinite number of stories that can possibly emerge with each (re)reading.

We will finish, then, our montage with our own conclusions of what we have learned in our study of migrant students, conclusions that are constructed in relationship to our own epistemological and ontological baggage. Nonetheless, we recognize the "radical irretrievability" (Spivak, 1995) of the migrant subject, and we acknowledge that we are unreliable narrators (Britzman, 1997) telling or constructing a story, one of the many possible stories about the migrant population.

Taken holistically, we learned that migrant workers are the poorest of this country's poor: a population of our own citizens who are living a Third World reality in the backyard of the richest, most powerful nation in the world. We learned that migrant families—including children as young as ten years old—often work 14- to 15-hour days under extreme, demanding, and hazardous working conditions. We learned that migrants and migrant families have an unprecedented work ethic and that migrant labor is literally the backbone of a multimillion dollar agricultural industry, yet migrants are typically compensated with low wages and no job security. We learned that migrant labor contributes substantially to the affordable food on our dinner tables, yet most of us would rather not think about them when we sit down to eat.

We learned that migrant students come from hard-working, close-knit families, families that migrate together—often experiencing the harsh realities of hunger, poverty, exploitation, racism, and classism as a family unit. We learned that migrants face the irony of being one of the most isolated groups in this country, yet are simultaneously one of the most dependent populations: often relying on others—for example, employers, recruiters, crew leaders, and so forth—for their livelihood. We learned that migrants live in overcrowded, slum-housing conditions and that their health is deteriorating faster than any other population in the county, yet they manage to celebrate life and not dwell on the demeaning and destructive negativity that surrounds them. We learned that migrants are the most likely candidates for a safety net, yet they do not typically rely on governmental agencies for welfare assistance. We learned that they believe in schooling as a vehicle for economic and social success, yet their constant mobility—coupled with loopholes in child labor and minimum wage laws—places them at a higher risk for failure than other students in the country. In fact, we learned that migrants have one of the highest dropout rates, yet they are also on honor rolls, involved in extracurricular activities, and enrolling in prestigious four-year institutions. Despite the multiple odds against them, the most important story we learned was that migrants persevere.

In short, migrants demonstrate the core values of U.S. society (strong work ethic, commitment to education, powerful belief in their families, centrality of religion, etc.), yet are a very long way from being incorporated into the American

Dream. They are, indeed, a daily reminder of everything we want to be and of what we most fear. They are self and they are other — disrupting the fragile tension between signifier and signified.

Although this window/ventana into migrancy must come to an end, we hesitate to put closure to this text — for the notion of closure assumes finality, fixity, stability, and an authorial violence of reappropriating the final word, forcing the reader to look through our ventana. And although — to a great extent — you have had no other option but to look through our window, or the images we have chosen to present to you, as well as our interpretations of those images, we hope that you have had the opportunity to critically engage our representations by dialoguing, interacting, and making meaning of them for yourselves.

Chapter 9

Preface

Chapter 9 is drawn from the same material as chapter 8 and was also done by Gerardo, Miguel, and myself. Although there is a repeat in chapter 9 of some of the material in chapter 8, I include it because it is an example of how we used the material in an entirely different context, and in different ways. This was a 20-minute multimedia "presentation" at a session at the AERA conference (Maricela Oliva, a former student and now a professor at the University of Texas at Pan American assisted us in the presentation.) Simultaneously (remember it was a multimedia presentation), there is music playing that is popular among Mexican-American migrant agricultural workers, a video about migrant workers running on a television set, and a slide show playing. What I have provided in chapter 9 is the script we handed out to some audience members; thus, this is a kind of reader's theater. Again, we wanted to break out of conventional epistemological representational forms and to displace the audience's understanding of migrant children and their families.

Chapter 9

Racing Representation: A "Raza Realist" Narration of Migrant Students, Their *Educación* and Their *Contexto*

Gerardo Lopéz, Miguel Guajardo, Maricela Oliva, and James Joseph Scheurich

Introduction

Good afternoon. Our presentation today emerged from a manuscript that was published in a special issue on postmodernism in *Educational Administration Quarterly*. The original manuscript was intended to be a multivocal, or polyphonic narrative of the migrant story. Its goal was to challenge the social invisibility and limited understanding of migrants through intentional polyvocality. In other words, the aim of the paper was to resist creating a definitive, or authoritative, discourse of and about migrants by accessing as many windows or "ventanas" as possible. We wanted to create a manuscript — a very nontraditional manuscript — that would offer various ways of knowing about migrants. The end result was a nonlinear narrative that included prose, poetry, music lyrics, pictures, artwork, and other material that told the "story" of migrancy in unique and different ways.

The purpose of today's presentation is to bring that manuscript to life so that we can interrogate those social spaces of how we come to know and understand the Other. Writers as diverse as Clifford and Marcus and Mikhail Bakhtin long ago undermined the expectation that reality is closed, complete, unambiguous, or unitary. We do not disagree. Some of the images we displayed are personal narratives, some are fragments from literary works. Still others incorporate the theoretical discourses with which academics are often most familiar. More than a few of the images have been crafted with respect and care for the people represented; others through the unconnected distance of objectifying research. All of the images of migrants are offered with the expectation that you might challenge or critique them as you make them your own. The objective, if there is one, is to resist their disappearance through our forgetting and neglect. We want to echo Tomas Rivera in the hope "that the earth does not swallow" them.

Script

Reader 1   A Migrant Child's Story

When school ends, I go with my family to Indiana. We go in the back of a big black truck that is covered with a green tarpaulin. It takes us three days and two nights to get to Indiana.

In Indiana, we live in a little green house on the farm. At seven o'clock in the morning, we get up and go to work in the tomato fields. We are nine in our family, and we all work picking tomatoes. In the mornings, we take a big bag of lunch to the fields. We eat tacos of beans, potatoes, and steak pieces on tortillas and bread.

We work on the tomato fields until four o'clock. We pick a thousand hampers of tomatoes a day. We get paid twenty-five cents per hamper. Then we get home and take a bath and eat supper. We watch the movies on the little TV we bring from Dilley, Texas. (Gauna, 1982, p. 53)

Reader 2   Findings from An Ethnographic Study

The migrant families that I observed very seldom depended on outside agencies for help. They took pride in the fact that they could work and immediately sought work when arriving in a new location. Occasionally, especially when they first arrived and did not have money, some would go for food stamps. Two women who were sick went to receive unemployment benefits. But, many expressed their desire to work and not cause the government any problems. Some told me that there were people who needed help more than they did. (Prewitt, Trotter, & Rivera, 1989, p. 74)

Reader 3   I Am Afraid of Not Making It

I am afraid of not making it. What I mean is, I hope I can get a good job and make enough money to support me or my family. I don't want to get welfare or something like that.

When I think of all that could happen, it makes you want to cry. You see everybody has a job, and they make it look so easy. But I can tell it's not.

I always thought we had enough money, but now I know we are not the richest people in the world. (Carroll, 1982, p. 108)

Reader 4   Portrait of A Successful Migrant Student

Francelia has migrated annually to Hillsboro, North Dakota, and Warden, Washington, since she was three years old. Despite her very late enrollments

and early withdrawals, Francelia has maintained an 86 G.P.A. in college preparation classes. In addition to her busy academic schedule and her job,
Francelia found the time to be a member of Business Professionals of America, President of the Migrant Club, and Vice-President of Youth Club of San
Luis Gonzaga Church. When she resided in North Dakota, she worked as a
volunteer Reader for preschoolers. Francelia has applied for admission to The
University of Texas-Pan American in Edinburg and at St. Edward's University in Austin. (University of Texas Migrant Student Program, 1997, p. 4)

Reader 5   *A Migrant's Relationship to the Land*

When I work my land, the one I own, I work it the same way I work somebody else's land. It makes no difference; none, really. Land is land, and
when all is said and done, or, as we say, when the music is over, one leaves
the terrain—el terreno—for somebody else to occupy. But, one must leave
the land clean, weeded, and ready for that somebody else who comes to it
with that hope and that handful of seeds I spoke of. (Pogue, Hinojosa
Smith, & Garcia, 1984, p.6)

Reader 6   *Migrant and Seasonal Workers in Michigan's Agriculture*

It has been estimated that one farm worker produces an average of 107,000
pounds of food, equaling 53 tons of finished products each year. This same
farm worker creates jobs for more than five nonfarm people who process,
transport, and merchandise the crops as well as produce items farmers need.
By this measure, nearly 25% of America's total labor force is involved directly in the food industry. (Rochin, Santiago, & Dickey, 1989)

Reader 7   *Y No Se Lo Trago La Tierra: . . .*
              And the Earth Did Not Devour Him

"All right, since we're gonna catch the hottest part of the day hoeing up and
down on the chop by those knolls there, don't forget to drink the water. You
drink as much as you can, got that? Every now and then, okay? Don't go too
long without it. And listen, it doesn't matter what the grower says if he
comes over. If you're thirsty, you stop work and get yourself a drink. And do
it! Never mind the grower; you get yourself some water.

"I don't want you coming down sick, now. You start feeling bad, you
stop right there and do it! You just let me know . . . and as soon as you do,
we go straight home. Okay? You remember what happened to Papá? Huh?
You saw him, right? He overdid it, see? That sun'll eat you right up . . . it
will." (Rivera, 1987, pp. 80-81)

Reader 8   *From a Newspaper Article*

Question: How do pesticides make us sick?

Answer: The poison travels from your skin or lungs into your bloodstream
and then begins to affect you as it affects the insects it was supposed to kill. The poisons hurt the different organs and systems
in your body in different ways. For example, many insecticides,
which kill insects, stop your body from producing cholinesterase.
This natural chemical helps your body control your nerves and
your muscles. When you are poisoned, your body cannot produce enough of the natural chemical to control the nerves and
muscles. ("How do pesticides hurt me?," 1982, p. 8)

Reader 9   *Congressional Testimony*

A migrant farm worker child can be employed in agriculture even if they're
younger than the age of ten. OK? A "fluke" in the law allows for a child
younger than ten to work in agriculture. No other child can do that.

Even without parental consent, ten and 11-year-old migrant farm
worker children can be used as hand-harvesters if the employer gets a waiver
from the Department of Labor. No other child can do that.

A migrant farm worker child under the age of 12 can be employed on a
farm that does not pay minimum wage if the child has written consent from
his parent or person standing in the place of the parent. No other child can.

A migrant farm worker child can work in agriculture more than 40
hours a week, even during the school term. No other child can.

A migrant farm worker child can earn more than a 40-hour week, but
is not eligible for overtime pay. No other child can.

A migrant farm worker child can work an unlimited number of hours
performing agricultural services before school. No other child can.

And a migrant farm worker child 14 or younger can use knives, machetes, operate some machinery, and be exposed to dangerous pesticides,
but no other child can. (*Implementation of the Helsinki Accords*, 1993, p. 98)

Reader 10   *From Chicken Coops to Trailers*

"Chicken Coops. We used to live in houses that looked like chicken coops,"
María Elena says with a serious look on her face. She recalls three years before when she, her husband, and their five youngest children lived in a
one-room house while they worked the fields in Michigan. "I remember
when we first got there. I looked around and I said, 'Look at all the chicken

coops!'" she recalls, laughing. "It was dirty. There were a few portable toilets for quite a lot of people, and they were always filled to the top. I knew I was going to get sick." (Valle, 1994, p. 21)

Reader 11   Congressional Testimony

Why do the parents allow the children to work? Well the answer is very simple. It's a basic necessity of survival. if you can't make a decent wage and you want to provide for your children and have food on the table, they need a place to live, everybody in the family has got to work to contribute so that the family can survive. We in America have to allow a situation where farm workers are forced to bring their kids to the field so that the basic family can survive? Why is that? (*Implementation of the Helsinki Accords*, 1993, p. 100)

Reader 12   From a Research Study: True Statements Made About Migrants

Migrants are satisfied with their life. They are simple, childlike, happy, passive, easily controlled, complacent, docile, nongoal oriented, nonsuccess oriented. So they have low aspirations. They are fatalistic. (God wants us to suffer.) Migrants don't try hard enough to help themselves. After all, we were poor, and we made it. They could, too, if they just tried harder. Those who are second- and third-generation ought to be better off. We made it up the scale.

Migrants get a lot of welfare and government program aids. They depend too much on welfare. They are getting more aid than the people who live here all the time. The migrants just want charity and handouts. They cheat on food stamps.

If being a migrant is so bad, why don't they get different work? If they really tried, they could get a factory job.

Mexicans are dirty, lazy, and so on. The camp housing is plenty good for them because it is better than what they have in Texas. There is no point in fixing up the camp housing because in a week or two the screens are broken and things torn up. They did not take care of the flush toilets when we had them in our camp.

Why don't they go back to Mexico where they belong? Why don't they stay in Texas? Why doesn't Texas take care of the migrant people? It's Texas' responsibility, not Ohio's. (Hintz, 1981, pp. 7-9)

Reader 13   Challenges and Solutions for Educating Migrants

Migrant students are three years behind on average academically. Some can't speak, read, or write English as well as their mainstream counterparts. The system is rigged against migrant students. Many administrators don't know Spanish and don't have the means for testing language efficiency or correctness of any of the tutors and or teachers. (Leon, 1997).

Conclusion

In this montage of migrancy, we have attempted to re-present a multidimensional, polyphonic picture of the migrant subject. It is not intended to portray migrant students and/or their families as a nondifferentiated, uncomplicated mass—or to demonstrate that migrants not only speak, but that they also speak in the same voice. Rather, it aims to disrupt this assumption by evoking an ambivalent and multivocal reading of migrant historiography.

It is ambivalent because we have the luxury of reading their stories from this beautiful, air conditioned hotel—while many migrants are out in the fields today working to put food on our dinner plates for this evening's banquet or reception. The distance between us and them—not only in our reading but also in the very practices of our research—functions as a buffer or a safety zone. Distance can, and often does, hold much promise: by problematizing the assumptions of/about the content of research—of empathy and of knowing the Other. But, this very distance can also guard us against the recognition of the context of our own positionality. Distance, in other words, fails to interrogate the limits of our own enunciation. We can always seek refuge with/in our distances.

It is multivocal because it not only aims to demonstrate the multipositionality of the migrant subject, but because such a reading also opens up a discursive space that disrupts the fixity of signification. It not only represents a different story—of a host of many other "unreliable" stories of/about migrants—but also highlights the normative tendency for one story to circulate over others. It may subscribe to a particular regime of truth, but this story is no different than the stock-story that is circulated every day about migrants.

The purpose of our re-presentation was not to present a single image of migrancy, but to interrogate the possibilities and problematics of our own engagement with these images. If this engagement is bounded by our unreliableness on the one side and cheery sentimentalized empathy on the other, then how can we negotiate the distances between one reality and another?

Chapter 10

Preface

Chapter 10 is a brief description of a research-based video documentary, called *Labores de la Vida/The Labors of Life*. Miguel Guajardo, Patricia Sánchez, Elissa Fineman, and I collaboratively produced a video documentary of a group of adults who had grown up in migrant agricultural worker families. The four of us did all aspects of the work from first to last. We worked very carefully to produce a representation that was appreciative and respectful of the people being represented and of their culture and historical experiences. We worked carefully to produce a documentary that would be valued by them. As was mentioned previously, anyone can obtain a free copy of this documentary by mailing a blank 90-minute or 120-minute video to the Texas Education Agency, Division of Migrant Education, 1701 N. Congress, Austin, Texas 78701-1494 with a request for a copy of the documentary. Once again, I was doing research on people of color in collaboration with people of color, rather than trying to do it alone or just with other whites. Also, once again, the way we represented the research data was designed to disrupt white racist conceptions of children who had grown up in migrant worker families. Following the description is a commentary on the research project by Miguel Guajardo, one of the four who did the documentary and the one who was for me the heart of the project.

Chapter 10

Labores de la Vida/The Labors of Life: A Description of a Video Documentary of Mexican-American Adults Who Were Migrant Agricultural Workers as Children and a Commentary by Miguel Guajard

Miguel Guajardo, Patricia Sánchez, Elissa Fineman, and James Joseph Scheurich

This chapter is a brief discussion of a video documentary that four of us made—Miguel Guajardo, Patricia Sánchez, Elissa Fineman, and Jim Scheurich, but this discussion is written by just one of us (Scheurich); however, below Miguel adds his reflections on the video. This video was our attempt to do research that does not participate in white racism. This, of course, does not mean that the process resulted in no racism in the documentary. This is not true, and virtually impossible, given the context within which we all live. As mentioned in the "Introduction," Francisco, one of the participants in the documentary, suggested that though he thought the video was a valuable and respectful representation of the participants, still, the method in which it was done was exploitive. By this he meant the documentary still used the approach of the colonist whereby we came in, gathered data, and then went away to analyze and compose. He suggested that a nonexploitive approach would have more deeply involved the participants in the project and would have shared expertise with the participants so that when we, the researchers, left, the community would have new expertise that the members of the community could use to enhance the community. We cannot argue with his critique, and we appreciate that he did not leave us without this critique.

While we agree with and value Francisco's critique, we will discuss here what we did and why we did it. Jim Scheurich received a limited amount of funding to do it as part of a larger project funded by the Migrant Education Division of the Texas Education Agency (the state's education agency). The Project Directors of the project were faculty colleagues of Jim's, Pedro Reyes and Jay Scribner. The project was divided into several areas of focus, and Jim was assigned to study adults who had been children in migrant agricultural worker families, but had been able to attain some level of educational and economic "success." Jim requested that his research would result in a video documentary rather than the typical research report, and this request was granted.

Because of his conclusions about the way white racism works that were discussed in the "Introduction," Jim first set out to find an activist who had been in a migrant family and who would collaborate with Jim in making the documentary. He quickly found Miguel who has a strong history of working as an activist in the Austin, Texas, area and in the Rio Grande Valley area of Texas. Because neither Jim nor Miguel had any experience with making a documentary, Jim sought a student with some of that experience who could be paid to work halftime on the project. He found Elissa Fineman, who started out as a doctoral student in education, but during the project changed to become a doctoral student in "new media" in the Department of Radio-Television-Film. Although she was certainly no film or documentary expert, she had much more knowledge and experience than either Miguel or Jim.

Since there was enough financial resources on the project to hire a second student, Miguel was able to find Patricia Sánchez, who grew up in the El Paso, Texas, area and whose father had been a migrant worker, to work on the project. Once all four were identified and agreed to participate, virtually all decisions and everything else was done as equally and as collaboratively as possible, though since they were the paid students, Patricia and Elissa did develop more knowledge of the editing equipment, Media 100.

This project, the video documentary, was done as qualitative research. The four of us reviewed the results of an earlier literature review and then viewed several films that had been made in the past on migrant workers. We also read some related books. We then designed the research process and developed the interview protocol. We obtained participants through networks that Miguel and Patricia were involved in, and we used "snowballing," a sampling method whereby one person nominates others who nominate others, and so on. We then interviewed the participants on camera one-by-one or in focus groups. All four of us were at virtually every shoot, with Patricia and Miguel doing most of the interviewing and Elissa and Patricia doing most of the camera work.

In early discussions—the four of us were in constant conversation about the project from beginning to end—one of our main areas of discussion was that the research project required that we focus on those adults who had been children in migrant families but now had some economic and educational success. We were uncomfortable from the beginning with this focus because we knew that the overwhelming percentage of migrant families live extremely difficult lives, with little economic "success," and large percentages of their children do not finish school. In our view, we began the project with this conclusion: this "lack" of "success" is primarily a function of the racial, cultural, and linguistic prejudices of the dominant race and culture and of the economic exploitation by the farmers and corporations who hire them. Consequently, we worried that focus on a few "successful" adults would leave the "conservative" impression that success was due to individual motivation, skills, etc. so that the lack of success of everyone else would be seen as their fault. We felt, then, that we both had to honor what the funding agency wanted and develop a documentary that did not reproduce conservative individualism.

Our solution, which emerged in process, especially in response to the data we were collecting, was to have a major portion of the documentary directly focus on the powerfully difficult conditions all migrants faced. We wanted a major percentage of the video to document, in the words of the participants, these conditions. Another part of this solution, though, was to have another major portion of the video focus on the resources and strengths these adults drew on for their success.

A third part of the solution is that a third portion of the documentary focused on the participants' definition of success, a definition that was much different than mainstream white definitions of success. Thus, the interaction among us around the issue of effects of destructive conditions versus conservative individualism, on the one hand, and our analysis of the data, on the other, yielded the documentary.

The documentary begins, before the opening titles, with just a few shots of the participants making particularly resonant or metaphoric statements. Miguel then introduces the film. This is followed by each of the participants introducing who each is, where each is from, and what each is currently doing. The participants, in order of introduction, were Ricardo Peréz (a teacher), Christina Flores (a college student), Sylvia Celedón (a student at the time but then an assistant professor), Francisco Guajardo (teacher and community activist), Encarnción Garza (a principal), Elmira Cura (a teacher), Mario Rodriguez (a college student), Rebecca Flores Harrington (a union organizer), Frank Contreras (Director, Migrant Education Division, Texas Education Agency), Frances Rocha (Director, Elementary Education in a district), Ernesto Rodriguez (college student), Carmen Pacheco (high school principal), Pedro Reyes (professor), Lupe Rodriguez (college student), Antonia Irene Castaneda (professor), José Raúl Valdez (college student), Carina Araiza (college student), and Mary Alice Reyes (a superintendent).

Rebecca Flores Harrington introduces the next and longest part. This is the part on the difficult conditions. It is divided into seven themes: economics, the fields, housing, schooling, tracking in school, language, and racism. In each of these themes there is a focus on the typical conditions experienced by migrant workers and their families. Each of these themes is illustrated through the comments and stories of one to seven participants speaking to that theme. For example, in the housing theme Frank Contreras speaks about living in chicken coops and housing with dirt floors, José talks about having one bathroom for hundreds of people, and Elmira tells a story about living in what is basically a shed in which her father puts up cardboard as insulation for cold nights.

The third part of the documentary focuses, then, on the resources and strengths the participants drew upon for their "success." There were seven themes in this part: family networks, parental support, the earth, personal motivation, the Farmworkers Union, education, and resistance. Again, between one and several participants spoke to each theme. For example, Ricardo speaks about the support his parents gave him, Antonia addresses the continual resistance to oppression, and Rebecca discusses the Farmworkers union and its importance to migrant workers.

The fourth section is composed of several of the participants commenting upon what success is to them. They all recognized that they each had enjoyed some economic and educational "success," but in general they reframed what success meant to them. As Antonio said, they did not really feel successful because the overwhelming percentage of migrant families continue to be economically exploited and treated negatively, even in a racist manner, by the dominant racial group and culture. For the participants, then, success was giving back to their people by helping create the conditions in which migrant families could have decent lives.

The documentary ends with Rebecca talking about the fact that all Americans consume the product—food—that the migrants grow and harvest. The price of this food is artificially low because government rules permit economic exploitation of the farm workers. Thus, as Americans buy and eat cheap food, they are eating the exploitation of these workers. Consequently, since we all benefit, Rebecca calls all of us to act in ways that would change this economic exploitation. This is followed by Antonia talking about the strong spirit of migrant families, the spirit they use to survive difficult conditions, to struggle against those conditions, and to prevail with dignity.

Another issue that was significant about making the video was one that brought a thematic issue together with a technical issue. Technically, we had to decide how to communicate our themes. Most commonly, this is done is a linear story-telling fashion. For example, one person's story will be followed through from beginning to ending. Often times in documentaries while the person is telling their story, what the viewer is actually seeing are scenes related to the story being told. For example, when our participants talked about being sprayed from the air by poisonous pesticides, the typical documentary would show scenes of such spraying. One problem we had with doing this is that this approach costs considerably more in terms of the time and money to get the appropriate place at the appropriate time. We had neither the time nor the money for this, but we did not think a documentary composed of one storytelling after another would maintain audience attention and interest.

We also decided, based on our analysis of our interviews, that have one storyteller after another reinforced a portrayal of our participants as individuals when one of their main messages to us was that who they were and what "success" they had emerged out of family, community, and culture. Thus, we began to look for a way to present a more communal portrayal and to address the problem that all we had time and money for was videotaped interviews. Happily for us, we devised a solution that simultaneously addressed both problems in an innovative way.

Here's what we did: we searched our videotape data for "cuts" of participant comments about a theme, like tracking in school. We then gathered all the cuts that addressed this theme. Each of these cuts was from ten seconds long to a few minutes long. We then arranged the cuts in an order that seemed to make sense and ran them without any break in between cuts, in a kind of MTV style. This meant as you watched the sequenced cuts, you would see first one person talking about a theme, then another, then another, through up to seven participants addressing the same theme. We then further edited the sequenced cuts to eliminate any we thought did not contribute and to get them down to the smallest length that would serve communication of that theme.

This solved both of our problems. First, because we moved quickly from person to person, using different participant's words wherever needed; this communicated more of a communal "voice" than we would have if we had each person just tell her or his story. Second, the quick movement from voice to voice solved much of the problem of maintaining audience interest throughout a 45-minute documentary, which is a long time for people to watch with interest this kind of presentation.

One other issue we addressed was making sure that we had a variety of people by age (generation) and gender. We sought a reasonable balance around these two in selecting our participants and in using them on the actual video. In the beginning we worried about having mostly men's voices and not enough women's voices, but this did not happen. In fact, we found that Rebecca and Antonio were often the best at characterizing the conditions migrant workers and their families face and their strengths and resources. Consequently, these two are actually the two participants most used on the documentary.

That, thus, provides a brief summary of what is on the documentary and of how we did it. Of course, this summary is a construction, and, as with all qualitative research, the actual process was much messier. We sometimes argued over both technical and content issues, and we had some interpersonal conflicts along the way. However, as well as any collaboration, we maintained a good spirit and good relations as we collaboratively worked our way from the beginning until the documentary was shown to the participants and others who had been or still were our migrant workers. And their response has consistently been very positive that what we had to say and the way we said it were both excellent.

It has subsequently been shown in two film festivals and at several conferences. It is also being used by educators throughout Texas to help improve schooling for migrant children. It is, by the accounts of others, both those who have had or are having the migrant experience and those who have not, a powerful documentary. The best way to see this for yourself is to get a free copy and view it yourself. We would suggest it is an excellent tool both for educating people about migrant workers, their children, and their children's education and for "seeing" qualitative research. It is also an excellent tool for doing community action in communities that include migrant workers.

Miguel Guajardo's Reflections on the Process

The experience of making this video was a great deviation from the traditional sterile positivist research conducted by traditional academia. The experience was vibrant, emotional, challenging, and intellectual. Indeed, this experience was pedagogical in nature. The teacher and learner positions and rules were fluid and constantly changing. The expertise the team members brought with them were diverse and critical to the implementation and outcome of this process.

In this section I want to elaborate on the text presented above. And in a reflective manner share some of my learning experiences as I relived experiences I clearly remember of being a migrant laborer as a kid. The re-learning experience was physical, emotional, cognitive, economic, and spiritual.

But before going there, I will speak to the academic process at the university. In 1975 Bowles and Gintis (1986) wrote, "why in a democratic society, should an individual's first real contact with a formal institution be so profoundly anti-democratic?"(p. 36) They are referring to the grade school experience, but I would add that it gets worse when you get to higher education. Certainly, there will be an "amen" from the undergraduate or graduate students who might have stumbled into this text. It is truly a circus environment when a student attempts to navigate and juggle through the bureaucratic process. This unfortunately doesn't change (unless my experience is unique) when arriving at a classroom. Soon we find out that the whole semester is script for you: what you will read, what you will learn, and how you will be tested. You will also be told what you will write, how you will write it, and what to write if you want an "A."

The opportunity to create a project from the ground up is truly an exciting learning experience. It is especially admirable for a professor in a traditional research university to say " I want to do a video about farm workers, but I know nothing about video and I know less about farm workers, what do you think." At this point I laughed, and I knew the experience would be worth it. Clearly, the power dynamics in the room and the project shifted and they were much more equally distributed. This created the space for a democratic process to guide the project. We knew the product we wanted, but the process became totally negotiable, i.e., what we watched, read, who we interviewed, and what questions we asked. Indeed, the whole learning process was negotiated; the research was cocreated, including the analysis and selection of final cuts. For me this democratic process afforded me the space for critical reflection and building the relationship with the professor and fellow students that is necessary for critical dialogue to occur. Sharing stories with each other—not only the video participants, but our personal stories too—created this space. This was truly revolutionary pedagogy (McLaren, 2000).

But does it matter if the process is democratic on a campus level, if it is not at the community level? I carry Sofia Villenas (1996) article *The colonizer/colonized Chicana/o Ethnographer* in mind all the time. Does this mean I don't violate it?

Probably not, but as a Chicano, who does research, I am always cognizant of this dynamic; I always ask myself, what is the reciprocity in this venture? Am I taking the information and running? Is Francisco's critique to Jim targeted at me too or would he have overlooked it if I were at the table? Is the fact that I am a native of the region of South Texas, where we did much of the taping, and have shared the migrant experience omit me from being the colonizer? And at what point or with what methodology and process is it okay for me to conduct this research? Certainly, there is no one answer to any of these questions, but there is a point that I feel satisfied in this particular process. I know that during the time I've worked with this community group, who are part of the video, they have developed their critical skill to the level that they will not allow a project to take place without the appropriate reciprocity taking place. Thus, there is a level of awareness that communities rise to that can prevent them from being used. I feel certain that our partners are there. Obviously, they have surpassed this level of sophistication as evident in the line of question that took place when I was not at the table. They have the critical consciousness to disrupt the traditional discourse when the setting and space is appropriate. Thus, to me it is critical that the research work that took place had a certain reciprocity to it, and it is not always carried out through the specific research project taking place.

Another critical factor that I feel that must take place when doing anti-racist work is the need to create the space for organic intellectuals to share their thoughts, theories, experiences, stories, and humor. The power of oral story is difficult to translate into text especially when it comes from a culture that speaks with both their voice and hands. Media helped us solve part of this problem. Video as a tool for research has created the opportunity for a wider audience to benefit from these products. It expands the access for audiences who do not have access to academic publications. It expands the opportunity for diverse audiences to participate in the educational process.

And my final point is that we as researchers must always be aware of our own politics and ontological blind spots that can be very damaging to students and community partners. The answer is not in the good intentions, it is in the critical discourse that must take place for change to happen.

REFERENCES

Aguirre, P. (1997). Suffering roots. *Llano Grande Journal, 1(2),* 18.

Alarcón, N. (1990). The theoretical subject(s) of This *Bridge Called My Back* and Anglo-American feminism. In G. Anzaldúa (Ed.), *Making face, making soul hacienda cares: Creative and critical perspectives by feminists of color* (pp. 356-369). San Francisco: Aunt Lute Books.

Aiken, W. F. (1942). *The story of the eight-year study.* New York: Harper.

American Association of University Women. (1992). *How schools shortchange girls: Action guide. Strategies for improving gender equity in schools.* Washington, DC: AAUW Education Foundation.

American Association of University Women. (1993). *Hostile hallways.* Washington, DC: AAUW Education Foundation.

Anderson, M. L. (1993). Studying across difference: Race, class, and gender in qualitative research In J. H. Stanfield & R M. Dennis (Eds.), *Race and ethnicity in research methods* (pp. 39-52). Newbury Park, CA: Sage.

Anyon, J. (1995). Race, social class, and educational reform in an inner-city school. *Teachers College Record, 97(1),* 69-94.

Anzaldúa, G. (1990). (Ed.). *Making face, making soul: Hacienda Caras.* San Francisco: Aunt Lute Books.

Appiah, K. A. (1992). *In my father's house: Africa in the philosophy of culture.* London: Methuen.

Apple, M. (1992). The text and cultural politics. *Educational Researcher,* 21(7), 4-11.

Applebome, R. (1995, April 23). Keeping tabs on Jim Crow: John Hope Franklin. *The New York Times Magazine,* 3-37.

Arendt. H. (1963) *On Resolution* (New York: Penguin).

Asante, M. K. (1987). *The Afrocentric idea.* Philadelphia: Temple University Press.

Asante, M. K. (1988). *Afrocentricity.* Trenton, NJ: Africa World Press.

Asante, M. K. (1990). *Kismet, Afrocentricity and knowledge.* Trenton, NJ: Africa World Press.

Asante, M. K. (1991). The Afrocentric idea in education. *Journal of Negro Education, 60(2),* 170-180.

Asante, M. K. (1993). *Malcolm X as cultural hero and other Afrocentric essays.* Trenton, NJ: Africa World Press.

Ashcroft, B., Griffiths, G., Tiffin, H. (Eds.). (1995). *The post-colonial studies reader.* London: Routledge.

Au, K. H., & Kawakami, A. J. (1994). Cultural congruence in instruction. In E. R. Hollins, J. E. King, & W. C. Hayman (Eds.), *Teaching diverse populations: Formulating a knowledge base* (pp. 5-24). Albany: State University of New York Press.

Avis, J. (1988). White ethnicity, White racism: Teacher and student perceptions of FE. *Journal of Moral Education,* 17(1), 52-60.

Azibo, D. A. Y. (1990). Personality, clinical, and social psychological research on Blacks: Appropriate and inappropriate research frameworks. In T. Anderson (Ed.), *Black studies: Theory, method, and cultural perspectives* (pp. 25-41). Pullman, WA: Washington State University Press.

Barakan, E. (1992). *The retreat of scientific racism: Changing concepts of race in Britain and the United States between the world wars.* New York: Viking.

Bakhtin, M. M. (1968). *Rabelais and his world* (H. Isowolsky, Trans.). Cambridge, MA: MIT Press.

Bakhtin, M. M. (1986). *Speech genres and other late essays* (C. Emerson & M. Holquist, eds; V. W. McGee, trans.) Austin, TN: Texas University Press.

Baldwin, J. A. (1981). *Afrikan (Black) personality: From an Afrocentric framework.* Chicago: Third World Press.

Banks, J. A. (1989). *Multicultural education: Issues and Perspectives.* Boston: Allyn & Bacon.

Banks, J. A. (1993). The canon debate, knowledge construction, and multicultural education. *Educational Researcher,* 22(5), 4-14.

Banks, J. A. (1995). The historical reconstruction of knowledge about race: Implications for transformative learning. *Educational Researcher,* 24(2), 15-25.

Banks, W. C. (1992). The theoretical and methodological crisis of the Afrocentric conception. *Journal of Negro Education,* 61(3), 262-272.

Barber, B. R. (1992). *An Aristocracy of Everyone: The Politics of Education and the Future of America.* New York: Ballantine Books, Inc.

Baratz, S. S., & Baratz, J. C. (1970). Early childhood intervention: The social science base of institutional racism. *Harvard Educational Review,* 40, 29-50.

Beck, L. G. (1994). *Reclaiming educational administration as a caring profession.* New York: Teachers College Press.

Beck, L. G., & Murphy, I. (1996). *The four imperatives of a successful school.* Thousand Oaks, CA: Corwin Press.

Bell, D. (1992). *Faces at the bottom of the well: The permanence of racism.* New York: Basic Books.

Benhabib, S. (1992). *Situating the Self: Gender, Community, and Post-modernism in Contemporary Ethics.* (New York: Routledge).

Bereiter, C. (1994). Constructivism, socioculturalism, and Popper's world 3. *Educational Researcher,* 23(7), 21-23.

Berliner, D. C., & Biddle, B. J. (1995). *The manufactured crises: Myths, fraud, and the attack on America's public schools.* Reading, MA: Addison-Wesley.

Bernstein, H. T. (1985). The new politics of textbook adoption. *Phi Delta Kappan, 66*(77), 463-466.

Bernstein, R. J. (1992). *The new constellation: The ethical-political horizons of modernity/ postmodernity.* Cambridge, MA: The MIT Press.

Berry, W. (1989). *The hidden wound.* San Francisco: North Point Press.

Bhabha, H. K. (1985). Signs taken for wonders: Questions of ambivalence and authority under a tree outside Delhi, May 1817. *Critical Inquiry,* 12, 14-165.

Bhaskar, R. (1986). *Scientific realism and human emancipation.* London: Verso.

Bhaskar, R. (1989). *Reclaiming reality.* London: Verso.

Billingsley, A. (1968). *Black feminists in white America.* Englewood Cliffs, NJ: Prentice-Hall, Inc.

Bledstein, B.1. (1978). *The culture of professionalism: The middle class and the development of higher education in America.* New York: Norton.

Boden, D., Giddens, A., & Molotch, H. L. (1990). Sociology's role in addressing society's problems is undervalued and misunderstood in academe. *The Chronicle of Higher Education,* 36(23), B1, B3.

Bowles. S., & Gintis, H. (1986). *Democracy and capitalism: Property, community and the contradictions of modern social.* New York: Basic Books.

Boyer, E. (1994). The basic school: Focusing on the child. *Principal,* 73(3), 19-32.

Britzman, D. (1991). *Practice makes practice: A critical study of learning to teach.* Albany: State University of New York Press.

Britzman, D. (1998, April). *On tolerating the ambivalence of unreliable narrators: Literature, psychoanalysis and affect.* Paper presented at the annual meeting of the American Educational Research Association, San Diego, CA.

Burka, P. (1996, November). Carl C. Waitz Elementary. *Texas Monthly,* 24(11), 119.

Burns, J. M. (1978). *Leadership.* New York: HarperCollins.

Butler, J. (1993). *Bodies that matter: On the discursive limits of "sex."* New York: Routledge.

Carlson, D. (1992). *Teachers and crisis.* New York: Routledge.

Carroll, P. (1982). I am afraid of not making it. In S. Kafka & R. Coles (Eds.), *I will always stay me: Writings of migrant children* (p. 108). Austin: Texas Monthly Press.

Cassirer, E. (1944). *An essay on man: An introduction to a philosophy of human culture.* New Haven, CT: Yale University Press.

Cherryholmes, C. H. (1994). More notes on pragmatism. *Educational Researcher,* 23(1), 16-18.

Civil Rights panel to study issue of racism in schools. *Education Week* 11(14), 22.

Cizek, G. J. (1995). Crunchy granola and the hegemony of the narrative. *Educational Researcher, 24(2),* 1-17.

Clark, D. L., & Meloy, I. (1989). Renouncing bureaucracy: A democratic structure for leadership of schools. In T. J. Sergiovanni & J. H. Moore (Eds.), *Schooling for tomorrow: Directing reforms to issues that count* (pp. 272-294). Needham Heights, MA: Allen & Bacon.

Clifford, J. (1988). Identity in Mashpee. *The predicament of culture: Twentieth-century ethnography, literature, and art* (pp. 277-345). Cambridge, MA: Harvard University Press.

Coladarci, A. P., & Getzels, J. W. (1955). *The use of theory in educational administration.* Stanford, CA: Stanford University Press.

Collins, P. H. (1991). *Black feminist thought: Knowledge, consciousness, and the politics of empowerment.* New York: Routledge.

Comer, J. (1984). Home-school relationships as they affect the academic success of children. *Education and Urban Society, 16,* 323-337.

Comer, J. (1986). *Yale child study center school development program. Developmental history and long term effects.* New Haven, CT: Yale University Child Study Center.

Comer, J. (1988). Educating poor minority children. *Scientific American,* 259(5), 42-48.

Comer, J. (1993). *A brief history and summary of the School Development Program.* New Haven, CT: Yale University Child Study Center.

Contreras, P., Galan, S., & Valdez, D. (1968). *Brown-eyed children of the sun* [music recording]. Miami, FL: Warner Brothers Publications and Irving Music, Inc.

Cose, E. (1993). *The rage of a privileged class.* New York: HarperCollins.

Crenshaw, K, Gotanda, N., & Thomas, K. (Eds.). (1995). *Critical race theory: The key writings that formed the movement.* New York The New Press.

Cuban, L. (1989). The "at-risk" label and the problem of urban school reform. *Phi Delta Kappan,* 70, 780–784, 799–801.

Cummins, J. (1986). Empowering minority students: A framework for intervention. *Harvard Educational Review,* 56(1), 18–36.

Daniel, J. (1996, November). Pietzsch Elementary. *Texas Monthly,* 24(11), 116.

Davidson, D. (1984). *Inquiries into truth and interpretation.* Oxford, UK: Oxford University Press.

Darling-Hammond, L. (1991, June). *The implications of testing policy for educational quality and equity.* Paper presented at the American Educational Research Association Public Interest Invitational Conference on Accountability as a State Reform Instrument: Impact on Teaching, Learning, and Minority Issues and Incentives for Improvement, Washington, DC.

Darling-Hammond, L. (1996). The right to learn and the advancement of teaching: Research, policy, and practice for democratic education. *Educational Researcher,* 25(6), 5–17.

Darling-Hammond, L., & Wise, A. E. (1985). Beyond standardization: State standards and school improvement. *Elementary School Journal,* 85, 315–336.

Deal, T. E., & Kennedy, A. A. (1982). *Corporate cultures.* Reading, MA: Addison-Wesley.

Deal, T. E., & Peterson, K. D. (1990). *The principals' role in shaping school culture.* Washington, DC: Ontario Educational Research Institute.

Death of a farmworker could have been avoided. (1995, October). *Food and Justice — The Official Publication of the United Farm Workers of America, AFL/C10,* 9(3), 13.

Deckard, B. S. (1983). The self-fulfilling prophecy: Sex- role socialization. In B. S. Deckard (Ed.), *The women's movement: Political, socioeconomic, and psychological issues* (pp. 27–58). New York: Harper & Row.

Delandshere, G., Jr., & Petrosky, A. J. (1994). Capturing teachers' knowledge: Performance assessment. *Educational Researcher,* 23(5), 11–18.

Delgado, J. (1982). Work to do. In S. Kafka & R. Coles (Eds.), *I will always stay me: Writings of migrant children* (p. 56). Austin: Texas Monthly Press.

Delgado, R. (1990). When a story is just a story. Does voice really matter? *Virginia Law Review.* 76, 95–111.

Delgado, R. & Stefancic, J. (1997). *Critical white studies: Looking behind the mirror.* Philadelphia: Temple University Press.

Delgado-Gaitán, C. (1992). School matters in the Mexican-American home: Socializing children to education. *American Educational Research Journal,* 29(3), 495–513.

De Leon A. (1983). *They call them greasers: Anglo attitudes toward Mexicans in Texas, 1821–1900.* Austin TX: Texas University Press.

Derman-Sparks, L., & Phillips, C. B. (1997). *Teaching/learning antiracism: A developmental approach.* New York: Teachers College Press.

Derrida, J. (1977). *Of grammatology* (G. C. Spivak, Trans.). Baltimore: Johns Hopkins University Press.

Deutsch, K. W. (1971). On political theory and political action. *American Political Science Review,* 65(1), 11–27.

Dewey, J. (1937). Education and social change. *Social Frontier, 3,* 235-237.

Deyhle, D. (1991). Empowerment and cultural conflict: Navajo parents and the schooling of their children. *International Journal of Qualitative Studies in Education,* 4(4), 277-297.

Dixon, D. A. (1997). *Conceptions of democracy and school reform: A systematic analysis of prominent democratic education reformers' ideas.* University of Georgia.

Donmoyer, R. (1985). The rescue from relativism: Two failed attempts and an alternative strategy. *Educational Researcher,* 14(10), 13-20.

Donmoyer, R. (1997). Visions of educational research's past and future. *Educational Researcher,* 26(3), 4-16.

Donmoyer, R., Imber, M., & Scheurich, J. J. (1995). *The knowledge base in educational administration: Multiple perspectives.* Albany: State University of New York Press.

Dube, E. E. (1985). The relationship between racism and education in South Africa. *Harvard Educational Review,* 55(1), 86-91.

DuBois, W. E. B. (1903/1989). *The souls of Black folks.* New York: Bantam. (Original work—published 1903).

Dyer, R. (1988). White. *Screen,* 29, 44-64.

Edmonds, R. (1979). Effective schools for the urban poor. *Educational Leadership, 37(1),* 15-24.

Edwards, P. A. (1996). Before and after school desegregation: African American parents' involvement in school. In M. J. Shujaa (Ed.), *Beyond segregation: The politics of quality in African American schooling* (pp. 138-161). Thousand Oaks, CA: Corwin Press.

Eisner, E. (1988). The primacy of experience and the politics of method. *Educational Researcher,* 17(5), 15-20.

Ellison, R. (1972). *Invisible man.* New York: Vintage Books.

Ellsworth, E. (1989). Why doesn't this feel empowering? Working through the repressive myths of critical pedagogy. *Harvard Educational Review,* 59(3), 297-325.

Elmore, R. F. (1990). Introduction: On changing the structure of public schools. In R. F. Elmore & Associates (Eds.), *Restructuring schools: The next generation of educational reform.* San Francisco: Jossey-Bass.

Ernst, G., & Statzner, E. L. (1994). Alternative visions of schooling: An introduction. *Anthropology and Education Quarterly, 25(3),* 200-207.

Estes, N. (1994). Learning and caring. *Executive Educator, 51(1),* 28-30.

Evers, C. W., & Lakomski, G. (1991). *Knowing educational administration. Contemporary methodological controversies in educational administration research.* Oxford, UK: Pergamon Press.

Fact Sheet: America's Farmworkers. (1995). [On-line]. Available on the World Wide Web: http://www.ncfh,org/aboutEws/facts.htm.

Faltz, C. J., & Leake, D. O. (1996). The all-black school: Inherently unequal or a culture based alternative. In M. J. Shujaa (Ed.), *Beyond segregation: The politics of quality in African American schooling* (pp. 227-252). Thousand Oaks, CA: Corwin Press.

Feagin, J. R. (1991) Blacks still face the malevolent reality of White racism. *The Chronicle of Higher Education,* 38(14), A44.

Feagin, J. R., & Vera, H. (1995). *White racism.* New York: Routledge.

Ferguson, K. E. (1993). *The man question: Visions of subjectivity in feminist theory.* Berkeley: University of California Press.

Fine, M. (1991). Reclaiming the public sphere. In *Framing dropouts: Notes on the politics of an urban public high school* (pp. 205-230). Albany: State University of New York Press.

Flax, J. (1990). *Thinking fragments: Psychoanalysis, feminism, postmodernism in the contemporary west.* Berkeley: University of California Press.

Foster, M. (1994). Educating competence in community and culture: Exploring the views of exemplary African-American teachers. In M. J. Shujaa (Ed.), *Too much schooling, too little education: A paradox of black life in white societies.* Trenton, NJ: Africa World Press, Inc.

Foucault, M. (1970). *The order of things: An archeology of the human sciences* (A. Sheridan, Trans.). New York: Pantheon.

Foucault, M. (1972). *Archaeology of knowledge* (A. M. Sheridan Smith, Trans.). New York: Pantheon.

Foucault, M. (1979). *Discipline and punish. The birth of the prison.* New York: Vintage.

Foucault, M. (1980a). *The history of sexuality: Vol. 1.* An introduction. New York: Vintage.

Foucault, M. (1980b). *Power & Knowledge: Selected interviews and other writings, 1972-1977* (C. Gordon, Ed.). New York: Pantheon.

Foucault, M. (1984). *The Foucault reader* (P. Rabinow, Ed.). New York: Pantheon.

Foucault, M. (1988). *Madness and civilization: A history of insanity in the age of reason.* New York: Vintage.

Frankenberg, R. (1993). *The social construction of whiteness: White women, race matters.* Minneapolis, MN: University of Minnesota Press.

Frankenberg, R. (1997). *Displacing whiteness: Essays in social and cultural criticism.* Durham, NC: Duke University Press.

Freda, E. (1997). Happening. *Atlanta Journal,* Thursday, October 9, 1997, A19.

Freire, P. (1970). *Pedagogy of the oppressed.* New York: Continuum.

Freire, P., & Macedo, D. (1987). *Literacy: Reading the word and the world.* South Hadley, MA: Bergin & Garvey.

Frierson, H. T., Jr. (1990). The situation of Black educational researchers: Continuation of a crisis. *Educational Researcher,* 19(2), 12-17.

Fullan, M. G. (with Steigelbauer, S.). (1991). *The new meaning of educational change.* New York: Teachers College Press.

Fuller, S. *(1998).* *Social epistemology.* Bloomington, IN: Indiana University Press.

Gage, N. L. (1989). The paradigm wars and their aftermath: A historical sketch of research on teaching since 1989. *Educational Researcher,* 18(7), 4-10.

Gage, N. L. (1991). The obviousness of social and educational research results. *Educational Researcher,* 20(10), 1-16.

Galbraith, J. R., Lawler, E. E. III, and Associates (Eds.). (1993). *Organizing for the future: The new logic of managing complex organizations.* San Francisco: Jossey-Bass.

Garcia, E. (1986). Bilingual development and the education of bilingual children during early childhood. *American Journal of Education, 95,* 96-121.

Garcia, E. (1994). Attributes of effective schools for language minority students. In E. R. Hollins, J. E. King, & W. C. Hayman (Eds.), *Teaching diverse populations: Formulating a knowledge base* (pp. 93-104). Albany: State University of New York Press.

Gardiner, M. (1992). *The dialogics of critique: M. M. Bakhtin and the theory of ideology.* New York: Routledge.

Gardner, J. W. (1964). *Self-renewal: The individual and the innovative society.* New York: Harper & Row.

Gates, H. L., & West, C. (1996) *The Future of the Race.* New York: Vintage Books.

Gauna, R. (1982). Work. In S. Kafka & R. Coles (Eds.). *I will always stay me: Writings of migrant children* (p. 53). Austin, TX: Texas Monthly Press.

Gideonse, H. D. (1990). Organizing schools to encourage teacher inquiry. In R. F. Elmore & Associates (Eds.), *Restructuring School: The next generation of educational reform.* San Francisco: Jossey-Bass.

Glickman, C. D. (1993). *Renewing America's Schools: A Guide to School-based Action.* San Francisco: Jossey-Bass.

Glickman. C. D. (1996). Education as democracy: The pedagogy of school renewal. Invited presentation to the annual meeting of the American Educational Research Association, New York, April.

Glickman, C. D. (1998a). Educational leadership for democratic purpose: What do we mean? *International Journal of Leadership in Education,* 1(1), 47–53.

Glickman, C. D. (1998b). *Revolutionizing America's Schools.* San Francisco: Jossey-Bass.

Goldberg, D. T. (1993). *Racist culture. Philosophy and the politics of meaning.* Oxford, UK: Blackwell.

Good, T. (1981). Teacher expectations and student perceptions: A decade of research. *Educational Leadership, 38(5),* 415–422.

Good, T., & Brophy, J. (1987). Classroom complexity and teacher awareness. In *Looking in classrooms* (pp. 26–54). New York: Harper & Row.

Goodlad, J. I., & Keating, P. (Eds.). (1994). *Access to knowledge: The continuing agenda for our nation's schools.* New York: College Entrance Examination Board.

Gordon, B. M. (1990). The necessity of African-American epistemology for educational theory and practice. *Journal of Education,* 172(3), 88–106.

Gordon B. M. (1993). Toward emancipation in citizenship education: The case of African-American cultural knowledge. In L. A. Castenell Jr. & W. F. Pinar (Eds.), *Understanding curriculum as racial text: Representations of identity and difference in education* (pp. 263–284). Albany: State University of New York Press.

Gordon, E. W. (Ed.). (1992). Afrocentrism and multiculturalism: Conflict or consonance? *The Journal of Negro Education,* 61(3).

Gordon, E. W., Miller, F., & Rollock, D. (1990). Coping with the communicentric bias in knowledge production in the social sciences. *Educational Researcher,* 19(3), 14–19.

Gould, S. J. (1981). *The Mismeasure of man.* New York: W. W. Norton Co.

Grant, C., & Sleeter, C. (1989). *Turning on learning: Five approaches for multicultural teaching plans for race, class, gender, and disability.* Columbus, OH: Merrill.

Grunsell, A. (1991). *Let's talk about racism.* New York: Gloucester.

Guba, E. G., & Lincoln, Y. S. (1994). Competing paradigms in qualitative research. In N. K. Denzin & Y. S. Lincoln (Eds.), *Handbook of qualitative research* (pp. 105–117). Thousand Oaks, CA: Sage.

Guerrero, A. G. (1987). *A Chicano theology.* New York: Orbis.

Gutherie, J. W., & Reed, R. J. (1991). *Educational administration and policy: Effective leadership for American education.* Boston: Allyn & Bacon.

Gutting, G. (1989). *Foucault's archaeology of scientific reason.* Cambridge, UK: Cambridge University Press.

Gwaltney, J. (1980). *Drylongso: A self portrait of black America.* New York: Random House.

Haberman, M. (1995). *Star teachers of children in poverty.* West Lafayette, IN: Kappa Delta Pi.

Hacker, A. (1992). *Two nations: Black and white, separate, hostile, unequal.* New York: Scribner's Sons.

Halpin, A. W. (1966). *Theory and research in administration.* New York: MacMillan.

Harris, C. (1993). Whiteness as property. *Harvard Law Review,* 106(8), 1707–1791.

Henderson R. D., Greenberg, N. M., Schneider, J. M., Uribe, O., Jr., & Verdugo, R. R. (1996). In M. J. Shujaa (Ed.), *Beyond segregation: The politics of quality in African American schooling* (pp. 162–184). Thousand Oaks, CA: Corwin Press.

Henry, A. (1992). African Canadian women teachers' activism: Recreating communities of caring and resistance. *Journal of Negro Education,* 61(3), 392–404.

Henry, M. (1996). *Parent-school collaboration: Feminist organizational structures and school leadership.* Albany: State University of New York Press.

Herrnstein, R. J., & Murray, C. (1994). *The bell curve: Intelligence and class structure in American life.* New York: Free Press.

Heshusius, L. (1994). Freeing ourselves from objectivity: Managing subjectivity or turning toward a participatory mode of consciousness? *Educational Researcher,* 23(3), 15–22.

Higham, J. (1971). Toward racism: The history of an idea. In N. R. Yetman & C. H. Steele (Eds.), *Majority and minority: The dynamics of racial of ethnic relations* (pp. 230–252). Boston: Allyn & Bacon.

Hill, N. (1993) Reclaiming American Indian education. In S. Elam (ed.), *The State of the Nations' Public Schools* (Bloomington: Phi Delta Kappa Society), 171–173.

Hill, P. T., Foster, G. E., & Gendler, T. (1990). *High schools with character.* Santa Monica, CA: RAND.

Hill, R. B. (1972). *The strengths of black families.* New York: Emerson Hall Publishers, Inc.

Hilliard, A. G., Jr. (1992). Behavioral style, culture, and teaching and learning. *Journal of Negro Education,* 61(3), 370–377.

Hintz, J. (1981). *Poverty, prejudice, power, politics: Migrants speak about their lives.* Columbus, OH: Avonelle Association Publishers.

Hollins, E. R., King, J. E., & Hayman, W. C. (Eds.). (1994). *Teaching diverse populations: Formulating a knowledge base.* Albany: State University of New York Press.

Hollins, E. R., & Spencer, K. (1990). Restructuring schools for cultural inclusion: Changing the schooling process for African American youngsters. *Journal of Education,* 172(2), 89–100.

hooks, b. (1990). *Yearning: Race, gender, and cultural politics.* Boston: South End Press.

hooks, b. (1995) Teaching to transgress. *Education as the Practice of Freedom* (New York: Routledge).

Hopfenberg, W. S., Levin, H. M., Chase, C., Christensen, S. C., Moore, M., Soler, P., Brunner, I., Keller, B., & Rodriguez, G. (1993). *The Accelerated schools: Resource guide.* San Francisco: Jossey-Bass.

House, E. (1994). Is John Dewey eternal? *Educational Researcher,* 23(1), 1–16.

Howard, G. R. (1993). Whites in multicultural education: Rethinking our role. *Phi Delta Kappan,* 75, 30–41.

How do pesticides hurt me? (1982, January). *Nuestra Lucha: Hasta la victoria,* 5(1), 8–9.

Howitt, D., & Owusu-Bempah, J. (1990). The pragmatics of institutional racism: Beyond words. *Human Relations,* 43(9), 885-899.

Huggins, J. (1991). Black women and women's liberation. In S. Gunew (Ed.), *A reader in feminist knowledge* (pp. 6-12). London: Routledge.

Implementation of Helsinki accords: Migrant farmworkers in the United States: Briefings of the Commission on Security and Cooperation in Europe. (1993, May). Washington, D.C.: U. S. Government Printing Office.

Jaeger, R. M. (1991, June). *Legislative perspectives on statewide testing: Goals, hopes, and desires.* Paper presented at the American Educational Research Association Public Interest Invitational Conference on Accountability as a State Reform Instrument: Impact on Teaching, Learning, and Minority Issues and Incentives for Improvement, Washington, DC.

Jensen, R. (1998, August 3). White people need to acknowledge benefits of unearned privilege. *Baltimore Sun,* pp. 1C, 4C.

Joyce, B., McKibbin, M., & Weil, M. (1977) *Teaching and learning: demonstration of alternatives.* Washington: Association of Teacher Educators.

Joyce, B., & Weil, M. (1996). *Models of Teaching,* 5th ed., (Needham Heights, MA: Allyn & Bacon).

Keith, N. Z. (1996). A critical perspective on teacher participation in urban schools. *Educational Administration Quarterly, 32(1),* 45-79.

Kershaw, T. (1989). The emerging paradigm in Black studies. *The Western Journal of Black Studies,* 13(1), 4-51.

Kershaw, T. (1992). Afrocentrism and the Afrocentric method. *The Western Journal* of *Black Studies,* 16(3), 160-168.

Killens, J. O. (1996) The Black psyche. *The New York Times Magazine,* April 14, p. 108 (first published in *The New York Times Magazine,* 7 June 1964).

King, J. E. (1991). Dysconscious racism: Ideology, identity, and the miseducation of teachers. *Journal of Negro Education,* 60(2), 133-146.

King, J. E. (1992). Diaspora literacy and consciousness in the struggle against miseducation in the Black community. *Journal of Negro Education,* 61(3), 317-340.

King, J. E. (1994). The purpose of schooling for African American children. In E. R. Hollins, J. E. King, & W. C. Hayman (Eds.), *Teaching diverse populations: Formulating a knowledge base* (pp. 25-60). Albany: State University of New York Press.

King, W. M. (1990). Challenges across the curriculum. Broadening the bases of how knowledge is produced. *American Behavioral Scientist,* 34(2), 16-180.

Kluegel, J. R., & Smith, E. R. (1986). *Beliefs about inequality: Americans' views of what is and what ought to be.* New York: de Gruyter.

Kovel, J. (1970). *Whim racism: A psychological history.* New York: Pantheon.

Kramer, J. R. (1970). *The American minority community.* New York: Crowell.

Krupat, A. (1993). Introduction. In A. Krupat (Ed.), *New voices in American literary criticism* (pp. xvii-xxv). Washington, DC: Smithsonian Institution Press.

Kuhn, T. (1970). *The structure of scientific revolutions* (2nd. ed.) Chicago: University of Chicago Press.

Kushner, T. (1994). *Angels in America, part two: Perestroika.* New York: Theatre Communications Group, Inc.

Kuykendall, C. (1992). *From rage to hope: Strategies for reclaiming Black & Hispanic students.* Bloomington, IN: National Education Service.

✗ Ladson-Billings, G. (1994). *The dreamkeepers: Successful teachers of African American Children.* San Francisco: Jossey-Bass.

✗ Ladson-Billings, G., & Tate, W. (1995). Toward a theory of cultural relevant pedagogy. *American Educational Research Journal,* 32(3), 46–491.

Laible, J. (1994, October). *Feminist analysis of sexual harassment policy: A critique of the ideal of community.* Paper presented at the annual convention of the University Council of Educational Administration, Philadelphia, PA.

Laible, J. (2000). A loving epistemology: What I hold critical in my life, faith, and profession. *International Journal of Qualitative Studies in Education,* 13:6, 683–692.

Lather, P. (1986). Issues of validity in openly ideological research: Between a rock and a hard place. *Interchange, 17*(4), 63–84.

Lather, P. (1991). *Getting smart: Feminist research and pedagogy with/in the postmodern.* New York: Routledge.

Lather, P. (1993). Fertile obsession: Validity after poststructuralism. *Sociological Quarterly,* 34(4), 673–693.

Laudan, L. (1990). *Science and relativism: Some key controversies in the philosophy of science.* Chicago: The University of Chicago Press.

Ledezma, M. (1996). Fiesta in the labor camp. In J. L. Flores (Ed.), *Children of la frontera: Binational efforts to serve Mexican migrant and immigrant students* (pp. 98–99). Charleston, WV: ERIC Clearinghouse of Rural Education and Small Schools.

Lee, C. D., Lomotey, K., & Shujja, M. (1990). How shall we sing our sacred song in a strange land? The dilemma of double consciousness and the complexities of an African-centered pedagogy. *Journal of Education,* 172(2), 45–61.

Lee, J. C. S. (1995). Navigating the topology of race. In K. Crenshaw, N. Gotanda, & K. Thomas, (Eds.). *Critical race theory: The key writings that formed the movement* (pp. 441–443). New York: The New Press.

Leistyna, P., & Woodrum, A. (1996). Context and culture: What is critical pedagogy? In P. Leistyna, A. Woodrum, & S. A. Sherblom (Eds.), *Breaking Free: The transformative power of critical pedagogy.* Cambridge, MA: Harvard Educational Review Reprint Series.

Leistyna, P., Woodrum, A., & Sherbloom, S. A. (Eds.). (1996). *Breaking free: The transformative power of critical pedagogy.* Cambridge, MA: Harvard Educational Review Reprint Series.

Lenzo, K (1995). Validity and self-reflexivity meet poststructuralism: Scientific ethos and the transgressive self, *Educational Researcher,* 24(4), 17–23.

Leon, E. (1997) *Challenges and solutions for educating migrants* [On-line]. Http:// www.jrsi.msu.edu/RandS/research/wps/WP28.html.

Levin, H. (1991). Accelerated schools for at-risk students: The case against remedial teaching. *Education Digest,* 56(9), 47–51.

Littlejohn-Blake, S. M., & Darling, C. A. (1993). Understanding the strengths of African American families. *Journal of Black Studies,* 23(4), 460–471.

Lima, E. S., & Gazzetta, M. (1994). From lay teachers to university students: The path for empowerment through culturally based pedagogical action. *Anthropology and Education Quarterly,* 25(3), 236–249.

Lincoln, Y. S., & Guba, E. G. (1985). *Naturalistic inquiry.* Beverly Hills, CA: Sage.

Lipka, J., & McCarthy, T. L. (1994). Changing the culture of schooling: Navaho and Yup-tik cases. *Anthropology and Education Quarterly,* 25(3), 266-284.

Loftin, J. D. (1991). *Religion* and *Hopi life in the twentieth century.* Bloomington, Indiana University Press.

Loman, M. (Executive Producer). (1997, March 21). *Sesame Street* (no. 36155). New York: Children's Television Workshop and Public Broadcasting Service.

Lomotey, K. (1989). *African-American principals: School leadership and success.* New York: Greenwood.

Lomotey, K. (1995). Social and cultural influences of schooling: A commentary on the UCEA knowledge base project, Domain I. *Educational Administration Quarterly, 31(2),* 294-303.

Lorde, A. (1990). I am your sister: Black women organizing across sexualities. In G. Anzaldúa (Ed.), *Making face, making soul: Haciendo caras: Creative and critical perspectives by feminists of color* (pp. 321-325). San Francisco: Aunt Lute Books.

Louis, K., & Miles, M. B. (1990). *Improving the urban high school: What works and why.* New York: Teachers College Press.

Lubiano, W. (1991). Shuckin' off the African American native other: What's "po-mo" got to do with it? *Cultural Critique, 20,* 149-186.

Lucas, T., Henze, R., & Donato, R. (1990). Promoting the success of Latino language-minority students: An exploratory study of six high schools. *Harvard Educational Review,* 60(3), 315-340.

Lynch, M., & Woolgar, S. (Eds.). (1990). *Representation in scientific practice.* Cambridge, MA: MIT Press.

Lyotard, J.-F. (1984). *The postmodern condition: A report on knowledge* (G. Bennington & B. Massumi, Trans.). Minneapolis: University of Minnesota Press.

Lytle, L. H. (1992). Prospects for reforming urban schools. *Urban Education,* 27 (2), 109-131.

Madaus, G. F. (1991, June). *The effects of important tests on students: Implications for a national examination or system of examinations.* Paper presented at the American Educational Research Association Public Interest Invitational Conference on Accountability as a State Reform Instrument: Impact on Teaching, Learning, and Minority Issues and Incentives for Improvement, Washington, DC.

Maier, P. (1997) *American Scripture, the Making of the Declaration of Independence* (New York: Alfred A. Knopf).

Mann, C. R. (1993). *Unequal justice: A question of color.* Bloomington: Indiana University Press.

Mann, J. (1994). *The difference: Growing up female in America.* New York: Warner Books.

Marks, C. C. (1993). Demography and race. In J. H. Stanfield (Ed.), *Race and ethnography in research methods* (pp. 159-171). Newbury Park, CA: Sage.

Massaro, T. (1991) *Constitutional literacy: A core curriculum for a multi-cultural nation.* Durham, NC: Duke University Press.

Mattai, P. R. (1992). Rethinking multicultural education: Has it lost its focus or is it being misused? *Journal of Negro Education, 61(1),* 65-77.

McCarthy, C. (1988). Rethinking liberal and radical perspectives on racial inequality in schooling: Making the case of nonsynchrony. *Harvard Educational Review,* 58, 265-279.

McCarthy, C. (1993). Beyond the poverty of theory in race relations: Nonsynchrony and social difference in education. In L. Weis & M. Fine (Eds.), *Beyond silenced voices: Class, race, and gender in United States schools* (pp. 325–346). New York: State University of New York Press.

McCarthy, C., & Crichlow, W. (1993). Introduction: Of identity, theories of representation, theories of race. In C. McCarthy & W. Crichlow (Eds.), *Race identity and representation in education* (pp. xiii–xxix). New York: Routledge.

McIntosh, P. (1992). White privilege and male privilege. In J. Andrzejewski (Ed.), *Human relations: The study of oppression and human rights* (3rd ed., pp. 235–238). Needham Heights, MA: Ginn.

McKissack, P., & McKissack, F. (1990). *Taking a stand against racism and racial discrimination.* New York: Franklin Watts.

McLaren, P. (1989). *Life in schools: An introduction to critical pedagogy in the foundations of education.* New York: Longman.

McLaren, P. (1995). *Critical pedagogy and predatory culture: Oppositional politics in a postmodern era.* New York: Routledge.

McLaren, P. (2000). *Che Guevara, Paulo Freire, and the pedagogy of revolution.* Lanham, Md.: Rowman & Littlefield.

Mercer, C. D. (1988). Students with learning disabilities. Columbus, OH: Merrill.

Meter, D. (1992). Reinventing teaching. *Teachers College Record,* 93(4), 594–609.

Merino, B. J. (1991). Promoting school success for Chicanos: The view from inside the bilingual classroom. In R. R. Valencia (Ed.), *Chicano school failure and success: Research and policy agendas for the 1990s* (pp. 119–148). London: Palmer.

Meyer, J. W., & Rowan, B. (1983). *Organizational environments: Ritual and rationality.* Beverly Hills, CA: Sage.

Minh-ha, T. T. (1989). *Woman native other.* Bloomington: Indiana University Press.

Minh-ha, T. T. (1990). Not you/like you: Post colonial women and the interlocking questions of identity and difference. In G. Anzaldúa (Ed.), *Making face, making soul: Hacienda caras: Creative and critical perspectives by feminists of color* (pp. 371–375). San Francisco: Aunt Lute Books.

Minnesota Women's Fund. (1991). *Reflections of Risk.* Minneapolis: Author.

Mohrman, S. A. (1994). High-involvement management in the private sector. In S. A. Mohrman, P. Wohlstetter, & Associates (Eds.), *School-based management: Organizing for high performance.* San Francisco: Jossey-Bass.

Mohrman, S. A., & Mohrman, A. M., Jr. (1993). Organizational change and learning. In J. R. Galbraith, E. E. Lawler III, and Associates (Eds.), *Organizing for the future: The new logic of managing complex organizations* (pp. 87–108). San Francisco: Jossey-Bass.

Morrison, T. (1992). *Playing in the dark: Whiteness and the literary imagination.* Cambridge, MA: Harvard University Press.

Moss, P. A. (1994). Can there be validity without reliability? *Educational Researcher,* 23(2), 5–12.

National Advisory Commission on Civil Disorder. (1968, May 1). *Report of the National Advisory Commission on Civil Disorder,* Publication No. 1968, 291–729). Washington, DC: U. S. Government Printing Office.

Nelson, J. S., Megill, A., & McCloskey, D. N. (Eds.). (1987). *The rhetoric of the human sciences.* Madison: University of Wisconsin Press.

Newmann, F. M., Marks, H. M., & Gamoran, A. (1995). *Authentic Pedagogy: Standards that boost student performance: Issues in restructuring schools. Report No. 8.* Madison: Wisconsin Center for Education Research.

Newmann, F. M., & Wehlage, G. G. (1995). *Successful school restructuring: A report to the public and educators by the Center on Organization and Restructuring of Schools.* Madison: Wisconsin Center for Education Research.

Nicolaides, N., & Gaynor, A. (1989). The knowledge base informing the teaching and administrative and organizational theory in UCEA universities: Empirical and interpretive perspectives. In *Improving the preparation of school administrators: Notes on reform.* Charlottesville, VA: National Policy Board for Educational Administration.

Nieto, S. (1996). *Affirming diversity: The sociocultural context of multicultural education* (2nd ed.). White Plains, NY: Longman.

Nieto, S., & Rolon, C. (1995). The preparation and professional development of teachers: A perspective from new Latinos. Paper presented to the CULTURES conference, "Defining the Knowledge Base for Urban Teacher Education," Emory University, Decatur, GA.

Noddings, N. (1984). *Caring: A feminine approach to ethics and moral education.* Berkeley: University of California Press.

Noddings, N. (1992). *The challenge to care: Alternative approaches to education.* New York: Teachers College Press.

Noddings, N. (1994). Foreword. In L. G. Beck (Author), *Reclaiming educational administration as a caring profession.* New York: Teachers College Press.

Nolly, G. L. (1997). *Effective instructional practices for teaching mathematics to African American students.* Unpublished doctoral dissertation, University of Texas at Austin.

Oakes, J. (1985). *Keeping track: How schools structure inequality.* New Haven, CT: Yale University Press.

Ogbu, J. U. (1978). *Minority education and caste: The American system in cross-cultural perspective.* New York: Academic Press.

Ogbu, J. U. (1990). Racial stratification and education. In G. E. Thomas (Ed.), *U. S. race relations in the 1980s and 1990s: Challenges and alternatives* (pp. 3-34). New York: Hemisphere.

Oliva, M. (1997). *Zones of influence and discourses of preference in North American higher education collaboration.* Unpublished doctoral dissertation, University of Texas, Austin.

O'Neill, K., & Shoemaker, J. (Eds.). (1989). *A conversation between James Comer and Ronald Edmonds: Fundamentals of effective school improvement.* Okemos, MI: Kendal/Hunt.

Ortiz, A. (1986). Recognizing learning disabilities in bilingual children: How to lessen inappropriate referrals of language minority students to special education. *Journal of Reading, Writing, and Learning Disabilities International, 2(1),* 43-56.

Ortiz, A. A., García, S. B., Wheeler, D. S., & Maldonado-Colon, E. (1986). *Characteristics of limited English proficient students served in programs for the speech and language handicapped: Implications for policy, practice, and research.* Austin, TX; The University of Texas, Department of Special Education, Handicapped Minority Research Institute on Language Proficiency (ERIC Document Reproduction Service No. ED 283 314).

Ouchi, W. G. (1981). *Theory Z.* New York: Avon.

Our best schools. (1996, September). *Texas Monthly,* pp. 112–119, 155, 157, 159–160.

Outlaw, L., Jr. (1996). *On race and philosophy.* New York: Routledge.

Padilla, A. M. (1994). Ethnic minority scholars, research, and mentoring. Current and future issues. *Educational Researcher, 23*(4), 24–27.

Page, R. (1987). Teachers' perceptions of students: A link between classrooms, school cultures and the social order. *Anthropology and Education Quarterly, 18,* 77–99.

Paredes, A. (1977). On ethnographic work among minority groups. A folklorist's perspective. *New Scholar, 6,* 1–32.

Paredes Scribner, A. (1996, November). *Psychoeducational assessment of linguistically diverse students in Texas borderland schools.* Paper presented at the 1996 Migrant Education Conference, South Padre Island, TX.

Parry, B. (1995). Problems in current theories of colonial discourse. In B. Ashcroft, G. Griffiths, & H. Tiffin (Eds.), *The post-colonial studies reader* (pp. 36–44). London: Routledge.

Peters, T. (1992). *Liberation management.* New York: Knopf.

Peters, T. J., & Waterman, R. H., Jr. (1982). *In search of excellence.* New York: Harper & Row.

Pettigrew, T. F., & Martin, J. (1987). Shaping the organizational context for Black American inclusion. *Journal of Social Issues, 43*(1), 41–78.

Phillips, D. E. (1987). *Philosophy, science, and social inquiry.* New York: Pergamon Press.

Pine, G. J., & Hilliard, A. G. III. (1990). Rx for racism: Imperatives for America's schools. *Phi Delta Kappan, 71,* 593–600.

Pogue, A., Hinojosa Smith, R., & Garcia, R. (1984). *Agricultural workers of the Rio Grande and Rio Bravo Valleys: A portfolio.* Austin, TX: Center for Mexican American Studies, University of Texas.

Popkewitz, T. S. (1997). A changing terrain of knowledge and power: A social epistemology of educational researcher. *Educational Researcher, 26*(9), 18–29.

Primis: The UCEA catalog. (1994). New York: McGraw-Hill.

Prewitt, J. O., Trotter II, R. T., & Rivera, Jr., V. A. (1989). *The effects of migration on children: An ethnographic study.* State College, PA: Centro do Estudios Sobre la Migración.

Putnam, H. (1983). *Realism and reason.* Cambridge, UK: Cambridge University Press.

Quine, W. V. O. (1960). *Word and object.* Cambridge, MA: MIT Press.

Ransford, H. E. (1977). *Race and class in American society: Black, Chicano, Anglo.* Cambridge, MA: Schenkman.

Raywid, M. A. (1990) Rethinking school governance. In R. F. Elmore and Associates (Eds.), *Restructuring Schools: The Next Generation of Educational Reform.* San Francisco: Jossey-Bass.

Raywid, M. A. (1993). Community: An alternative accomplishment. In G. A. Smith (Ed.), *Public schools that work. Creating Community* (pp. 23–44). New York: Routledge.

Rebolledo, D. (1990). The politics of poetics: Or, what am I, a critic, doing in this text anyhow? In G. Anzaldúa (Ed.), *Making face, making soul hacienda caras: Creative and critical perspectives of feminists of color* (pp. 346 355). San Francisco: Aunt Lute Books.

Reyes, M. L, & Halcon, J. J. (1988). Racism in academia: The old wolf revisited. *Harvard Educational Review, 58*(3), 299–314.

Reyes, P. (1993, October). *Cultural citizenship and social responsibility: A call for change in educational administration.* Presidential address presented at the annual convention of the University Council for Educational Administration, Houston, TX.

Reyes, P. (1996, November). *Effective classroom practices in mathematics.* Paper presented at the 1996 Migrant Education Conference, South Padre Island, TX.

Reyes, P., & Scribner, J. D. (Eds.). (1996). *Final report of research findings: Effective border school research and development initiative.* Edinburg, TX: Regional One Educational Service Center.

Reyes, P., Scribner, J. D., Pazey, B., Scheurich, J. J., Laible, L., Paredes Scribner, A., Wagstaff, L., Fusarelli, L., Young, M., Pedroza, A., Brooks, A., Kavanaugh, P., Kazal-Thresher, D., & Fuller, E. I. (1996, April). *An interactive symposium on how schools can be successful with students of color (based on research on low SES, linguistically different, Mexican-American students).* Symposium conducted at the American Educational Research Association Annual Meeting, New York.

Richardson, V., Casanova, U., Placier, P., & Guilfoyle, K. (1989). *School children at-risk.* New York: Palmer.

Rivera, T. (1987). *Y no se lo trago la tierra* [And the earth did not devour him]. (R. Hinjosas, Trans.). Houston: Arte Publico.

Rizvi, R (1993). Children and the grammar of popular racism. In C. McCarthy & W. Crichlow (Eds.), *Race identity and representation in education* (pp. 126-139). New York: Routledge.

Rochin, R., Santiago, A., & Dickey, K. (1989). *Migrant and seasonal workers in Michigan's agriculture: A study of their contributions, needs, characteristics and services* [On-line]. Http://www.jsri.msu.edu/RandS/research/irr/rr01.html.

Rorty, R. (1982). *Consequences of pragmatism.* Minneapolis: University of Minnesota Press.

Roscoe, W. (1991). *The Zuni man-woman.* Albuquerque: University of New Mexico Press.

Roueche, I. E., & Baker, G. A. III (1986). *Profiling excellence in America's schools.* Arlington, VA: American Association of School Administrators.

Rumberger, R. (1991). Chicano dropouts: A review of research and policy issues. In R. Valencia (Ed.), *Chicano school failure and success: Research and policy agendas for the 1990s* (pp. 64-89). New York: Palmer.

Sadker, M., & Sadker, D. (1994). *Failing at fairness: How America's schools cheat girls.* New York: Scribner.

Said, E. W. (1979). *Orientalism.* New York: Vintage.

Saldivar, R. *Chicano narrative: The dialectics of difference.* Madison: Univeristy of Wisconsin Press.

Salinas, R. R. (1970). Un trip through the mind jail. *Can Safos, 6,* 39-42.

Sangari, K. (1995). The politics of the possible. In B. Ashcroft, G. Griffiths, & H. Tiffin (Eds.), *The post-colonial studies reader.* London: Routledge.

Sarason, S. B. (1982). *The culture of the school and the problem of change* (2nd ed.). Boston: Allyn & Bacon.

Sarris, G. (1993). Hearing the old ones talk: Reading narrated American Indian lives. In E. Colson's *Autobiographies of Three Pomo Women.* In A. Krupat (Ed.), *New voices in Native American literary criticism* (pp. 419-452). Washington, DC: Smithsonian Institution Press.

Scheurich, J. J. (1991, April). *The knowledge base in educational administration: Postpositivist reflections.* Paper presented at the annual meeting of the American Educational Research Association, Chicago, IL.

Scheurich, J. J. (1993). Toward a white discourse on white racism. *Educational Researcher,* 22(8), 5-10.

Scheurich, J. J. (1994a). Policy archaeology. A new policy studies methodology. *Journal of Education Policy, 9(4),* 297-316.

Scheurich, J. J. (1994b). Social relativism. A postmodernist epistemology for educational administration. In S. J. Maxcy (Ed.), *Postmodern school leadership: Meeting the crises in educational administration* (pp. 17-46). Westport, CT: Praeger.

Scheurich, J. J. (1995) Highly successful and loving public pre-K schools populated mainly by low SES children of color: Core beliefs and cultural characteristics. Unpublished paper. Department Educational Administration, University of Texas at Austin.

Scheurich J. J. (1996, November). *Best programmatic and organizational practices in effective border schools.* Paper presented at the 1996 Migrant Education Conference, South Padre Island, TX.

Scheurich, J. J. (1997). *Research method in the postmodern.* London: Falmer.

Scheurich, J. J. (1998). The grave dangers in the discourse on democracy. *International Journal of Leadership in Education,* 1(1), 55-60.

Scheurich, J. J., & Imber, M. (1991). Educational reforms can reproduce societal inequities: A case study. *Educational Administration Quarterly,* 27(3), 297-320.

Scheurich, J. J., & Laible, J. (1995). The buck stops here—In our preparation programs: Educative leadership for all children (no exceptions allowed). *Educational Administration Quarterly,* 31(2), 313-322.

Scheurich, J. J., & Young, M. D. (1997). Coloring epistemology: Are our research epistemologies racially biased? *Educational Researcher,* 27(4), 4-16.

Schiele, J. H. (1990). Organizational theory from an Afrocentric perspective. *Journal of Black Studies,* 21(2), 145-161.

Schneider, G. (1992). UCEA annual presidential address,1991: Looking back—Moving forward. *UCEA Review, 33(1),* 1, 4-5, 8-9.

Schofield, J. W. (1996). Promoting positive peer relations in desegregated schools. In M. J. Shujaa (Ed.), *Beyond segregation: The politics of quality in African American schooling* (pp. 91-112). Thousand Oaks, CA: Corwin Press.

Schuman, H. (1971). Free will and determinism in public beliefs about race. In N. R. Yetman & C. H. Steele (Eds.), *Majority and minority: The dynamics of racial and ethnic relations* (pp. 332-390). Boston: Allyn & Bacon.

Schwandt, T. A. (1994). Constructivist, interpretivist approahes to human inquiry. In N. K. Denzin & Y. S. Lincoln (Eds.), *Handbook of qualitative research* (pp. 118-137). Thousand Oaks, CA: Sage.

Scores count. (1996, September 8). *The New York Times Magazine,* pp. 41-45.

Scribner, J. D. (1996, November). *Effective school and community involvement strategies.* Paper presented at the 1996 Migrant Education Conference, South Padre Island, TX.

Sergiovanni, T. L. (1996). *Leadership for the schoolhouse.* San Francisco: Jossey-Bass.

Shakeshaft, C. (1986). A gender at risk: The lack of educational equality for women. *Phi Delta Kappan, 67,* 499-504.

Shakeshaft, C., Barber, E., Hergenrother, M. A., Johnson, Y., Mandel, L., & Sawyer, J.

(1994, October). *Conceptions of community: Peer harassment and the culture of caring in the schools.* Paper presented at the annual convention of the University Council of Educational Administration, Philadelphia, PA.

Shepard, L. (1991, June). *Will national tests improve student learning?* Paper presented at the American Educational Research Association Public Interest Invitational Conference on Accountability as a State Reform Instrument: Impact on Teaching, Learning, and Minority Issues and Incentives for Improvement, Washington, DC.

Shepardson, D. P., & Pizzini, E. L. (1992). Gender bias in female elementary teachers' perceptions of the scientific ability of students. *Science Education, 76,* 147–153.

Shipley, D. (1992). What is a community? A principal's view of James Comers's School Development Program. *Equity and Choice,* 8(3), 19–23.

Shockley, W. (1992). Society has a moral obligation to diagnose tragic racial IQ deficits. In R. Pearson (Ed.), *Shockley on eugenics and race: The application of science to the solution of human problems.* Washington, DC: Scott-Townsend.

Shor, J. (1992). *Empowering education: Critical teaching for social change.* Chicago: University of Chicago Press.

Shuey, A. (1958). *The testing of Negro intelligence.* Lynchburg, VA: Ben.

Shujaa, M. J. (Ed.). (1994). *Too much schooling, too little education: A paradox of black life in white society.* Trenton, NJ: Africa World Press, Inc.

Shujaa, M. J., & Afrik, H. T. (1996). School desegregation, the politics of culture, and the Council of Independent Black Institutions. In M. J. Shujaa (Ed.), *Beyond segregation: The politics of quality in African American schooling* (pp. 253–268). Thousand Oaks, CA: Corwin Press.

Shulman, S. (1990). The causes of black poverty: Evidence and interpretation. *Journal of Economic Issues, 24,* 995–1016.

Siddle Walker, E. V. (1993). Caswell county training school, 1933–1969: Relationships between the community and school. *Harvard Educational Review,* 63(2), 161–182.

Silberman, C. E. (1964). *Crisis in black and white.* New York: Vintage.

Simon, H. W. (Ed.). (1989). *Rhetoric in the human sciences.* London: Sage.

Simon, R. J. (1992). *Teaching against the grain: A pedagogy of possibility.* New York: Bergin-Garvey.

Sleeter, C., & McLaren, P. (1995). *Multicultural education, critical pedagogy, and the politics of difference.* Albany: State University of New York Press.

Smircich, L. (1983). Organizations as shared meanings. In L. R. Pondy, P. Frost, G. Morgan, & T. Dandridge (Eds.), *Organizational symbolism* (pp. 55–65). Greenwich, CT: JAI Press.

Smith, G. A. (1993). Introduction. In G. A. Smith (Ed.), *Public schools that work. Creating community.* New York: Routledge.

Smith, J. K. (1997). The stories researchers tell about themselves. *Educational Researcher,* 26(5), 4–11.

Spivak, G. C. (1988). *In other worlds: Essays in cultural politics.* New York: Routledge.

Spivak, G. C. (1995). Can the subaltern speak? In B. Ashcroft, G. Griffiths, & H. Tifflin (Eds.), *The postcolonial studies reader* (pp. 24–28). New York: Routledge.

Stanfield, J. H. II. (1985). The ethnocentric basis of social science knowledge production. In E. W. Gordon (Ed.), *Review of research in education* (Vol. 12, pp. 387–415). Washington, DC: American Educational Research Association.

Stanfield, J. H. II. (1993a). Epistemological considerations. In J. H. Stanfield & R. M. Dennis (Eds.), *Race and ethnicity in research methods* (pp. 16–36). Newbury Park, CA: Sage.

Stanfield, J. H. II. (1993b). Methodological reflections. In J. H. Stanfield & R. M. Dennis (Eds.), *Race and ethnicity in research methods* (pp. 3–15). Newbury Park, CA: Sage.

Stanfield, J. H. II. (1994). Ethnic modeling in qualitative research. In N. Denzin & Y. Lincoln (Eds.), *Handbook of qualitative research* (pp. 175–188). Thousand Oaks, CA: Sage.

Stanfield, J. H. II, & Dennis, R. M. (Eds.). (1993). *Race and ethnicity in research methods.* Newbury Park, CA: Sage.

Stevenson, R B., & Ellsworth, J. (1993). Dropouts and the silencing of critical voices. In L. Weis & M. Fine (Eds.), *Beyond silenced voices: Class, race, and gender in United States schools* (pp. 259–271). Albany: State University of New York Press.

Stake, R. E. (1991, June). *The teacher, standardized testing, and prospects of a revolution.* Paper presented at the American Educational Research Association Public Interest Invitational Conference on Accountability as a State Reform Instrument: Impact on Teaching, Learning, and Minority Issues and Incentives for Improvement, Washington, DC.

St. Pierre, E. A. (1997). Methodology in the fold and the irruption of transgressive data. *International Journal of Qualitative Studies in Education,* 10(2), 175–189.

Stroud, B. (1984). *The significance of philosophical scepticism.* Oxford, UK: Oxford University Press.

Takaki, R. (1993). *A different mirror: A history of multicultural America.* Boston: Little, Brown.

Tatum, B. D. (1992). Talking about race, learning about racism: The application of racial identity development theory in the classroom. *Harvard Educational Review, 62,* 1–24.

Taylor, R. L. (1987). The study of black people. A survey of empirical and theoretical models. *Urban Research Review, 11(2),* 11–15.

Terry, B. (1992). The White male club. In J. Andrzejewski (Ed.), *Human relations: The study of oppression and human rights* (3rd ed., pp. 49–56). Needham Heights, MA: Ginn.

Thompson, S. (1992). Redefining roles and relationships. *Equity and Choice,* 8(3), 22–33.

Teirney, T. T. (1997). *Academic outlaws: Queer theory and cultural studies in the academy.* Thousand Oaks, CA: Sage.

Trueba, H. T. (1991). From failure to success: The roles of culture and cultural conflict in the academic achievement of Chicano students. In R. R. Valencia (Ed.), *Chicano school failure and success: Research and policy agendas for the 1990s* (pp. 151–163). London: Palmer.

Trueba, H. T. (1994). Reflections on alternative visions of schooling. *Anthropology and Education Quarterly,* 25(3), 376–393.

Tyack, D., & Hansot, E. (1982). *Managers of virtue: Public school leadership in America, 1820–1980.* New York: Basic Books.

United Farm Workers of America, AFL-CIO. (1986). *The wrath of grapes* (narrated by Cesar Chavez). Keene, CA: Author (15 minutes).

University of Texas Migrant Student Program. (1997). *1997 Exemplary migrant students.* Austin: Author.

Valdez L. (1971). *Actos* [Acts]. San Juan Bautista, CA: Cucaracha.

Valencia, R. (1997). *A critical appraisal of deficit theory in education.* London: Palmer.

Valencia, R. R. (1991). The plight of Chicano students: An overview of schooling conditions and outcomes. In R. R. Valencia (Ed.), *Chicano school failure and success: Research and policy agendas for the 1990s* (pp. 3–26). London: Falmer Press.

Valenzuela, A. (1999). *Subtractive schooling: U.S.–Mexican youth and the politics of caring.* Albany: State University of New York Press.

Valle, I. (1994). *Fields of toil, a migrant family's journey.* Pullman: Washington State University Press.

Van Dijk, T. A. (1993). *Elite discourse and racism.* Newbury Park, CA: Sage.

Villegas, A. M. (1988). School failure and cultural mismatch: Another view. *The Urban Review,* 20(4), 253–265.

Villenas, Sofia. (1996) The colonizer/colonized Chicana ethnographer: identity, marginalization, and co-optation in the field. *Harvard Educational Review, 66,* 711–731.

Wagstaff, L. (1996, November). *Best leadership and organizational practices.* Paper presented at the 1996 Migrant Education Conference, South Padre Island, TX.

Warfield-Coppock, N. (1995). Toward a theory of Afrocentric organization. *Journal of Black Psychology, 21(1),* 30–48.

Watkins, W. H. (1996). Reclaiming historical visions of quality schooling: The legacy of early 20th-century black intellectuals. In M. J. Shujaa (Ed.), *Beyond segregation: The politics of quality in African American schooling* (pp. 7–28). Thousand Oaks, CA: Corwin Press.

Webster, Y. O. (1992). *The racialization of America.* New York: St. Martin's Press.

Weinberg, R. (1993). IQ correlations in transracial adoptive families. *Intelligence,* 17(4), 541–556.

Weiner, B. (1986). *An attributional theory of motivation and emotion.* New York: Springer-Verlag.

Wellman, D. T. (1977). *Portrait of white racism.* New York: Cambridge University Press.

West, C. (1988). *Prophetic fragments.* Grand Rapids, MI: William B. Eerdmans Publishing Company.

West, C. (1989). *The American evasion of philosophy: A genealogy of pragmatism.* Madison: The University of Wisconsin Press.

West, C. (1990). The new cultural politics of difference. *October,* 53, 93–109.

West, C. (1993a). *Keeping faith: Philosophy and race in America.* New York: Routledge.

West, C. (1993b). *Beyond Eurocentrism and Multiculturalism,* Vol. 1 (Monroe, Maine: Common Courage).

West, C. (1993c). *Race Matters.* New York: Vintage Books.

West, C. (1995). Foreword. In K. Crenshaw, N. Gotanda, & K. Thomas (Eds.), *Critical race theory: The key writings that formed the movement* (pp. xi–xiii). New York: The New Press.

Wilder, M. A. (1995). Professional development schools: Restructuring teacher education programs and hierarchies. In H. G. Petrie (Ed.) *Professionalization, partnership and power: Building professional development schools* (Albany: State University of New York Press), 263–268.

Wiley, M., & Eskilson, A. (1978). Why did you learn in school today? Teachers' perceptions of causality. *Sociology of Education, 51,* 261–269.

Willie, C. V. (1993). Social theory and social policy derived from the black family experience. *Journal* of *Black Studies*, 23(4), 451–459.

Williams, J. (1989). Reducing the disproportionately high frequency of disciplinary actions
against minority students: An assessment-based policy approach. *Equity and Excellence*, 24(2), 31–37.

Williams, R. (1991). Base and superstructure in Marxist cultural theory. In C. Mukerji &
M. Schudson (Eds.), *Rethinking popular culture: Contemporary perspectives in cultural
studies* (Berkeley: University of California Press) pp. 407–423.

Williams-Dixon, R. (1991). Disproportionate mental retardation placement of minority
students. *Reading Improvement*, 28(3), 133–137.

Winfield, L. F. (1986). Teacher beliefs toward academically at risk students in inner urban
schools. *The Urban Review*, 18 (4), 253–268.

Winfield, L. F. (Ed.). (1991). Resilience, schooling, and development in African-American
youth. *Education and Urban Society*, 24(1), 5–165.

Wohlstetter, P., & Smyer, R. (1994). Models of high-performance schools. In S. Mohrman, P. Wohlstetter, & Associates (Eds.), *School-based management: Organizing for
high performance* (pp. 81–107). San Francisco: Jossey-Bass.

Wright, L. (1994, July 25). One drop of blood. *The New Yorker*, 46–55.

Yetman, N. R., & Steele, C. H. (Eds.). (1971). *Majority and minority: The dynamics of racial
and ethnic relations*. Boston: Allyn & Bacon.

Young, M. D. (1995a, May). *Diverse women. The ethics of cross-group feminist research*.
Paper presented at the Second Annual Gender Studies Conference, University of
Texas at Austin.

Young, M. D. (1995b, November). *Putting on paradigms and perspectives: Using multiple
frames in our search for women*. Paper presented at the Southwest Conference on
Gender Studies, Trinity University, San Antonio, TX.

Young, R. (1990). *White mythologies: Writing history and the West*. London: Routledge.

CONTRIBUTORS

W. B. Allen is Professor of Political Science at Michigan State University. He recently completed, with Carol M. Allen, *Habits of Mind: Ethics and Change in Higher Education.*

Elissa Fineman is working on her Ph.D. at The University of Texas at Austin in the Department of Radio-Television-Film. She is a visiting assistant professor at Trinity University in San Antonio, where she teaches classes on web design and media criticism. She has presented papers at the Association of International Communication Association and the Association of Internet Researchers. She is also the co-author of the video documentary, *Labores de la Vida (The Labors of Life).*

Carl D. Glickman is President of The Institute for Schools, Education, and Democracy, Inc., and University Professor Emeritus of Social Foundations of Education at the University of Georgia. He is on the Board of the National Commission of Learning In Deed, a countrywide initiative to revitalize democratic citizenry by connecting student academic learning with service to local communities. He is the chair of collaborations focused on democratic education including the League of Professional Schools, author of twelve books, and is currently completing two books, *Leadership for Learning* and *Holding Sacred Ground: The Hidden Story Behind Successful Progressive Public Schools.*

Miguel A. Guajardo, a teacher by training, has worked with neighborhoods, nonprofits organizations, and schools to develop effective youth community development strategies. He is presently a graduate student (A.B.D.) in the Educational Administration program at The University of Texas. He has co-authored a number of articles that focus on youth community development and community change issues. Miguel has been a Fellow with the Kellogg International Leadership Program (Class II) and the Salzburg Seminar's Urban Youth Session. He is committed to the training and development of public intellectuals. Miguel is a Project Coordinator with the Urban Issues Program at The University of Texas at Austin.

James W. Koschoreck is an Assistant Professor in the Educational Administration Program at the University of Cincinnati. Identifying as a social dissident, he engages in the ongoing battle against the windmills of bigotry and intolerance. His current research agenda includes the examination of lesbian and gay issues in public education. He has most recently published in *Education and Urban Society, Educational Administration Quarterly,* the *Journal of Curriculum Theorizing,* and

International Journal of Qualitative Studies in Education. He is currently working as co-editor on a special issue of the *Journal of School Leadership* that will focus on gay and lesbian issues in educational administration.

Julie Laible was an Assistant Professor at the University of Alabama before she was killed. She was a highly active, anti-racist scholar and teacher. She also was an active anti-racist in her community. She was a close friend to many of us, always setting a loving, caring example in all of her relationships. This book is dedicated to her and her work.

Gerardo R. Lopéz is an Assistant Professor in the department of Educational Leadership and Policy Analysis at the University of Missouri-Columbia. His specializations are educational policy, parental involvement, and school-community relations. He has published in the *American Educational Research Journal, Harvard Educational Review, Educational Administration Quarterly,* and *International Journal of Qualitative Studies in Education* and is currently working on an edited book on racism in qualitative research methodology.

Kanya Mahitivanichcha is a third-year doctoral student in Educational Policy and Planning at The University of Texas at Austin. She is a recent graduate of Harvard College (A.B., Economics) and Harvard Graduate School of Education (Ed.M.). She has lived in four countries and worked in a variety of cultural settings. Her research interests include economics of education, research methods, program evaluation, and educational reform. She has co-authored articles in the *American Journal of Educational Research* and *Educational Administration Quarterly.* Her current dissertation addresses human capital accumulation and the occupational outcomes of women.

Steven I. Miller is Professor in the Department of Foundations, Leadership and Counseling Psychology, School of Education, and Adjunct Department of Philosophy at Loyola University, Chicago. His areas of research interest include: social epistemology and education, philosophy of social science, philosophical issues in educational research, and qualitative research methods. He has authored articles in *Proto Sociology: Journal of Mind, Philosophy of Science, Social Epistemology, Analytic Teaching,* and *Synthese.* Recent areas of publication include the relationships of contexts to events and the ontological commitments of Null Hypothesis Statistical Testing.

Patricia Sánchez is a doctoral student in Social and Cultural Studies at the Graduate School of Education at the University of California, Berkeley. She is one of the co-founders of the Center for Popular Education and Participatory Research. Her most recent work on transnationalism and Chicana feminist theory can be found in the Australian journal, *Discourse: Studies in the Cultural Politics of Education.* She is also the co-author of the video documentary, *Labores de la Vida (The Labors of Life): Voices of Tejano Migrant Farm Workers.* Her next project includes working with Latina youth on a research-based children's book on transnationalism.

Jay D. Scribner holds the Ken McIntyre Professor for Excellence in School Leadership at The University of Texas at Austin. His studies focus on large urban areas, such as Los Angeles and Philadelphia, and in smaller communities throughout the state of Texas, particularly in the Borderland Schools. Scribner has been President of the University Council for Educational Administration, the Politics of Education Association and the Pennsylvania Educational Research Association. He served a year at Harvard University as an Alfred North Whitehead Fellow for Advanced Study in Education. He has co-edited books, authored chapters, and published articles in leading educational journals.

Christine E. Sleeter is a Professor in the Center for Collaborative Education and Professional Studies at California State University, Monterey Bay, where she directs the Institute for Advanced Studies in Education. She consults nationally in multicultural education and multicultural teacher education. Dr. Sleeter has received several awards for her work including the National Association for Multicultural Education Research Award, the AERA Committee on the Role and Status of Minorities in Education Distinguished Scholar Award, and the University of Wisconsin-Parkside Research Award. She has published numerous books and articles in multicultural education; her most recent books include *Culture, Difference and Power*, which is a multimedia electronic book; *Multicultural Education as Social Activism;* and *Turning on Learning* with Carl Grant.

Cynthia A. Tyson is an Assistant Professor in the School of Teaching at Learning at the Ohio State University where she teaches courses in social studies/global and multicultural education. Her research interests include an examination of race/racism in qualitative research, the development of socio-political identity in civic education, and the impact literature written for children and young adults has on student social activism. She has published articles in *Educational Researcher, International Journal of Qualitative Research in Education, Journal of Literacy Research,* and other books and journals.

Michelle D. Young is the Executive Director of the University Council for Educational Administration and a former professor of policy, planning, and leadership studies at the University of Iowa. Her scholarship focuses on how school leaders and school policies can ensure equitable and quality experiences for all students and adults who learn and work in schools. Her work has been published in the *Review of Educational Research, Educational Researcher,* the *American Educational Research Journal, Educational Administration Quarterly,* the *Journal of School Leadership,* and the *International Journal of Qualitative Studies in Education,* among other publications.

INDEX

A

academy · 1, 26, 27, 28, 29, 31, 32, 34, 65, 180

administration · 10, 15, 16, 101, 103, 105, 106, 107, 134, 135, 136, 137, 138, 139, 140, 141, 144, 145, 146, 148, 151, 181

AERA · 11, 13, 14, 17, 23, 75, 218

affirmative action · 25, 97, 122, 123

Afrocentric · 15, 64, 65, 85, 86, 95, 167, 188

ageism · 143

Alarcón · 63

anti-racist · 1, 2, 3, 8, 9, 10, 11, 12, 13, 14, 15, 16, 19, 21, 23, 26, 33, 42, 49, 54, 63, 68, 73, 90, 92, 97, 99, 111, 153, 234

anti-racist scholarship · 1, 2, 9, 11, 13, 14, 23, 49

Anyon · 188

Apache · 61

apartheid · 120, 123, 125, 141

apolitical · 10, 16, 153, 156, 157

Asante · 64, 79, 188

Au · 175

axiologies · 57, 58, 59, 61, 62, 76, 79

axiology · 17, 56, 63, 71

B

Bakhtin · 122, 198, 199, 220

Banks · 48, 51, 54, 55, 57, 59, 60, 62, 64, 71, 88, 92, 106, 107, 122, 188

Bell · 55, 63, 75, 105, 122, 123, 188, 198, 200

Bell Curve · 55, 105

Bhaskar · 69

bilingual · 38, 39, 186

Bledstein · 31, 32

border · 169, 178, 185, 186

Britzman · 201, 202, 215, 216

Butler · 69, 94, 96, 122

C

Cherokee · 59, 61

Cherryholmes · 92

children of color · 4, 5, 6, 7, 89, 97, 98, 109, 124, 125, 145, 146, 150, 156, 161, 165, 166, 167, 168, 169, 170, 172, 174, 177, 178, 183, 184, 185, 187, 190, 191

civilizational racism · 57

class · 29, 30, 31, 32, 33, 35, 36, 42, 48, 53, 56, 58, 67, 94, 95, 96, 103, 104, 105, 106, 107, 108, 109, 134, 137, 145, 150, 151, 176, 180, 183, 184, 185, 187, 210, 214

classism · 8, 103, 143, 189, 216

Clifford · 56, 220

collaborative · 168, 181, 183, 192

collaboratively · 18, 108, 181, 182, 226, 229, 232

Collins · 57, 59, 60, 61, 64, 78, 85

colonial · 57, 128, 189, 191

Comer · 106, 129, 166, 173, 176, 179, 181, 182

commitment · 31, 33, 53, 68, 72, 86, 93, 105, 106, 109, 136, 143, 148, 151, 161, 166, 167, 175, 176, 177, 178, 179, 181, 183, 184, 185, 187, 188, 192, 196, 216

communities of color · 167, 168, 169, 174,
   184, 185, 188, 190, 193
community · 7, 11, 12, 19, 46, 54, 57, 61,
   76, 78, 79, 80, 81, 82, 86, 103, 109,
   113, 114, 115, 116, 117, 118, 126, 129,
   136, 137, 138, 144, 147, 167, 172, 173,
   175, 176, 177, 178, 179, 182, 185, 189,
   192, 201, 228, 230, 231, 232, 233, 234
conservative · 10, 96, 140, 157, 229, 230
conspiracy · 60, 61, 83
constructivism · 48, 199, 200
co-researcher · 161
Cose · 57, 68, 188
critical dialogue · 65, 233
critical pedagogy · 167, 188, 189
critical race theory · 65, 75
critical theorist · 73, 94, 128, 158, 159
critical theory · 63, 69, 136, 142, 158
critical tradition · 52, 55, 59, 63, 68, 69
critique · 9, 10, 12, 15, 16, 21, 40, 44, 45,
   46, 47, 69, 79, 81, 86, 89, 90, 91, 92,
   93, 94, 97, 98, 101, 120, 126, 129, 136,
   142, 153, 157, 158, 159, 167, 168, 169,
   187, 189, 199, 220, 228, 234
Cuban · 29, 55, 88
cultural · 3, 15, 29, 35, 38, 39, 43, 44, 48,
   54, 56, 59, 60, 61, 62, 63, 64, 69, 72,
   73, 81, 83, 84, 86, 94, 103, 113, 115,
   116, 118, 122, 128, 145, 166, 167, 171,
   174, 175, 177, 199, 210, 229
cultural tradition · 60
culturally disadvantaged · 54
culture · 7, 18, 30, 32, 35, 39, 44, 53, 54,
   56, 57, 60, 61, 62, 63, 64, 66, 67, 69,
   72, 73, 75, 80, 81, 83, 84, 85, 86, 87,
   90, 104, 128, 150, 156, 166, 167, 168,
   169, 174, 175, 176, 181, 182, 183, 184,
   185, 187, 188, 189, 192, 201, 214, 226,
   229, 231, 234
culture-based epistemologies · 67
culturocentric · 167, 168, 191
Cummins · 54, 88, 104, 106

D
Darling-Hammond · 129, 165, 173, 179,
   182, 192
Delgado · 1, 191, 198, 204
democracy · 2, 3, 10, 16, 113, 114, 115,
   116, 117, 118, 119, 120, 121, 122, 123,
   124, 125, 126, 127, 128, 129, 145, 146
democratic · 3, 15, 46, 84, 109, 111, 113,
   116, 117, 118, 120, 121, 122, 123, 126,
   127, 136, 143, 148, 151, 168, 233
depoliticized · 44
Derman-Sparks · 89
Derrida · 8, 69, 94, 96, 202
Deyhle · 65, 191
dialogic · 133
dialogue · 10, 14, 15, 21, 42, 49, 64, 65, 67,
   77, 85, 86, 89, 133, 137, 148, 151, 183,
   201, 233
disadvantage · 56
disadvantaged · 54, 185
discourse · 7, 9, 19, 34, 36, 37, 38, 39, 40,
   42, 43, 45, 46, 71, 73, 77, 81, 94, 95,
   120, 122, 126, 137, 142, 147, 168, 189,
   198, 201, 220, 234
diversity · 44, 117, 136, 137, 138, 139,
   141, 149, 151
documentary · 11, 12, 13, 18, 226, 228,
   229, 230, 231, 232
dominant · 7, 10, 30, 31, 54, 56, 57, 58, 59,
   60, 61, 62, 64, 66, 72, 73, 76, 77, 81,
   83, 84, 85, 86, 87, 90, 91, 92, 96, 121,
   122, 123, 124, 125, 126, 127, 157, 166,
   167, 168, 169, 184, 187, 189, 199, 200,
   229, 231
dominant epistemologies · 62, 66, 91
dominant group · 30, 31, 58, 59, 61, 72,
   76, 123, 124, 187
domination · 65, 92, 118, 123, 126, 143
Donmoyer · 15, 77, 92, 101, 107, 134,
   135, 136, 137, 140, 141, 144, 145, 148
double consciousness · 27, 30, 32, 36
DuBois · 25, 27, 28, 36, 39, 40, 72, 73, 78

E

Edmonds · 106, 171, 181, 183

educational administration · 10, 15, 16, 101, 103, 105, 106, 107, 134, 135, 136, 137, 138, 139, 140, 141, 144, 145, 148, 151

educational leadership · 108, 114, 115, 126, 128

Educational Researcher · 9, 14, 23, 49, 87

Eisner · 92

Ellsworth · 62, 63

Elmore · 175

emancipation · 79, 120, 128, 158

emancipatory · 63, 65, 69, 86, 120, 121, 124

embargo · 161, 163

epistemological · 15, 17, 51, 52, 54, 55, 56, 57, 59, 60, 61, 62, 63, 64, 65, 66, 68, 69, 71, 73, 76, 77, 78, 79, 81, 82, 83, 84, 85, 86, 133, 135, 136, 137, 140, 141, 143, 146, 149, 150, 157, 194, 216, 218

epistemological racism · 51, 52, 54, 55, 56, 57, 60, 61, 62, 68, 69, 71, 73, 77, 78, 82, 83, 84, 85, 86

epistemologies · 10, 14, 49, 51, 52, 53, 54, 55, 57, 58, 59, 60, 61, 62, 63, 66, 67, 68, 71, 73, 76, 77, 79, 80, 81, 82, 85, 87, 89, 90, 91, 92, 93, 95, 98, 135, 142

epistemology · 7, 14, 49, 54, 55, 56, 60, 62, 63, 64, 65, 67, 71, 75, 76, 78, 79, 81, 82, 85, 86, 91, 155, 156, 157, 159

equality · 48, 72, 75, 106, 115, 116, 151, 185

equity · 2, 25, 84, 92, 121, 128, 138, 139, 140, 143, 145, 146, 148, 149, 151

ethical · 3, 4, 15, 53

ethnic · 25, 29, 37, 40, 41, 44, 67, 77, 79, 81, 113, 117, 127, 174, 175, 187, 188

ethnicity · 37, 41, 44

ethnographic · 16, 17, 221

ethnography · 155, 156, 157, 214

exploited · 125, 205, 231

F

fallacy · 38, 95

Feagin · 35, 54, 55, 56, 58, 72, 75, 188

Ferguson · 202

Fine · 104, 106

Fineman · 12, 18, 98, 226, 228, 229

Foster · 17, 125, 174, 181

Foucault · 57, 69, 71, 72, 94, 96, 197, 199, 202

framework · 81, 143, 197, 201

Frankenberg · 1, 4, 8, 57, 58, 63

freedom · 31, 84, 85, 113, 115, 116, 128, 151

Freire · 188

Fullan · 180

G

Gage · 51, 107, 134

Garcia · 175, 187, 205, 222

Gates · 127

gender · 8, 29, 31, 32, 35, 36, 45, 48, 81, 96, 103, 104, 105, 106, 107, 108, 109, 117, 127, 151, 184, 185, 187, 232

Goodlad · 105, 129

Gordon · 29, 35, 51, 54, 59, 60, 61, 62, 63, 64, 76, 77, 90, 92, 188

Grant · 40, 106

Guajardo · 11, 12, 13, 17, 18, 19, 194, 196, 201, 203, 208, 220, 226, 228, 230, 233

Guba · 69, 93, 171

H

Hacker · 54, 55, 56, 58, 72, 165, 188

Handbook · 10, 16, 99, 131, 133, 134, 135, 137, 139, 140, 141, 142, 144, 145, 146, 147, 149, 150, 151

Herrnstein · 55, 105, 165

heterosexism · 8, 9, 143

hierarchy · 4, 7, 29, 30, 31, 32, 33, 52, 77, 79, 104, 114, 156

high performance · 170, 171, 172, 175, 178, 187
high-stakes · 166, 168, 182, 186, 192, 193
Hilliard · 25, 29, 35, 36, 54, 68
HiPass · 166, 169, 171, 173, 174, 175, 177, 178, 179, 180, 181, 182, 183, 184, 187, 191
historicize · 198
Hollins · 15, 175, 187, 188, 191
homophobia · 128
hooks · 25, 29, 35, 48, 62, 63, 94, 96, 125, 126, 188
Hopi · 57, 66, 72
hybrid · 167, 168, 169
hybridity · 169, 189

I

identity · 38, 174, 176, 200
individual · 3, 27, 28, 29, 30, 31, 32, 33, 34, 38, 43, 46, 48, 52, 53, 54, 55, 62, 66, 72, 73, 81, 82, 83, 104, 116, 120, 122, 124, 139, 140, 143, 157, 180, 184, 186, 229, 233
individual racism · 53, 55, 72
individualism · 29, 30, 31, 32, 34, 36, 40, 43, 73, 143, 151, 167, 230
individuality · 32, 48, 59
inequalities · 2, 46, 72, 104, 105, 106, 108
inequality · 7, 107, 128, 156
inequities · 29, 34, 69, 96, 105, 122, 127, 147, 151
inequity · 15, 34, 121, 155, 157, 158, 189
institutional racism · 54, 55, 127, 151
intelligence · 30, 31, 55, 97, 114, 150

J

James · 25, 46, 51, 54, 56, 59, 71, 77, 79, 88, 103, 120, 129, 133, 134, 136, 138, 142, 144, 147, 149, 155, 165, 196, 220, 228
Joseph · 25, 46, 51, 77, 79, 88, 103, 120,

128, 133, 138, 144, 149, 155, 165, 196, 220, 228

K

Kershaw · 64, 65
King · 54, 64, 88, 118, 175, 187, 188
knowledge production · 62
knowledge-base · 15, 101
knowledge-base project · 15, 101
Koschoreck · 16, 131, 133, 136, 140, 141, 142, 143, 144, 146, 147, 148, 149, 151
Kovel · 30, 36
Kuhn · 197

L

Lacan · 157
Ladson-Billings · 15, 54, 64, 67, 74, 78, 118, 172, 174, 175, 178, 184, 187
Laible · 10, 15, 63, 88, 99, 101, 103, 104
language · 7, 36, 44, 45, 61, 69, 80, 85, 104, 128, 150, 157, 167, 168, 174, 175, 184, 186, 198, 202, 210, 213, 214, 215, 225, 230
Lather · 69, 79, 201, 202
leadership · 11, 15, 56, 72, 103, 108, 111, 113, 114, 115, 118, 126, 128, 134, 135, 136, 145, 146, 166, 168, 169, 170, 177, 189
Leistyna · 188, 189
Lenzo · 51
liberal · 96, 114, 115, 139
liberty · 115, 116, 118, 126, 127, 128
Lincoln · 69, 93, 171
lived reality · 97, 147, 149
Lomotey · 15, 54, 103, 104, 105, 106, 107, 108, 167, 175, 193
love · 63, 78, 118, 167, 173, 178, 179, 185
loving · 158, 159, 165, 166, 168, 169, 171, 172, 173, 174, 178, 179, 181, 184, 185, 187, 191
Lubiano · 198

M

margins · 59, 143

McCarthy · 33, 35, 54, 55, 62, 169, 174

McIntosh · 42

McLaren · 188, 233

metaphor · 71, 176, 183

methodologies · 61, 62, 65, 73, 76, 77, 79, 81, 89, 91, 93, 95, 97, 134, 155

methodology · 10, 16, 65, 71, 78, 79, 82, 85, 86, 91, 153, 155, 156, 157, 159, 198, 234

migrant · 11, 12, 13, 17, 18, 191, 194, 196, 197, 198, 199, 200, 202, 204, 205, 206, 209, 210, 211, 212, 213, 214, 215, 216, 218, 220, 221, 222, 223, 224, 225, 226, 228, 229, 230, 231, 232, 233, 234

migrant farm worker · 210, 211, 212

Minh-ha · 35, 59, 61, 63, 136, 141, 168, 198

modernism · 56, 57, 58, 59, 60, 69, 73, 129, 157, 158

modernist · 57, 58, 72, 73, 202

Mohrman · 179, 192, 193

multiculturalism · 25, 38, 48, 107, 109

multivocal · 196, 197, 198, 225

N

narrative · 61, 175, 183, 198, 199, 202, 220

neorealisms · 52, 68

Nietzsche · 78

Noddings · 173, 185

Nolly · 187, 191

norm · 56, 176

normativity · 122, 123, 124, 125, 126, 128

norms · 3, 56, 58, 60, 77, 83, 84, 122, 151, 187, 188, 202

O

Oakes · 104, 171, 172

Ogbu · 28, 29, 35, 36, 48, 53

Oliva · 17, 198, 199, 202, 218, 220

ontologies · 57, 58, 59, 60, 61, 62, 76, 79

ontology · 7, 56, 63, 71, 73, 157, 158

oppressed · 35, 38, 69, 78, 79, 127, 189

oppression · 38, 76, 78, 79, 88, 95, 96, 123, 124, 125, 155, 198, 231

organization · 117, 172, 175, 178, 184, 188, 192, 202

organizational · 15, 52, 54, 135, 166, 169, 173, 175, 176, 181, 182, 183, 187, 188

organizational culture · 54, 166, 175, 176, 181, 182, 183, 188

Ortiz · 55, 104

Other · 16, 35, 84, 120, 161, 183, 187, 206, 220, 225

Outlaw · 91

P

Padilla · 65, 67

paradigm · 77, 79, 107, 135, 150, 155, 178, 197

paradigmatic · 51, 135, 142, 146, 202

Paredes · 54, 61, 170

Paredes Scribner · 170

participatory · 113, 114, 115, 117, 118, 126, 129, 136

participatory democracy · 114, 115

pedagogies · 88, 97, 116

pedagogy · 105, 115, 116, 118, 121, 127, 145, 167, 172, 173, 174, 175, 186, 188, 189, 192, 233

people of color · 1, 2, 3, 4, 10, 11, 12, 13, 16, 17, 18, 26, 27, 28, 29, 30, 32, 33, 35, 36, 39, 43, 45, 51, 61, 62, 63, 66, 67, 71, 73, 76, 77, 91, 92, 94, 95, 97, 120, 123, 124, 125, 156, 161, 168, 194, 226

pluralistic · 134, 148

Pogue · 17, 205, 222

Policy Archaeology · 71

political · 3, 15, 17, 33, 34, 35, 38, 46, 56, 58, 97, 114, 115, 124, 128, 129, 135, 137, 143, 155, 156, 158, 161, 174, 189, 191, 194, 197

political correctness · 38, 143

politics · 23, 48, 79, 123, 124, 125, 126,
    135, 136, 139, 141, 155, 201, 234
politics of reality · 123, 124
polyphonic · 198, 202, 220, 225
Popkewitz · 92
positivism · 52, 59, 61, 62, 64, 66, 67, 68,
    69, 85
postcolonial · 73, 168, 169, 189
postcoloniality · 168
postmodern · 11, 17, 194, 201
postpositivism · 69
postpositivisms · 52, 59, 68, 69
poststructural · 59, 61, 67, 68, 69, 201, 202
poststructuralism · 136
poststructuralisms · 59, 61, 67, 68, 69
power · 5, 8, 29, 30, 31, 32, 33, 34, 38, 40,
    43, 44, 45, 48, 72, 77, 96, 120, 121,
    123, 124, 125, 127, 140, 141, 142, 149,
    157, 168, 189, 200, 208, 233, 234
principal · 83, 85, 89, 91, 120, 170, 172,
    173, 176, 178, 179, 180, 181, 182, 186,
    187, 191, 192, 230
problematic · 35, 68, 69, 72, 105, 141, 155,
    200, 201
problematize · 139, 168
public · 3, 6, 14, 36, 49, 53, 56, 60, 65, 67,
    84, 95, 97, 105, 113, 114, 115, 117,
    118, 121, 123, 136, 143, 148, 165, 168,
    169, 182, 183, 199, 210

Q
qualitative research · 51, 76, 198, 229, 232
Quine · 80, 94, 98

R
race · 5, 6, 7, 8, 15, 16, 27, 28, 29, 31, 32,
    33, 35, 36, 37, 39, 42, 44, 45, 48, 51,
    53, 54, 55, 56, 58, 60, 61, 62, 63, 64,
    65, 66, 67, 68, 69, 72, 73, 75, 76, 77,
    78, 79, 81, 88, 89, 90, 91, 92, 93, 94,

    95, 96, 103, 104, 105, 106, 107, 108,
    109, 117, 122, 127, 142, 145, 151, 156,
    165, 167, 168, 183, 184, 185, 187, 188,
    198, 200, 229
race war · 95
race-based epistemologies · 63, 66, 67, 73,
    76, 77, 79
race-based epistemology · 64, 65, 76, 78
racial bias · 5, 51, 52, 63, 71, 89, 92, 109,
    139, 151
racial group · 27, 32, 33, 34, 36, 45, 48, 55,
    57, 61, 62, 105, 124, 186, 231
racial profiling · 5
racialized · 28, 30, 34, 36, 46, 48, 88, 90,
    91, 122, 139, 140, 141, 142
racially segregated · 4, 88
realism · 69, 199, 200
reality · 3, 8, 26, 56, 59, 60, 66, 71, 83, 86,
    88, 90, 91, 92, 95, 96, 97, 113, 123,
    124, 125, 126, 127, 134, 137, 140, 147,
    149, 155, 157, 158, 159, 184, 187, 197,
    198, 199, 200, 201, 216, 220, 225
reason · 2, 17, 40, 53, 81, 89, 118, 192,
    194, 198, 201, 206
relativism · 38, 80, 81, 82, 84, 86, 94, 95
representation · 13, 18, 56, 108, 139, 141, 142,
    197, 198, 199, 202, 216, 220, 226, 228
re-presentation · 17, 194, 197, 199, 225
reproduction · 2, 30, 34, 55, 105, 147, 158
research epistemologies · 10, 51, 52, 53, 54,
    55, 57, 59, 60, 61, 62, 63, 67, 71, 73, 76,
    77, 80, 82, 89, 90, 91, 92, 93, 95, 98
Reyes · 11, 26, 35, 53, 54, 61, 103, 106,
    107, 108, 170, 188, 191, 228, 230
Rizvi · 53, 68
Roueche · 177

S
Sadker · 104
Said · 35, 57, 59, 121
Sarris · 61

Scheurich · 15, 25, 37, 40, 42, 43, 46, 51, 53, 63, 71, 75, 76, 77, 78, 79, 80, 81, 82, 83, 84, 85, 86, 88, 89, 101, 103, 107, 109, 118, 120, 122, 126, 127, 133, 138, 140, 141, 142, 143, 144, 146, 147, 148, 149, 151, 155, 165, 170, 171, 188, 196, 201, 202, 220, 228

Schwandt · 69

Scribner · 11, 16, 131, 133, 134, 139, 141, 142, 144, 146, 148, 149, 150, 170, 188, 191, 228

Sergiovanni · 173, 176, 177, 178, 179, 181, 187

SES · 89, 165, 166, 169, 170, 171, 178, 179, 182, 183, 184, 185, 186, 187, 191, 192

sexism · 8, 9, 45, 103, 143

sexual orientation · 35, 48, 96, 150, 185

Shakeshaft · 104, 106, 109

Shujaa · 54, 167

Siddle Walker · 176

Sleeter · 14, 23, 42, 46, 47, 48, 106, 188

social class · 42

social construction · 58, 59, 60, 68, 123, 157, 199

social constructions · 58, 59, 60, 157, 199

social group · 27, 28, 30, 31, 32, 33, 38, 57, 60, 61, 69

social practice · 56, 60, 109, 121, 122

social problem · 25, 26, 34, 147, 151

social science · 14, 16, 49, 54, 55, 65, 69, 71, 77, 80, 92, 93, 94, 95, 96, 153, 156, 159, 198, 201

societal racism · 51, 52, 55, 56, 62, 83, 145

space traders · 122

spirituality · 2, 196

Spivak · 25, 29, 35, 202, 216

St. Pierre · 202

standards · 3, 30, 62, 81, 83, 85, 86, 92, 95, 96, 97, 98, 115, 134, 172, 181

standpoint · 64, 85, 86, 136

Stanfield · 28, 29, 30, 35, 39, 51, 54, 56, 57, 58, 59, 60, 61, 62, 63, 72, 77, 91

students of color · 7, 10, 11, 36, 54, 55, 67, 72, 90, 92, 109, 131, 156, 165, 166, 167, 170, 171, 182, 183, 186, 187

subjectivity · 7, 8, 51, 73, 140, 141, 158, 159

superintendent · 53, 230

T

Takaki · 58, 188

Tatum · 47, 53, 71

Texas · 12, 17, 18, 58, 103, 104, 155, 169, 170, 178, 185, 186, 191, 201, 203, 205, 213, 218, 221, 222, 224, 226, 228, 229, 230, 232, 234

Tierney · 137

totality · 198

totalized · 1, 35, 94, 95

transformation · 103, 108, 125, 128, 158, 179

Trueba · 15, 16, 125, 153, 174, 175, 186, 188, 192

trust · 10, 176, 178

trustworthiness · 171

U

union · 174, 175, 208, 230, 231

United Farm Workers · 17

V

Valencia · 11, 88, 89, 91, 125, 188

Valenzuela · 11

values · 2, 56, 59, 91, 148, 149, 176, 177, 179, 181, 187, 188, 216

video documentary · 11, 13, 18, 226, 228, 229

Villegas · 104

Villenas · 65, 233

W

Wagstaff · 11, 98, 170, 187, 188

West · 25, 33, 35, 36, 48, 57, 58, 59, 60,
    62, 63, 65, 72, 88, 91, 94, 96, 125, 126,
    127, 128, 174, 188
white discourse · 34, 42, 46
white people · 4, 5, 18, 25, 30, 43, 45, 62,
    89, 94, 98, 128
white privilege · 7, 8, 96, 97
white racism · 1, 2, 3, 4, 6, 7, 8, 9, 10, 11,
    12, 13, 14, 15, 16, 17, 18, 19, 23, 25,
    33, 34, 35, 39, 41, 42, 43, 44, 45, 46,
    47, 48, 49, 58, 71, 75, 88, 89, 90, 91,
    92, 93, 94, 95, 96, 97, 98, 131, 153,
    157, 159, 161, 163, 228, 229
White racism · 3, 7, 12, 18, 38, 39, 40, 56, 88
white racist · 2, 3, 8, 9, 10, 19, 39, 97, 157,
    158, 163, 226
white scholars · 1, 8, 9, 10, 13, 15, 16, 17,
    62, 63, 65, 89, 90, 93, 95, 98, 99, 111,
    153, 157, 161, 163
white skin privilege · 2, 9, 97, 158
white supremacy · 44, 45, 58, 124
whiteness · 7, 42, 44
Wohlstetter · 171, 182, 192
Wolcott · 10, 16, 99, 153, 155, 159

Y

Young · 9, 10, 14, 21, 33, 35, 49, 51, 75,
    76, 77, 78, 79, 80, 81, 82, 83, 84, 85,
    86, 88, 89, 122, 188

Z

Zero · 6